Messenger to the Spirits

MESSENGER TO THE SPIRITS

MICHAEL J. WHITAKER

RTP
Research Triangle Publishing, Inc.

This novel is a fiction. Any reference to historical events; to real people, living or dead; or to real locales are intended only to give the fiction a sense of reality and authenticity. Names, characters, places, and incidents either are the product of the author's imagination or are used fictitiously, and their resemblance, if any, to real-life counterparts is entirely coincidental.

Published by
Research Triangle Publishing, Inc.
PO Box 1130
Fuquay-Varina, NC 27526

Copyright © 1996 by Michael J. Whitaker
All rights reserved.
This book, or parts thereof, may not be reproduced in any form without permission.

ISBN 1-884570-60-7

Jacket Design and illustrations by Kathy Holbrook

Library of Congress Catalog Card Number: 96-70836

Printed in the United States of America
10 9 8 7 6 5 4 3 2 1

This book is printed on acid-free paper. ∞

*This book is dedicated to the memory of my parents,
Maxine and Preston Whitaker,
with whom it all began.
Thank you for the wonderful memories.
You are truly loved and painfully missed.*

I am indebted to many people;

Donna Whitaker, my wife, for her many hours of patience and understanding, at least most of the time. To my many friends who are too numerous to list but know who they are, I send my gratitude for their continued support and encouragement. Finally, I am indebted to the follow people for their help in making this book a reality: The publishers, Liz and Dave Anderson, for the opportunity, as well as their hard work, wisdom, and dedication; Debra Bailey, for her detail, pointed comments, helpful suggestions, thoroughness, and professional critique; Kathy Holbrook, for her insight and extraordinary talent in capturing the essences of the novel in her wonderful design; and to the photographer Byron Williams, for his valuable time and professional expertise.

Chapter 1

May 30
Alaska Interior

Today would be Max Saylor's last hunt. There was only one more day left to bear-hunting season, at least until the following September when the killing would start again. But Max wouldn't be part of that.

He was considered to be the best guide in Alaska when it came to tracking down the fearsome grizzly. His daddy, whom most folks called Whitie, had taught him everything he knew about hunting, trapping, and surviving, in the northern wilderness. Alaska was a beautiful country, yet to those who denied it respect, it could be extremely hostile, even deadly.

Max had officially been registered as a big-game guide since he was twenty. That had been twelve years ago, and now he was ready to do something else with his life, something that had more of a future than hunting down animals. He was thinking about it now more than ever, because he was getting married in two days and would soon be starting a family. That wasn't the only reason though. For the past couple of years the thrill of the hunt had lost its excitement. It was still fun, but that special something that had been there before, was gone now.

About the same time, he and his best friend, Jerry Hudson, began to talk about doing something else with their lives. In addition to being the best hunting guides in Alaska, they were both excellent pilots. After many hours of lip-flapping, over steamy cups of black coffee at the Trading Post in Two Forks, their discussions started to focus on their flying skills. They decided to open their own charter airline service. In July, they would start providing the public with regular flight service out of Fairbanks, flying to many of the smaller towns and communities located in the interior of Alaska. Max was excited about the new venture and glad that today would be his last professional hunt.

Fortunately, he was guiding two experienced hunters, Harry O'Brien and John Cummings, whom he'd led several times before. Both were in their early fifties and were successful businessmen from the mid-west.

Reaching the east ridge of Hazard Creek, an area frequently roamed by the giant grizzly, he landed his helicopter. The three men slowly worked their way down the steep slope to the bottom of the ravine, where wildlife, including the bears, watered from the rapidly flowing stream that cut its way down through the gorge walls.

Max was in the lead as they descended. As he reached out and grabbed a spruce branch for balance, he noticed a tiny tremble quaking through the small limb. He glanced over his shoulder at his two clients close behind. They didn't seem to notice the earth's little shiver and he didn't see any need to bring it to their attention. It was important that they totally focus on the hunt, or they could very quickly become the prey instead of the predators. Besides, seismic activity in Alaska was fairly common and was nothing to be alarmed about. It had been several years since the last big one, and even then, most of the damage was along the coast.

"This sure is a beautiful morning," Harry O'Brien said in a low voice as he came up beside Max. "What's the temperature?"

"It was about forty-eight when we left the airport at Two Forks," Max whispered back. "This spring's been kind of warm. Lots of snow melt . . . lots of water." He tilted his head toward the bottom of the ravine and cupped his hand around his right ear. The river was yet to be seen, but at this distance, if he listened closely, he could hear the roar of the water as it raced down the gorge and crashed against the boulders.

John Cummings had moved up on his other side. "How much farther until we're there?"

"About two hundred yards," Max answered, putting his finger to his lips to indicate silence. "From here on we don't want to be heard." Both men nodded their heads in acknowledgment, and he gestured with his hand to continue their descent down the steep ravine wall.

Fifteen minutes later and three-fourths of the way down the slope, the ground shuddered and bucked as if an arctic chill had trickled down Mother Earth's spine and reached her very core.

"Whoa! Did you guys feel that?" Harry blurted out.

Max simply said, "Yeah," and raised his hand for his two clients to stop. They were ten feet behind him, standing close together.

"What the hell was that?" John asked. There was a slight quiver in his voice. "Is someone blasting in a mine around here this early in the morning?"

"No. That old mine we passed on the way down, has been closed for years. It was just a tremor," Max replied calmly, trying not to show his own apprehension. His eyes quickly scanned the terrain for signs of more seismic activity. That was a pretty solid hit, stronger than he'd felt in two or three years.

"A tremor . . . as in earthquake?" John asked, his voice two octaves above his normal tone.

"I don't like this. Maybe we should go back to the chopper and get the hell out of here," Harry pleaded. His right arm was wrapped around the trunk of a medium sized spruce, and he looked like a child clinging to a security blanket.

Max gazed down through the forest of white and black spruce, to the turbulent stream fifty yards below. Harry might be right, he thought. Maybe they should get out of here. But that would mean he'd have to bring them back tomorrow, because that was the last day of bear season. He didn't want to come back tomorrow, or any other day. He had promised his future wife that today would be his last hunt.

"I think it'll be all right, guys," Max said reassuringly, as he looked back over his shoulder at the two of them. "We have these little ripples every now and then. It's nothing to worry about. But I'll leave it up to—"

"What's that?" John Cummings squeaked. "That noise. Do you hear it?".

Max cocked his head and listened closely. He could hear a faint rumbling over the roar of the stream.

"I'm gettin' the hell out of here!" John yelled, tearing up the slope toward the helicopter at the top of the ridge.

"Me too!" Harry echoed, hot on the heels of his hunting companion.

The dull rumble got progressively louder. Max's eyes darted toward the belly of the ravine. His body stiffened and a cold shiver ran across the back of his neck. "Oh shit! Run, guys! Run like hell!" he shouted. Max spun around, dug the toes of his Wolverine hunting boots into the loose soil, and began to charge up the mountainside.

Near the stream's edge the earth began to crack open. The stress and pressure of the earth's crust had finally become too great. The ground began to tremble and split open like the torn seam of a ragged dress. It cut a jagged forty-five degree path up the slope and rapidly came toward the three of them.

Harry looked over his shoulder, as he scurried on all fours up the steep incline. His face was red from exertion, his eyes were wide with fear, and his forehead was spattered with cold beads of sweat.

John was a much thinner man, obviously more conscious about his health than his friend Harry. He sprinted toward the top of the ridge, slightly slumped over, with arms pumping along his sides, in sync with his legs, which were moving like the pistons of a revved-up engine. He set a sizzling pace and was now several yards in front of his hunting companion.

The entire mountainside shook violently, as the earth twisted, turned, and bucked. Large boulders began to break loose on the slope above them, and as they fell toward the bottom of the gorge, they pulverized anything in their way. Max stopped for a moment and glanced back in awe, just as the ground shifted along the crack and pitched the near side of the tear, six or seven feet into the air. Dust and debris belched from the opening. He had never seen such devastation. For thirty feet on each side of the earth's rip, the trees lay broken and mangled as if they were wooden matches.

The sound of snapping and crunching slapped Max out of his trance. He jerked his head around just in time to see a large rock plummeting toward him. He tried to dive out of its way and landed, with a painful cracking thud, on his right side, on an outcropping of small rocks. Air whistled through his mouth as it gushed from his lungs. Ignoring the pain, he managed to roll out of the boulder's path. It thundered by with the force of a Red-Ball-Special freight train, missing him by inches.

He lay on his back, staring up at the quaking trees. The sharp pain in his side felt like someone had driven a railroad spike into his lung. He struggled to lift his head and look toward the bottom of the ravine. The tear in the earth was speeding up toward them like some kind of monster.

"Oh God, help me!" Harry screamed in terror.

Max snapped his head to the side and glared up the incline. Ten feet above him to his left, the bucking earth had slammed Harry to the ground. The frightened man rocked back on his large, rounded stomach, lifted his head, and clawed desperately with his fingers at the dirt, while staring up at a huge monolith that had been torn loose by the earthquake. It was as big as a full-sized pickup. Flipping end over end, it was heading directly for Harry.

"Roll out of the way, Harry!" Max yelled. Knifelike pain stabbed at his right side. The enormous rock was in the middle of a flip high in the air, as he continued to holler at his client to get out of its way. The man seemed to be deaf to his warning. As the oblong monolith swung over, Max stared in horror at the lower half of John Cummings's smashed body, which was pressed into the end of the rock.

When that end hammered into the ground, dirt, dust, and small stones exploded in all directions. Trees toppled behind it, snapping, breaking, and up-rooting, as if a hurricane had just delivered its cataclysmic destruction.

Through the haze of pulverized stones and dust, he continued to yell his warnings. Harry, frozen with fear, continued to ignore them. From his angle, Max could see that Harry had his teeth clenched together. Blood flowed from his lips. Harry's tongue was partially bitten in two, and it dangled down onto his chin by a thin thread of crimson tissue.

The other end of the monolith speared down toward the earth. Its jagged edge caught Harry just below the shoulder blades, severing his arms and head from the rest of his body.

"Holy Mother of God!" Max screamed in revulsion. He turned his head away from the horrendous scene.

He lay there on the bucking ground, gasping for air, paralyzed with shock. Momentarily, he had forgotten about the split in the earth that was ripping up toward him at lightning speed. A second later there was a loud boom. The earth under him surged up like a rocket, then abruptly stopped, catapulting him into the air. Three seconds later Max Saylor was dead.

Later that afternoon, screams echoed across the vast land, etching an old man's pain into the granite walls of the nearby canyons. Max's father, Whitie, had found his son's body, spread-eagled and face up, impaled on the splintered trunk of a small spruce. The old man remained slumped there for hours, weeping over the body.

Meanwhile, hundreds of feet below the eastern slope of Hazard Creek, an ancient reservoir, millions of years old, began to seep up through the rock formations. Hairline fissures caused by the earthquake, provided the way. Carried within its waters, were billions of microscopic organisms starving for the rich minerals of the surface environment.

Chapter 2

**December 1, four years later
Ely, Minnesota**

T*HE COLD DISMAL DAY HAD STRETCHED* into the longest one Grant Rawlings could remember in the twenty-six years of his life. He sat snuggled in the overstuffed La-Z-Boy chair his father had given him, his feet propped on the footrest. The blank screen of the 486 notebook computer, which was perched on his lap, stared back at him. His eyes had been glued to the small 8½ inch screen since six o'clock that morning. He had taken only short breaks at eleven and three, with intermittent stops to refill his cup with stale coffee. It was now twelve hours later, and his hazel-colored eyes burned. They felt gritty and strained as if he had spent the day in a smoke-filled bar.

Grant blinked a few times to clear the blurriness, but it didn't seem to help much. He sluggishly rolled his head left toward the living room window of his small three-room apartment. It was dark outside, but in the parking lot, he could see the powdery glistening snow swirling about under the amber-colored sodium lights. When he listened carefully, he could hear the small pecking and scratching sounds of sleet mixed in with the snow, as it brushed against the glass panes.

It had been twenty minutes since he'd made his last entry. One more time, Grant's tired eyes reread the last paragraph he had written. This time the words didn't seem to be flowing or reading as well as when he'd first typed them in.

He saved the file, used the trackball to move the pointer to the word count icon, then clicked on it. A small window appeared in the upper right-hand corner of the screen. Its display read 3017 words. He was disappointed and could hardly believe that all he had produced in twelve hours were 3017 words. At this rate it would take him a year to write his thesis.

This was his first day of formally documenting his research on the gray wolf, other than what was in his field notebooks. He had worked on the introduction all day, and he still had at least that much, and maybe more to write, before entering and describing his research results.

"That's all she wrote," Grant said to himself, chuckling at the unintended pun. The phrase reminded him of his father, who'd said the same thing all the time, when Grant was growing up. No doubt that's where he'd picked up the saying.

Grant was tapped out—his brain hurt, his eyes burned, and his fingers ached. That was more than enough reason to call it quits for the day. Grant closed the file, exited the word processor, turned off the notebook, and laid it on the small table beside the La-Z-Boy. The computer was a graduation gift from his parents. They gave it to him when he received his B.S. degree in biology from Southwest Missouri State University.

As he sat there trying to clear his mind, his stomach growled loudly. The only things he'd eaten all day were an apple, a few pretzels, and two slices of left-over pizza zapped in the microwave. Of course, he'd drunk what seemed like forty gallons of coffee. The bitter taste in his mouth, was clear evidence that he'd had too much.

Grant had come to Ely, to the University of Minnesota, to acquire his master's degree in wildlife biology. Actually, the University of Minnesota was located in Minneapolis, but he had spent most of his time in Ely, working under the guidance of one of the world's experts on wolves, Dr. Johnny Boy Jackson, otherwise known by his peers as the Wolfman. Grant had studied gray wolves for two years in their natural habitat on Isle Royale, in Lake Superior. Now he was writing his thesis on the predator/prey relationship of the wolf and moose in that park.

During those two years, Grant had lost more than 20 pounds. Normally his five-ten stocky frame carried around 175 pounds. But for a farm-bred boy from Missouri, he was a little on the puny side right now. And it never failed—when his mother phoned each week, the subject came up. First, she would ask if he was going to church every Sunday; then, if he'd met any nice Christian girls; and finally, the topic of whether he'd been eating properly would always squeeze into the conversation.

It was December 1. He had elected to stayed in Minneapolis for Thanksgiving to get his thesis started and planned to go home for Christmas. This would give his mother the opportunity to pamper him, as she loved to do, and feed him three meals a day of her fabulous cooking. There wasn't enough money or time to fly back to Missouri for both holidays. As a graduate student, his stipend barely paid the rent and bought the groceries.

His parents offered to send what money they could, but he always refused. He knew they were struggling just to pay the taxes on the farm. That was one of the reasons he felt guilty about having the notebook computer. His parents had bought it on credit and were still making payments. It was the only way they could afford to get it. It would have hurt them deeply if he hadn't accepted it and shown a great deal of excitement. He didn't fail them.

Grant closed his eyes for a moment, leaned back in the La-Z-Boy, and smoothed his light brown, shoulder-length hair against the headrest. His thoughts focused on an image of his mother in the kitchen, cooking up a storm. Almost immediately, he could smell pork roast with fresh home-baked rolls. He envisioned mashed potatoes smothered with brown gravy, green beans, corn on the cob, and blackberry cobbler covered with vanilla ice cream, for dessert. His mouth watered from the savory aroma, even though it was imagined, and he unconsciously licked his lips. He opened his eyes and said, "The woman I marry will have to be a good cook, just like mom. That's all there is to it."

At that moment he felt a wave of homesickness and a quick flash of tears in his eyes. He rubbed the dampness away with the heels of his hands and composed himself. Farm work had forced him to be tough, building the muscles in his body and planting calluses on his hands, but he had always kept his sensitive heart. "God, I miss them. I'll be glad when Christmas gets here."

Grant lowered the footrest and crawled out of the La-Z-Boy. He raked his fingers through his tangled hair, scratched the scraggly whiskers on his square chin, then leaned over and tucked his woolen socks into the legs of his sweatpants. Picking up the remote control from the floor next to the chair, he turned on the television.

Within seconds, Dan Rather's face appeared on the screen. The news commentator was in the middle of reporting about a new health-care bill Congress had voted on before the holidays. As usual, the elected officials had voted strictly down party lines, and the bill was defeated. Grant scrunched up his face and shook his head in disgust at the bureaucratic folly of the government. He headed toward the kitchen and slipped his right hand under the UM sweatshirt, patting his noisy stomach as if that would stop the growling.

Just as he opened the freezer door, he heard Dan Rather's smooth voice take on a serious tone. "The wolf-control controversy in Alaska continues, and a nation is dismayed and outraged. I warn you, the video we are about to show is very graphic and may not be appropriate for children under thirteen years of age—"

When Grant heard the words "wolf control," he froze, and the uncontrollable flutters in his stomach replaced the hunger pangs. His heart began to thump loudly, and he felt a sick feeling growing deep inside of him.

Dan Rather continued, "The video was taken on Tuesday by an—"

Grant's moment of paralysis gave way to an urgent need to see what was about to be aired on the television. He charged toward the living room, leaving the freezer door wide open, and stood in front of the TV, waiting to see what Dan Rather meant by "very graphic."

"—animal-rights activist who was joined by two members of the media. This video shows one of the methods used to control the Alaskan wolf. Later in the day, the three men were joined by a representative from the Alaska Department of Fish and Game. I would like to repeat that the video we are about to show, is very graphic and may not be appropriate for children under thirteen years of age to watch."

There was a couple of seconds where Mr. Rather stared into the TV camera. His face had taken on a grim look, and his dark piercing eyes seemed to be looking directly into Grant's. Grabbing the remote, Grant turned up the volume and leaned close to the screen, his hands propped against his knees.

The TV flickered, and then the back of a man appeared. He was clad in heavy winter clothing, and the parka of his coat was pulled up over his head as he waded in knee-deep snow. The snow was coming down hard, giving the appearance of a thick fog. The person videotaping, apparently the animal activist, trailed the man with the parka. The camera jostled up and down, and Grant could hear the labored breathing of the individual taping the scene.

Grant's eyes scanned the screen, darting from side to side and top to bottom. He had not seen any evidence of a wolf yet, only the falling snow, the ground, some spruce trees, and the back of the man trudging through the snow. Grant guessed that he was probably the agent from the Alaska Department of Fish and Game. He felt his insides tighten, afraid of what was about to be shown.

After two years in Minnesota studying the gray wolf, he had learned a great deal and felt connected in some way, to the magnificent animal. He had also learned about the sad tragedy, worldwide, of this misunderstood predator, which resulted from human fears and superstitions. By the early 1900s, the wolf had been eradicated in the lower forty-eight states. At the moment, Minnesota was the only one of those states that had a healthy population of wolves, with numbers ranging from fifteen hundred to two thousand animals.

Grant felt good to be part of a group of people dedicated to protecting and studying this isolated population of wolves. In Minnesota, in just the past couple of years, their status had been upgrade from endangered to threatened.

Alaska was the only state where the wolf was not protected under the Endangered Species Act. There, it was still hunted as big game and trapped as a furbearing animal. The estimated population of wolves in Alaska ranged from four thousand to seven thousand, depending on whom you talked to. Alaska was also the only state that had a control program in place, where wolves were harvested so hunters would have larger herds of caribou and moose to hunt. From Grant's point of view, there was something morally wrong about killing one animal, to provide better hunting of other animals, for an elite group of individuals.

On the television, the man with his back to the camera stopped abruptly. Grant thought he saw something in the man's right hand as he lifted it up, but he couldn't be sure. He'd only gotten a brief glimpse. The man's body was now blocking his view.

The cameraman stepped to one side and panned ahead of the man. There, in front of him, was a gray wolf with a wire snare trap around its chest. It was still alive, struggling to get free. Grant estimated the wolf to be this year's crop, a pup no more than six months old. Then he saw the pistol in the man's hand. It looked like a .22 and the barrel was aimed directly at the wolf pup.

Unconsciously, Grant slipped his lower lip between his teeth and began to bite down on it. At the same time, he clenched his fingers so tightly into his knees that even through the sweatpants, his fingernails left marks in his flesh.

A muffled crack came from the television. The wolf jumped and jerked to one side. It was obviously in pain, but it was still alive. "Oh Jesus!" Grant cried out. Even though he'd seen the pistol, the shot still caught him off guard.

This is ludicrous, he thought. Why don't they just let the wolf go? How could any sane person be so cruel to an animal?

The sound of another shot came from the television. The wolf leaped in the air and was immediately yanked back down by the wire snare around its chest. Steam rushed from the pup's mouth and nostrils as it continued its battle for freedom.

Grant flinched and jerked with the animal. His fingernails dug even deeper into the sweatpant material and his skin. A drop of blood trickled from his lip and down his chin.

Three more shots were fired. With each volley, the defenseless animal lurched in pain, trying to get away from the crazy human being. Grant winced along with the wolf pup, at each crack of the firearm, as if the bullets were piercing his own flesh. When the wolf's lifeless body finally dropped into the bloodstained snow, tears began to stream down Grant's cheeks. In his entire life he'd never felt such deep sorrow for another creature, as he did right now for the wolf pup. Nor had he ever felt such revolting disgust and embarrassment to be a member of the human race.

Grant dropped his head in sadness, and stared at the worn beige carpet on the living room floor. He didn't want to see any more. The crushing pain in his heart brought him to his knees. Tears rolled from his cheeks and onto the floor. The wolf's killing had taken less than thirty seconds, but it seemed as if he'd witnessed a terrible massacre that went on for hours and hours.

He felt many things at once—lonely, helpless, angry, violated. His eyes were burning worse than ever, but that didn't matter right now. Grant took a deep breath, trying to regain some level of composure. His stomach churned from the acid inside. He felt like vomiting.

"Over there! Look over there!" a man's tinny voice yelled from the television.

Just as Grant looked up, the video camera scanned toward the trees, left of where the men were standing with the dead wolf. At the edge of the woods were three more wolf pups—a white one, a black one, and gray one. They all looked to be about the same age as the one that had just been killed and were most likely from the same litter. All three animals were facing the camera, looking at the three men and what had just taken place. The white wolf raised its head into the falling snow and began to howl a mournful wolf-song. A few moments later the other two joined the pitiful wailing. Their eerie cries seemed to slice through the frigid air of that far north country and seep from the television screen into Grant's living room, where they filled it with a bone-chilling presence.

Grant shuddered. A flow of tears surged from his eyes, and the knot in his throat was about to strangle him.

"I'll be damned. A silver-blue," one of the men on the TV said.

The camera swung back and zoomed in on an adult wolf about thirty feet in front of them. The animal was caught by the foot in a snare trap. Part of the creature's foot looked to be chewed away. It was bloody and raw.

There was another tug at Grant's heart. He was certain this wolf was the mother of the four pups. He'd never seen a wolf with a more beautiful pelt. In the falling snow, it seemed to be surrounded by a glowing aura. He'd heard of the rare silver-blue wolf, but had never seen one.

The man Grant thought was the agent, raised the pistol and moved toward the snared animal.

"No! I'm not going to let you kill the silver-blue! Not the silver-blue!" the cameraman yelled. He began running toward the man with the gun.

Grant stopped crying. His eyes were wide and glued to the television. He was praying that another wolf would not be killed. But he knew it was illegal for the cameraman to interfere with a fish and game official. By law, it was the man's job to kill the wolf.

His eyes gravitated toward the silver-blue wolf in the upper right-hand corner of the TV screen. It was tugging and jerking at the wire snare, trying to break free. But the situation looked grim for the beautiful creature.

The man cocked the hammer on the pistol, stretched out his arm and took aim at the wolf. The animal's golden eyes peered up at the man. Its expression seeming to understand that its life was about to be taken. The wolf began to twist and turn and chew at the snared foot, desperately trying to break free. The three wolf pups at the edge of the woods stop howling and started a high-pitch yelping.

Grant turned his head away from the television. He couldn't watch another cold-blooded killing. He began to pace back and forth across the living room floor, tears streaming down his face. His chest heaved up and down, kind of a half cough, half sigh.

Dan Rather's voice and image came back on the TV. "The animal activist videotaping the scene you just saw, was Dr. Albert Goode. Dr. Goode was arrested and charged with interfering with a state official while trying to perform his duties. It is not known at this time, if the other wolf caught in the snare trap was shot and killed. The governor of Alaska—"

Grant pressed the off-button on the remote. There was a flicker that narrowed down to a single white dot, and then the television screen went black.

Chapter 3

May 30
Alaska Interior

It was late in the day on Monday, as Grant peered out the airplane window at the expanse of wilderness below. He was flying over the largest state in the union, Alaska, and he could hardly believe it. His life was changing pretty fast.

Three weeks ago—in just under five months— he'd finished his master's degree thesis on the predator/prey relationship of the wolves and moose on Isle Royale. Even though other biologists had already studied the relationship, continued research was considered important because the relationship was such a dynamic one. The research could help scientists determine the multiple factors in an ever-changing environment.

Leaning back against the headrest, Grant closed his eyes and began to think about the past couple of years. He had always thought it was an interesting story, maybe even an act of fate, how the two animals appeared on that isolated island in the first place.

For some reason, early in the century, several moose swam twenty miles through the frigid waters of Lake Superior, to reach Isle Royale. No one was ever able to explain the reason for the migration. The large herbivore found the island to be one big gourmet salad. For thirty to forty years, they browsed and reproduced without the threat of predators.

In the winter of 1949, two wolves from Canada, crossed the ice to the island. The holiday for the moose came to an end. They had overgrazed and overproduced, so both the stressed vegetation and the starving ungulates were in sorry condition. Like the moose, the wolves found the island to be a bonanza. With the large numbers of prey available, their population grew to as high as fifty by the early 1980s.

But due to Lyme disease and parvovirus, which were brought to the island on the soles of human boots, the wolf population had plummeted to only twelve by 1989. So far, in the 1990s, their numbers had not recovered significantly.

Because of its isolation, the primary concern at present, was the genetic diversity of the wolf population. The remaining wolves appeared to be the offspring of one alpha female. Because of that, they could lose ten to fifteen percent of their genetic variability with each generation. If the gene pool continued to shrink, the pack's health would likewise diminish. As good health was needed to survive, something like this could ensure their eventual extinction. The future looked grim for the island's wolves.

About the same time that Grant finished his thesis, the Isle Royale management decided that they could learn a great deal more by simply letting nature take its course. So, after finalizing everything at the university, Grant went back to Ely for a week to finish packing and say good-bye to all his friends, especially Dr. Johnny Boy Jackson.

Dr. Jackson was an amazing person, and it was he who had made Grant's trip to Alaska possible. Grant had found out in early March that he had been accepted into the University of Alaska's doctoral program in wildlife biology, focusing on the predation of gray wolves. He hadn't even submitted an application to the university. It had all been arranged by Dr. Jackson. Grant was still in a state of shock.

"Excuse me, Sir," a female voice said.

Grant's eyes snapped open to see an attractive flight attendant standing in the aisle next to his seat. She appeared to be about his age.

"Can I get you anything?" she asked, with a smile. "This is the last call before we land."

"No, I don't think so," he said. "Thanks." Closing his eyes again, his thoughts drifted back to the exciting events of the last few months.

At the end of March, he had flown to Fairbanks for an interview with his new major professor, Dr. Dale Barlow, to discuss his doctoral research project while at UA. To his surprise, the director of the Alaska Wildlife Management Commission, Linsey Hogan, was at the interview as well. Miss Hogan told Grant that Dr. Jackson had contacted her personally, to recommend him highly and to inform her that his particular experience and upcoming research with Dr. Barlow, might be useful to her and the AWMC. She further explained that she had discussed with Dr. Barlow, the possibility of Grant working for the AWMC as a field agent, while conducting his research at the same time.

Miss Hogan gave him a brief synopsis of the job, which seemed to follow the program he and Dr. Barlow had outlined for his Ph.D. project. The only drawback was that it would extend the doctoral program to three years instead of two. However, Miss Hogan made a point of telling him that he would be paid as an entry level field agent with a master's degree. She added, that once he completed his doctorate, they could discuss his remaining with the AWMC in a supervisory capacity. Of course the final decision for all of this, was up to him.

It was like a dream come true. Grant would never forget that moment of exhilaration when Miss Hogan made him the offer. He was so happy he wanted to jump in the air, kick his legs out, flail his arms around, and scream at the top his lungs like a crazy man. But he didn't. Instead, he maintained his composure like a cool level-headed professional and calmly said that he would like to think about it for a few days. Then as soon as he got to the university parking lot, he leaped into the air and screamed for joy.

Of course he would accept the offer. Only a fool would turn down something like that. The job would provide him with the extra money to send to his folks when they needed it, give him plenty to live on, and still allow him to continue his education.

Before leaving for Alaska, Grant had spent the last two weeks visiting his parents. He wasn't sure if he'd gained back the twenty pounds he'd lost, but it certainly wasn't from lack of eating. He and his father took advantage of the time of year and went fishing while the crappie were on their spawning beds. Other than that, he had pretty much been a couch potato and just enjoyed the time with his folks.

Now, sitting on the plane thinking of these things, feeling relaxed and wearing a slit of a smile, Grant's brain took an unexpected turn down a dark corridor, to a more sinister memory. Since Grant had seen the horrible TV clip of the wolf that was caught in the snare trap and shot to death, the newly elected governor of Alaska had stopped all formal programs to control the population of wolves in the state. This was definitely a step in the right direction, as far as Grant was concerned. Even though he had sent numerous letters to various organizations and state departments in Alaska, he was never able to find out if the silver-blue wolf in the videotape had been killed.

For some reason, the image of that beautiful animal had stuck in his mind. Many of his nights were filled with dreams of the silver-blue wolf, though not of its being shot. He could only remember bits and pieces of the dreams, but somehow, in a strange way that he couldn't explain, he knew that the magnificent creature was still alive. Surely someone within the organization or in the state system would know what had happened to the silver-blue wolf.

He heard the familiar gong and opened his eyes. The seatbelt sign flashed on, and the captain asked over the speaker system, for the attendants to prepare for landing.

The Delta flight from Anchorage was on time, putting him into Fairbanks at 9:20 that evening. Dr. Barlow, who preferred to be call Dale, was waiting for him in the off-ramp lobby. He looked to be about the age of Grant's dad, fifty-five, and was a short round balding man, with sandy hair and a well-trimmed beard that was gray around his mouth and chin.

"Hey, Grant! Good to see you again," Dale said, holding out his hand to take one of the bags. "How was the flight?"

Grant handed Dale the smaller of the three tote bags and answered, "Fine. No problems. It's good to be here."

"Great!" Dale said with a genuine smile. They began to walk down the corridor to the airport parking lot. "You remember Helen, my wife?"

"Certainly."

"She's spent most of the weekend getting the guest room ready for you," Dale said. "It'd sure make her feel good if you'd mentioned how nice it looks."

"I'm sure she worked very hard," Grant replied as they walked along. "And I do appreciate her efforts and your hospitality. I'll be sure to say something." He didn't say it to Dale, but he would have complimented Helen without the coaching.

After they reached the Barlows', the three of them had a late dinner then stayed up for a bit, drinking white wine and talking. When they finally turned in at 11:45, he was ready. It had been a long day.

It was a little after ten on Tuesday morning when they finished breakfast. Mrs. Barlow cleared away the dishes, while Grant and Dale remained at the kitchen table sipping their coffee. So far, his first impression of Dr. Barlow was good. He liked the man. Their chemistry seemed to work—an important criterion in the relationship between a graduate student and the major professor—and he thought they were going to get along just fine.

"Well, lets get down to business," Dale said.

"Sounds good to me," Grant replied. "I'm ready."

"I think we should get together at least once a month," Dale began. "This will be like your situation at UM. You'll be doing your research on location instead of at the university. That sound all right to you?"

"Sure," Grant said. "We can meet more often if you like."

"Well, let's see how it goes. It's about ninety miles by highway, from Fairbanks to Two Forks. It's a good road, so it'll take about two hours. By plane, it's twenty minutes."

"Okay."

Dale took a sip of his coffee, leaned back in his chair, and stared hard across the kitchen table at Grant. "I don't operate like Johnny Boy does," he said flatly. "I've known Dr. Jackson for a long time, and I know he runs a pretty loose ship. But I'm the type that likes to hold the reins in my hands so I can tug back on them when I see fit. When I see students straying off in the wrong direction, I want to be able to pull them back on track."

Grant stiffened in his chair and stared back at the man. "I don't have a problem with that," he said firmly. Dr. Barlow was right. Johnny Boy was pretty free-wheeling with his grad students. As long as you were focused and motivated, like he was, that style was okay. If you weren't, it was usually a disaster for the student.

"Good," Dale said. A slight grin crept across his lips. "I require each of my students to keep a detailed daily journal of all their research activities, and to write a summary report once a month."

Grant could see that Dale was watching him, probably to see if Grant would flinch at his statement.

"The reports will give us something to talk about in our monthly meetings," Dale continued, "and will let me know just what you're up to. Also, I expect all notebooks and any other documents, to be kept in a scientific journal-quality format. Do you have a problem with any of this?"

"I don't think so," Grant answered. "In fact, I agree that accurately documenting research is very important." While working on his master's degree, he had gotten in the habit of taking elaborate notes.

"Good," Dale said again. The smile was complete this time. "Johnny Boy said you learned your research and study habits from someone other than him."

After lunch, Dale brought him back to the Fairbanks airport, and Grant caught the 1:30 flight to Two Forks, the small community where he would be living for the next few years. M & J Flying Service was the only commercial service to the town. Dr. Barlow had already made arrangements with a local businessman there, Charlie Sanford, to rent Grant a small cabin for his stay.

To his amazement, the town, with a population of only 500 people, had its own airstrip. Maybe it was because of Denali National Park and Preserve, he thought. It was just a few miles up the road, and no doubt attracted thousands of visitor every year. The main attraction, of course, was Mount McKinley, also part of the Denali National Park system, and the tallest mountain in the United States.

Grant peered out the airplane's small oval window. The plane appeared to be heading for a bank of black clouds which were dead ahead. Below, there were fewer trees than he had expected.

He thumbed through the Alaskan almanac, to page 142. He had purchased it in Ely to bring himself up to date on some of the basic facts about the state. According to the almanac, the tree line in this area was around twenty-five hundred to twenty-eight hundred feet. He lifted his eyes from the book and gazed out the window again, at the wild land below, making a mental note of the many streams and rivers that laced the bellies of the steep gorges. Most of the trees were grouped around and along these tributaries, and their growth continued halfway up the mountainsides.

This would be a much tougher and more rugged country to observe, learn, and do his research in, he thought. Determining such things as the wolf's social structure and communications; its hunting and territory habits; and its interaction with its prey and other animals in this environment, were going to be a lot more difficult than on Isle Royale. He was already beginning to get the feeling that three years to complete his research was a conservative estimate.

Slumped in the seat across the aisle from him, was an elderly man that he guessed was in his mid-sixties. The old codger was pretty rough looking, too, with scraggly long gray hair and a beard. Both were dingy yellow, apparently from lack of bathing. His scruffy clothes were just as filthy. Clumps of the mud, caked on his boots and legs of his faded jeans, had flaked off and crumbled into a fine powder on the floor of the plane. The old fellow had started snoring loudly five minutes after the plane lifted off. He had no teeth, and his lips fluttered like a dirty rag in a stiff breeze every time he exhaled. Perched atop his head was a red and black lumberjack cap with earflaps. The left earflap dangled down along the side of his face, while the other stretched across the top of the hat, which was cocked down over his forehead so the frayed bill shaded his eyes.

Grant chuckled to himself at he looked at the man, then turned his attention out the window again. The plane had veered away from the dark clouds and was beginning to descend. Just then the noisy aircraft dropped from the sky like a slab of granite. The seat belt dug into his mid-section as his body floated upward. He immediately grabbed the armrests and let out a small yelp. His stomach slapped against the back of his throat. Then the plane caught hold again and slammed him back down into the seat. The entire episode hadn't lasted more than three seconds, but to Grant it seemed to have gone on for several minutes.

The old gentlemen in the seat across the aisle grunted a couple of times, blinked his eyes, and straightened himself up in the seat. He gazed over at Grant, wiped drool from the corner of his mouth, and said, "What's the matter, sonny, got a few jet-stains in your shorts?" He cackled loudly like a barnyard roaster.

"No, not quite," Grant responded in a quiet voice, looking around to see if anyone heard the old guy.

"Won't do you much good to hold onto them armrests. If she goes down, that's it, Bub. Lights out and good night, Miss Sweet Georgia Brown. Armrests ain't going to help you none if this Beaver slams into the side of these mountains. Anyway, you best get used to flying if you're going to get around up in this country. Bet you didn't know that Alaska is the flyingest state in the whole blame Union."

"No, I guess I didn't know that," Grant said, a little shocked that the man had now turned into a jabber-box.

"That's right. It is," said the old guy. "There's one plane for every fifty-eight Alaskans. Bet you didn't know that either. According to the FAA, there's six times as many pilots and sixteen times as many airplanes per capita, as the rest of the US. Hell, there's over seven hundred airports in this state. And that's the blame truth of it."

"How do you know all this?" Grant asked, amazed that this rough looking character was spitting out all these facts like an encyclopedia of air travel.

The elderly man's eyes fluttered, and his face went sad for a second or two, as if a painful memory had called, unannounced. He glanced down at the floor of the plane for a moment, then slowly lifted his gaze back to Grant and began to talk again. The sad look was still on his face. "My son . . . He was a big-game guide and bush pilot. Damn good one, too. Maybe the best there ever was. Got killed a few years back." The old fellow gazed at Grant. "You look like you probably don't know much of anything about this country. Anyway, it wasn't the flying that sent my boy to hell, it was an earthquake that got him. He was guiding a hunting party when it happened. My son and the guy that owns this airline, were going to go into business together. That's why it's named M & J. My boy's name was Max. His buddy's name is Jerry."

"I'm sorry, Sir," Grant said. He offered his hand to the old man. "My name is Grant Rawlings. Pleased to meet you."

The crusty old guy reached into the side pocket of his dirty jeans-jacket, pulled out a business card, and handed it to Grant. The card was dingy gray and badly wrinkled. It read:

Willie (Whitie) Saylor
Experienced Guide
P.O. Box 12
Two Forks, Alaska 99743

"Been doing this line of work for nearly forty years," Whitie added. "Ain't nobody in this whole country that knows the area between Yanert Fork and Wood Creek better than old Whitie here." The old man wiped his callused wrinkled hand on his dirty jeans and stuck it across the aisle. "Pleased to meet you, Grant" he said. "If you ever need a damn good guide, or need some damn good advice, I'm your man. Just leave a note in my mail box. Number's there on the card. I check the P.O. every now and again."

"I just might do that, Mr. Saylor," Grant said. He slipped the old man's business card in his shirt pocket, then reached across the aisle and shook his hand.

"Everyone calls me Whitie. That's why it's in parentheses on the card."

"Okay, Whitie. Thanks."

While he and Whitie had been talking, the pilot landed at Two Forks Airport. The pilot unloaded everyone's luggage from a compartment at the back of the small plane and set it out on the tarmac to be picked up. Whitie was the first one off the plane, followed by Grant. Grant grabbed his three bags and headed for a small Quonset style building just beyond the plane. That's the direction Whitie was limping toward, also. Grant figured that building was the Two Forks airport.

Miss Hogan had told him there would be a field agent from the Alaska Wildlife Management Commission, waiting for him at the airport. She indicated the man was a native Alaskan, would be his helicopter pilot, and was one of the more experienced field men she had in her organization. Miss Hogan told him the field agent would take him to the vehicle the commission was providing and direct him to the cabin he had rented. Grant had forgotten the man's name. So much was happening and so fast, that he was having trouble keeping up with everything, especially people's names. He did remember, however, that it was an odd name.

When Grant walked through the door of the small building, there was only one person in the room, a tall slender man holding up a rectangular piece of cardboard that was large enough to hide the man's face. In large handwritten block letters scrawled across the cardboard, was his name, GRANT RAWLINGS.

He found it comical to see his name plastered up like that. After all, there had only been eight people on the plane, and this guy was the only person waiting for anyone. With a smile on his face, Grant walked up to the man holding the sign, set his luggage down, held out his hand, and said, "Hi, I think I'm the one you're looking for. I'm Grant Rawlings."

When the man lowered the sign, Grant's eyes drifted upward. He caught his breath and stepped back, not knowing whether this was a joke and he should laugh, whether this guy was for real and he should be in awe, or whether he should be just plain frightened.

The man had to be at least six-seven and had bright red hair that was neatly braided and laced with multiple colored beads. Each braid hung down below the breast pockets of his green AWMC jacket. The most striking feature of the man's chiseled high-cheeked face, was a long ugly scar. It began just above the left eyebrow, sliced across the eyelid, continued down the cheek, and finally stopped at the jawline. Peeking out from behind the man's head, were two black feathers shaped like a V.

The tall Indian lifted his right hand, palm outward, just like in the old western movies, and slowly said in broken syllables, "How. My name is Victor Trnavsky." Victor lowered the large hand and offered it to Grant, continuing to speak in a slow broken fashion. "It is good to meet you, Grant Rawlings."

Grant slowly accepted Victor's hand and just looked up. That's when Victor started laughing. Bent over, with his hands on his knees, Victor laughed so hard he began to cough.

Grant just stood there, in a state of shock, watching the back of Victor's head bob around. Red hair? Victor? Miss Hogan had said the man was a native Alaskan, but Grant wasn't sure what to think.

Still bent over, the man whooped and sputtered, while the two long braids dangling in front, swung back and forth. One of the feathers pinned in his hair, jarred loose from all the commotion and floated to the floor. The remaining feather was ajar and cocked to one side. It became apparent to Grant that this had all been a practical joke.

Grant wondered what kind of person this man would be like to work with. Obviously he was a jokester, something Grant wasn't too fond of. There was serious work to be done, and there wasn't any time for funny business.

When Victor finally stood up, his face matched the color of his fiery red hair and tears trickled from the corners of his eyes. He continued to chuckle for a few more moments, then finally got command of his voice enough to mumble a few words. "Man, you should have seen your face. I wish I had a picture of it." He laughed a little more, then said, "This all the gear you have?" His speech was no longer slow and broken.

Grant said, "That's all I brought on the plane. I shipped the rest of my things. They should be here in a few days." He reached down for his luggage and grabbed two of the bags.

"I'll get this one," Victor said, grabbing the third before Grant could get to it. Victor wiped the tears from his eyes with the palm of his free hand. "Come on. Let's throw these in your truck, and I'll show you where you're staying."

They crossed the room, which was about thirty steps wide, and walked out the door. Two light green late-model Suburbans, with AWMC decals on the sides, were parked nearby. The only other vehicles, were a few cars and pickups about sixty yards to their right. They were parked along the sides of two airplane hangars that were each large enough to accommodate three or four small planes. Behind the two buildings, there were three helicopters, and several airplanes resembling Piper Cubs.

"This one's yours. The keys are in it. I gassed her up for you," Victor said, pointing to the shiny Suburban on the right. He handed Grant his bag and headed to the second car, which was completely covered with gray mud. "Yours will look like mine in a day or two," he said with a grin as he climbed into the truck. "Follow me and I'll take you to your cabin. It's about ten miles from here."

Grant nodded. He was still shocked that he was getting a truck, and nearly a new one at that. He tossed his bags in the back seat and climbed in. Cranking up the huge vehicle, he backed out and followed his new coworker.

He hadn't noticed it before, but as he pulled away from the small airstrip, he saw the Alaska Range peaks in the distance, looming up in the blue sky. The highest of them was Mount McKinley, at over twenty thousand feet. Their barren slopes were beautiful and majestic, with something almost spiritual about them. The gloomy bank of clouds he had seen earlier from the airplane, had moved farther north, leaving the snow-covered summits of the mountains, unveiled for the onlooker's pleasure.

It was a short distance from the airport to State Highway 3. They crossed it and continued on the narrow paved road. He compiled mental notes of the new area for future reference.

About a mile after crossing the highway, a Two Forks city limit sign came up on his left. With a population of only five hundred people, there wasn't much to the main drag—a Conoco gas station on the right, Marie's Grocery, the Two Forks Laundromat, a post office, and Sally's Wilderness Diner. That was it. That was Two Forks, Alaska.

Just as he passed two empty buildings on the outskirts of town, he caught a movement out of the corner of his right eye. He glanced over and saw a bull moose casually strolling between the buildings, gawking each way as if it were looking out for traffic. He slowed down for a moment, chuckled to himself, then sped up to catch Victor.

Grant smiled as he turned right onto another narrow paved road about a half-mile out of town. The street sign indicated he had been on Main Street and was now turning onto Crooked Creek Road. He liked small, out-of-the-way places like this, free from the hustle and bustle of large cities, with their crime, poverty, and violence.

He checked the mileage on the odometer. He'd been on Crooked Creek Road now for just over two miles. To his left, a business had carved out a spot in the middle of a grove of white spruce. Burned into the wooden sign hanging over the front door, were the words: TRADING POST. The log-cabin style building was about twice the size of the airport building. There were three gas pumps out front, and all were in use. The white gravel parking lot was nearly full, and the place was like a beehive, with people coming and going in their pickups and Suburbans. There seemed to be more business going on here than in the whole town of Two Forks.

Still following Victor, and just a few feet beyond the Trading Post, he crossed a bridge that spanned the Nenana River, which was several hundred feet wide. Two and a half miles past the Trading Post, the pavement ran out. Grant could now see where the name Crooked Creek Road came from. The road mirrored every curve and bend in the stream that roared along its right side. The stream was a tributary of the Nenana River.

He reached down for the lever in the floorboard of the Suburban and slipped it into four-wheel drive, to accommodate the muddy rutted road. To his left, aspens, and white and black spruce covered the steep slopes of the wild landscape. He recalled reading in his almanac, that this type of forest was called "taiga," a name given by the first Russian trappers in Alaska. It meant "land of little sticks."

Three miles down the road, the stream split. Victor turned right onto the narrow side road that followed the right-hand fork in the stream. Close behind, Grant slowed when Victor pulled up by a wooden bridge that crossed Crooked Creek. It was badly in need of repair, and he was doubtful as to whether the bridge would accommodate the weight of both vehicles. He brought his truck to a halt and waited until Victor was safely on the other side. Before crossing the dilapidated structure, he checked his shoulder harness and seat belt. Swallowing hard, he tightened his grip on the steering wheel and drove very carefully. Where in the world was this Alaskan taking him, anyway?

They had gone another two miles, when the dirt road they were on veered off to the left. Victor continued straight, on what looked like an old logging trail that hadn't been used for many years.

When Dale Barlow told Grant the cabin he had found for him was isolated, he certainly wasn't kidding. This place was really in the wilderness. Grant began to get visions of a run-down prospector's shack built in the late 1800s, with an old fellow traveling to town with pack mules for his monthly supplies.

It was another mile and a half before he finally pulled up to the small, one-room, log cabin. To his surprise, the building and the immediate surroundings looked to be well cared for. The cabin was about twenty feet square. The front door, which was in the center of it, had a small covered stoop and windows on each side of it. A rick of wood was stacked just to the right of the door.

By the time Grant stepped from his car, Victor stood in the doorway, with a cheerful smile plastered on his face. The lanky Indian anxiously waved for him to come and inspect the inside of the cabin.

When Grant walked through the doorway he could hardly believe how neat and clean everything was. "Man, this place is nice. I didn't expect this. How much is it going to cost me, anyway?"

"Don't worry about it," Victor said. "Charlie'll treat you fair. Charlie's dad, Hank, used to live here. That's why it's in such good shape. They were close. Real close. He's been dead for a couple of years now."

"This is really great. Out in the sticks, but great," Grant said as he walked through the cabin. To his left, the wall was solid native stone. Molded in the center of the wall was a huge fireplace. Sitting in front of it was a large beige sofa. There was a handmade pine end table at one end of the sofa, and atop it was a lamp made of a unique wood that Grant had never seen before. Earlier, he had noticed that Victor wore an Indian pendant laced on a leather tether around his neck, and he now realized it was made of the same wood.

Stretched out over the fireplace was a beautifully designed black and white Indian blanket. Sitting at an angle against the far corner of the stone wall, was a wood cookstove. To the right of that was a tidy kitchen area, that included cabinets and a small counter with a sink. Behind the front door and to his right, was a bed. It was small, but large enough for a single adult.

"From the look on your face, I take it you approve of the cabin?" Victor asked.

"Approve? You bet I approve," Grant said enthusiastically. His eyes continued to scan the room. In the center of the wall on the far right, was an antique dresser with a mirror. Beside it was a blue and white pitcher sitting in a large dark blue bowl that was cradled in an ornately carved wooden washstand. There was a door in the center of the back wall, and like the one in the front of the house, it had two windows evenly spaced on each side of it.

Victor had wandered to the back of the cabin and stood next to a small wooden desk. Looking down at it, he slowly moved his finger around the glass lip of the kerosene lamp's chimney. "Charlie's dad spent many hours at this desk before he died," Victor said with obvious sadness in his voice. "He liked it because it overlooks the creek. He was a writer. Wrote frontier adventure novels. You know, gold rush stuff and all that. He was a real good man. A lot of him rubbed off on Charlie." Then Victor stared out the window, as if looking into the past and recalling a memorable moment.

Meanwhile, Grant had walked across the room and opened the back door. "My God. This is beautiful." Thirty feet from the back of the cabin, a crystal clear stream hurried along, gurgling and swirling. He closed his eyes and inhaled deeply, sucking in the pristine air. A few moments later, he asked, "What's the name of this creek?"

"Denning Fork," Victor answered as he walked over to Grant and stood next to him in the doorway. "Victor was quiet for a moment again then said, "I was just thinking about Hank and how many times he and I wetted flies while fishing that stream for trout. He loved this place, and he especially loved to hear the wolves howl. This creek used to be one of the wolves favorite places to den. That's why it's named Denning Fork."

Grant opened his eyes and looked at Victor. "You say that as if the wolves don't den there anymore."

"They don't. But we've got plenty of time to talk about that. Right now let me show you around the place." Victor went down the three wooden steps leading from the back door. He motioned with his hand and said, "Come on."

Grant followed. "Hey, what's that?" he asked, pointing to a structure that looked like a miniature log cabin mounted on stilts. It was located in a clearing, thirty to forty feet northeast of him.

"It's called a cache. That's c-a-c-h-e," Victor said. "It's a small storage building for just about anything you want to have on hand—extra fuel, bedding, whatever. Some people use them as food freezers in the winter. They're built on stilts, so animals like bears, dogs, foxes, or any other hungry or curious critters can't get to them. You can get up to it by using that ladder on the ground next to it."

That's when it dawned on Grant that he hadn't seen a refrigerator, or any other electrical appliance in the house. The lamp on the end table was the only electrical device he could remember seeing in the cabin. "Does this cabin have electricity?" he asked. "I have a notebook computer I need to use for my research." The thought of not being able to use the computer his parents had given him, left an empty hole in his stomach.

"No electricity. No running water. No bathroom," Victor replied. He pointed behind Grant and said, "There is your john over there."

Grant glanced over his shoulder. Partially hidden behind a clump of willows, was an outhouse. You've got to be kidding, he thought to himself. No running water and no bathroom? That wasn't good, but he guessed he could live without those if he had to. But no electricity? That was a major problem. He brought his attention back to Victor.

"You can take a bath in the stream," Victor explained, "though you probably won't do that for a while because the water's too cold. Otherwise, you saw the washstand inside. You can use it with water from the stream to give yourself a sponge bath, or, if you like, you can just smell like a goat." Victor's face maintained its serious expression. After a moment, he grinned. "Just kidding."

"Right." Grant forced a smile. This place wasn't looking quite as attractive as it did at first.

Victor reached out and lightly tapped him on the shoulder. "Lighten up, Grant," he said. You're going to love it around here. We're kind of a laid-back bunch. Nothing exciting ever happens in Two Forks. It's just smooth going."

"Smooth going. Yeah, that sounds great," he replied, with a few doubts.

"Let's go get your luggage so you can get settled in." Victor pointed and said, "Let's go this way. I want to show you something else." He turned and headed for the southwest end of the cabin.

As they rounded the corner, Victor said, "If you want to use your computer you can fire this baby up."

There, next to the cabin, was a gas generator. "Oh, great! Does this thing work?" Grant asked hopefully.

"Of course it works. I had an old guy named Whitie take a look at it."

"I think met him on the plane. Long white hair and beard?" He pulled the wrinkled business card from his shirt pocket and looked at it. "Whitie Saylor, experienced guide."

"That's him, all right. Some of our local color," Victor said. "Anyway, I had him gas 'er up and install a new plug and points. There's more gas in a plastic five gallon can in your truck."

"Thanks, Victor. I really appreciate it," Grant said. "Believe me this will come in very handy."

"Nah, don't think anything of it. Let's go back to the trucks. I have a little surprise for you."

When they got there, Victor opened the back doors of his vehicle, leaned inside, and reached into a wooden box. He lifted out a large metal cooking pot, with a lid and wire handle over the top. "Here, take this. My wife cooked up a big batch of moose stew. Since it gets so cool around here at night, this ought to stay fresh for better than a week. This'll give you something to eat until you get to the grocery store."

Grant took the pot from his new working partner and said, "That was very thoughtful of you, Victor. Very thoughtful. Tell your wife I said thanks." Grant was touched that he had even thought of such a thing. This was something his mother would have done to welcome someone new in the community.

Just then the ground trembled. Grant's eyes darted down to the tinny rattle of the lid, as it vibrated off the pot and clanked to the ground. "What was that?" he asked, clutching the car door for balance. Then it was over. The ground had stop shaking, but his legs were still quivering. "An earthquake?"

Victor chuckled, "Ah, that was nothing. That was just a little tremor. We get quakes up here all the time."

"You're kidding. Here in Alaska?"

"Yeah, here in Alaska," Victor answered. "Most people don't know it, but Alaska is the most seismic of all fifty states."

"I didn't know that."

"Since 1900, there have been over seventy-five earthquakes that were 7 or higher on the Richter scale. The worst one of all, though, was Black Friday. Actually, it was on Good Friday, March 27, 1964. Man, I'll never forget that day. That baby hit 9.2. It was the strongest earthquake ever recorded in North America. The scientists say it was ten million times stronger than the bomb dropped on Hiroshima in World War II. During the next two months or so, there were twelve thousand jolts that were 3.5 or higher."

"Ten million times," Grant said, amazed at the fact. "What's the most recent one that's hit in the 7s?"

"Four years ago. It registered 7.6. That one was right around here, too. In fact, they say the epicenter was about three miles southeast of this cabin."

"Anyone get hurt?"

"Yeah, three men were killed," Victor answered. "One of them was Whitie's son. The old guy has never recovered from it either. At one time, Whitie was one of the best big-game guides in these parts. Now he's the town drunk. It's sad."

"I'm sorry to hear that," Grant said.

"Look, I'd better get going," Victor said. "I want to check out Flutter Butt before we head out in the morning."

"Who?" Grant asked, puzzled.

"Flutter Butt. That's what I call the chopper."

"Oh, okay. Flutter Butt," he said, thinking that was an unusual name for an aircraft.

"You remember seeing the Trading Post on the way to your cabin?"

"Yeah."

"Well, meet me there in the morning about seven, and I'll buy you breakfast," Victor said. "That'll give us a chance to talk about a few things before our meeting with Miss Linsey Hogan."

Grant noticed Victor's voice changed when he mentioned Miss Hogan's name, almost as if there was a lack of respect.

"Then we'll go up in Flutter Butt, and I'll show you from the air, the area you'll be studying."

"Okay, sounds great, Victor. I'll see you bright and early in the morning. Don't forget to thank your wife for me, for the moose stew."

Victor nodded as he got in his Suburban and drove away.

Chapter 4

It was a bone-shivering twenty-two degrees inside the cabin. Grant leaned over the kitchen sink and glared in disbelief at the thermometer that was tacked to the side of the cabinet, next to the window overlooking Denning Fork. The steam from his mouth and nostrils instantly frosted a circular imprint of his breath on the window.

He was bundled up in one of the three woolen blankets he had found neatly folded under the bed. Even though he'd covered his feet with two pairs of sweat socks, worn his long underwear, and scrunched up into a ball under the three blankets, the frigid temperatures nipped at him all night long.

"Man, it's cold in here," he said. Tugging the blanket tighter around his head and under his chin, he hobbled over to the wood cookstove. He shook all over from the cold in the room. Luckily his mother had gotten him a battery-powered digital alarm clock for his birthday last year. When it went off at 5:45, Grant's only thought as he lumbered out of bed, was HEAT. Last night he'd fired up the stove to warm up the moose stew, which he had to admit tasted incredible. Victor was absolutely right, though. As cold as it got here in the evenings, there would be no fear of the stew going bad for a long time, maybe even a month or two.

The warmth from last night's orange-glowing embers had been reduced to gray cold ashes, and he'd had to restart the fire earlier this morning. At the moment, the only place in this iceberg-of-a-cabin where there was any warmth at all, was near the stove. It was beginning to warm up just a little. Still cocooned in the blanket, Grant backed up as close as he dared, to the stove.

Atop the stove, was a small pan of water he was heating for coffee. He'd discovered some useful items on the kitchen counter yesterday afternoon, after he'd brought in his luggage—a gallon jug of bottled water, a jar of Taster's Choice, a jar of Coffee-mate creamer, and a small TUPPERWARE container of sugar. A hand-written note, propped up against the sugar bowl, read:

> Dear Grant,
> Here's the fixing's for your coffee in the morning. Hope instant is OK. I don't know about you, but I have to have a steamy cup of java first thing in the morning to get my motor started. Stop by the Trading Post when you get a chance, and we'll discuss the arrangements on the cabin. I'm looking forward to meeting you. If there's anything you need, let me know.
>
> Charlie

That was a thoughtful note. He liked this person already and hadn't even met him. Grant reached over from where he stood, picked up the note and inspected it a little closer. The handwriting was clean and delicate, with almost a feminine quality.

He noticed steam floating up from the pan on the stove. The water had just begun to boil. He pulled a brown mug from the cabinet, quickly made his coffee, and hurried back to the warmth of the woodstove, trying to wake up.

He had gone to bed late. After putting his things away and building a fire in the fireplace, Grant had wanted try out the gas generator and notebook computer. He'd forgotten that the daylight hours were longer here this time of year, than when he was in Minnesota. In fact, by June 22, the time of the summer solstice, this area would have nearly twenty-two hours of daylight. It was some time after ten before it had actually gotten dark, allowing him time to investigate the area outside the cabin a little more and start up the generator. To his relief, the computer worked fine.

This eased his anxiety because his handwriting was atrocious. Between making detailed daily notes on his research, and writing a monthly report, it would have been messy and slow-going without a computer. Also, Grant had been thinking about starting a diary to record his daily adventures while here in Alaska. So last night before turning in, he'd made his first entries, writing about his experiences of the past few days, about the people he'd met, and of course about Victor, his new work companion.

The cabin was beginning to warm slightly. Cradling his hot coffee, Grant shuffled over to the sofa in front of the fireplace and plopped down. The heavy woolen blanket was still draped over his shoulders. He set the mug on the end table and picked up a loose-leaf notebook and pen.

He'd had a dream of the silver-blue wolf again, and this time it was more intense. It had returned to him in his sleep last night, and before its memory completely evaded him, Grant wanted to jot down whatever fragments he could still remember. He would wait until this evening to enter them in the computer.

There was something in the dream about water. The silver-blue wolf was running and splashing in a mountain stream, stopping occasionally to lap up the cool, clear water. Suddenly, the landscape in the background shuddered, becoming twisted and distorted. The wolf tumbled into the stream, which had changed from a beautiful flowing brook, to something vile, stagnant, and stenchful. It had the crimson color and thick consistency of blood. The dark liquid hung from the wolf's snout like cold molasses on a frosty winter morning. The poor creature's head was the only part of its body that was above the surface of the putrid mess. In a desperate attempt to save its life, the animal struggled to lift its paws from the muck and dog-paddle to freedom. Surrounding the wolf were the rotting carcasses of hundreds of other animals, whose bodies were floating in the blood-water. That was all Grant could remember.

He reread what he'd just written. When he finished, a cold chill, unrelated to the temperature in the cabin, shot down his back. It was a horrible dream. He had heard or read somewhere, that dreams were messages from a person's subconscious. However, this dream was too weird to have any kind of an underlying message. He was sure of that. Yet the fact that he was still having these dreams of the silver-blue wolf after six months, was strange. He would ask Victor about the videotape he'd seen on TV last winter, and whether the silver-blue wolf had been killed or set free. Surely, he would know.

Grant laid the notebook back on the end table and pulled himself up from the sofa, leaving the crumpled blanket behind. Taking his mug, he walked toward the washstand. The battery-powered digital clock on the dresser next to the bed, read 6:10. He sipped the coffee and decided it was time to get ready for work, as he was supposed to meet Victor at the Trading Post by seven.

Setting the mug on the dresser, he picked up the pitcher from the washstand and headed toward the back door of the cabin. He'd just get some water from the stream and give himself, what Victor had called, a sponge bath. This wasn't really going to be so bad once he got into a regular routine. In fact, he kind of liked the idea of not having electricity or running water. Most of all, he liked being stuck out in the sticks by himself. Oh sure, it would be a little inconvenient, but he'd learn to improvise. He'd survive this less privileged environment with no problem.

After slipping his feet into cold boots, he opened the back door. Immediately, like a slab of ice, the frigid morning air slapped him in the face. As Grant hurried down the steps, he wondered just how cold the water in the stream was, and if he'd have to heat it up before washing.

A light fog had settled in the lowlands and hung over Denning Fork like a delicate garment swaying in a breeze. When Grant lifted his head and glanced toward the stream, he thought he saw a pair of golden eyes peering at him from across the brook. But just then a wave of thicker fog swirled over the water and erased the glaring eyes from view.

Grant stood there motionless, holding his breath, and not knowing exactly what he had seen, or even if he had seen anything at all. The seconds ticked by. He began to shiver in his long johns, as he stood there cradling the blue and white pitcher like a small infant.

Finally he exhaled, and a large cloud of steam rushed from his mouth and nostrils. Either he had imagined seeing something, or the animal went on its way. If he stood out here much longer, frostbite might settle into the tips of his fingers or other appendages. He chuckled about the "other appendages."

As he hurried to the stream, clutching the pitcher tightly to his chest, Grant wondered if it was just a memory fragment from the freaky dream he'd had last night. Dismissing the thought, he scanned the far bank of Denning Fork, hobbling around in his untied boots, which slid up and down on his heels. Nothing was there. Must have been his imagination. Reaching the edge of the cold rapidly flowing stream, he knelt down and plunged the pitcher into the water, filling it.

When Grant stood back up, his eyes automatically looked to the other side of Denning Fork. Mysteriously, the fog had parted as if it was an orchestrated special effect in a low-budget horror film. From out of the mist, came a large silver-blue wolf, head held high, staring directly at him.

With a start, Grant lurched back and sucked in a large gulp of frigid air, burning his throat down to his lungs. As before, he stood there like a granite statue, while his right hand quivered as it held the handle of the full pitcher. Freezing water dripped from his left hand, which was supporting the bottom of the pitcher, and splattered onto his right boot.

The wolf's penetrating eyes seemed to mesmerize him. Grant felt like they were looking inside him and probing his soul. In a flash, the magnificent creature spun on its hind legs and vanished into the ghostly murkiness, like a phantom apparition. Its movements were swift, but had such grace and agility. The loud screech of an eagle circling overhead, echoed through the ravine and jarred him out of his trance. The entire thing had happened so quickly, Grant wasn't really certain if he had seen a wolf or not.

Billy Jack Boone came to the Trading Post most mornings, to eat breakfast and pick up the day's clients. A big-game guide, he had taken over his father's hunting business at eighteen—the summer he graduated from high school. That was fourteen years ago—the year his father had taken a party of three out for a hunt and his plane malfunctioned, going down near Anderson Pass in the Denali National Park wilderness. All on board were killed.

Since Billy Jack was an only child and his mother had died giving birth to him, his father's death left him completely alone. There were no relatives or close friends he could rely on, for help or guidance. Whether Billy Jack liked it or not, he was forced to learn how to provide for himself.

He had always been an independent lad, but faced with taking care of himself at such an early age, he went deeper into his shell. What few friends he had from high school, he eventually drove away, and he was left totally alone. As time went on, he became more hardened and withdrawn, shying away from the local people. For social recreation, Billy Jack had gotten into the habit of flying to Anchorage once a week, where he had a number of business relationships, and a few personal friends. But to support himself, he maintained his father's local guide service, and he had turned it into a very profitable business.

At six-four and 220 pounds, Billy Jack was a big man. He had a wedge-like physique, short curly hair that was coal-black, and a full well-trimmed beard that he'd had since he was twenty-two. His crisp brown eyes were shadowed by thick eyebrows that had grown together. Where there were no whiskers, his chiseled face had the weathered appearance of an outdoorsman. Most of the time he was clad in high-top boots, blue jeans, a red and black checkered flannel shirt, and a dark-blue knit watch cap. He looked more like a lumberjack than a professional guide and businessman. His presence was intimidating to most folks in the area, and he had gained the reputation of being brash, inconsiderate, and a bully. But, he also had a reputation as one of the best guides in all of Alaska's interior.

Billy Jack opened the door of the Ford Ranger, peeled himself from the seat and rolled out of the vehicle. Immediately, the mouth-watering aroma of the Trading Post's kitchen, invaded his nose. It was a few minutes before seven. The parking lot was nearly full, like it was most mornings this time of year. He had stayed up later than usual with his hobby last night and was feeling the consequences of his passion, this morning. Today, he had two novice clients from the Midwest, who wanted to shoot caribou, moose, grizzly, and he supposed, anything else in the wild they could get in their sights.

There were two front doors to the Trading Post. The right one lead to the diner, while the left one went to the general store, where you could buy supplies for hunting, camping, fishing, cooking, hiking, and just about anything else a person might need in this part of the country.

He stepped inside the diner and heard the usual tinkle from the bell hanging just above the door. Billy Jack surveyed the L-shaped room. Only two of the eight stools at the counter were empty. Charlie was at the cash register waiting on a customer. The freak red-headed Indian, Victor, was sitting in the far corner sipping his coffee and staring at him, as if he was Satan himself. There were ten rustic pine tables, with four wooden chairs per table, neatly placed around the room. There were people eating their breakfasts at about half of them. There was a low rumble in the room from talk of yesterday's events and today's adventures. As usual, Jonah Irick, the cook's twelve-year-old son, was bussing tables, and Whitie Saylor, the local drunk, was sitting at the counter slouched over a cup of coffee.

The woman from a young couple sitting at a table on the north wall waved at Billy Jack and asked, "Mr. Boone?"

"Yes?" he responded.

"We're the Petersons, your clients for today," the woman said.

"Just a moment. Let me get a cup of coffee first." Billy Jack figured that she must have recognized him from the picture in the brochure he'd sent them. He really wasn't looking forward to taking these two pups out this morning. But he had to make a living.

Jonah hurried by with a tray of dirty dishes. He reached out and mussed the boy's hair. "What's up this morning, Brat?" Billy Jack teased.

Immediately the boy, pulled away and curtly said, "Jerk." Then he turned his back and started walking off toward the kitchen.

Billy Jack was in no mood for any smart talk this morning, especially from some kid. Quietly, he rushed up behind the boy and pinched him hard on the arm.

"Ouch!" Jonah yelled, dropping the tray of dishes. With a loud crash, greasy plates, juice glasses, coffee cups, and saucers shattered on the pinewood floor.

Whitie Saylor jumped from his stool as if someone had shot off a cannon. Spinning around to see the mess scattered all over the floor, he grumbled, "For crying-out-loud, what's going on around here? Can't an old man have some peace and quiet for Christ's sake? Man can't even drink his coffee in peace anymore!"

"Billy Jack made me do it, Whitie!" the boy hollered. "He pinched my arm. It was his fault."

With his lame leg slightly dragging across the floor, Whitie limped over to where Billy Jack stood, looked up into his face, and said, "Now most people around here might be afraid of you, Boy. But I'm not too danged old to turn you over my knee and give you a good walloping."

The old man's breath was so rich with stale alcohol, it made Billy Jack's eyes water. He could see that this was going to be a bad day. With a smirk, he glared right back at Whitie and said,

"You better sit down before you fall down, Old Man. Now get out of my way so I can get some coffee." He pushed past Whitie and marched up to the counter, crunching through the broken glassware on the floor. "How about a cup of coffee and one of those longjohns, Charlie?" he asked.

"Well good morning to you too, Billy Jack," Charlie said. "Looks like you are your usual personable self this bright morning. How about you helping Jonah there clean up that mess you made, first, and of course shell out some dough for the damages?"

Before he could reply to the sharp-tongued innkeeper, he felt someone tugging on the sleeve of his shirt. When he turned around, there was Whitie again, staring up at him through squinted eyes. The old man was swaying from side to side, obviously loaded up to the gills. Both of Whitie's fists were clenched and held up in front of him.

"You don't scare me, you big bully," Whitie blabbered. "I can remember when you were a snot-nosed little runt. You were meaner than snake oil then, and that part of you ain't changed one bit. Now you help this boy clean up this mess and pay Charlie the damages. Fifty dollars ought to do it. Then get your butt out of here and don't come back. Or I'm going to clean your plow."

Billy Jack was in a foul mood as it was, and he didn't need this, not this morning.

"It's okay, Whitie," Charlie said. "I can handle this on my own."

"That's all right, Charlie. It's about time someone showed this young pup a thing or two. He's got no consideration for anybody," Whitie slurred.

"That's it. I've had enough of this bull," Billy Jack said. He reached out and gripped Whitie by the arms, lifted the old man straight up in the air, then stuffed him down on a stool. "Now like I said, you old coot, drink your coffee or go sleep it off."

Grant checked his watch. It was 6:58. "Right on time," he said as he opened the door to the Trading Post.

Just as he stepped inside, a large, muscular man that looked like a lumberjack, slammed the old man he'd met on the plane, Whitie Saylor, down on a stool at the counter. It took Grant by surprise at first, and he wondered just what was going on. His eyes ran across the silent room. Everyone had stopped eating and talking, and their stares were directed to the counter area of the diner. Victor was getting up from his chair at a corner table. The Indian's face was twisted with anger. Directly in front of him, toward the counter, was a young boy scraping up broken dishes from the floor. The boy looked as if he was about to cry.

"Now give me some coffee and a longjohn," the lumberjack-looking character said. His back was to Grant, who had begun to ease toward the brute.

The lady at the cash register stomped out from behind the counter. Grant was immediately taken by her. The way her long legs carried her around the corner of the counter, made his stomach quiver. She looked to be in her early thirties, about 120 pounds, and kind of tall—around five-six. The way she confidently strode up to the man and placed her hands on her hips, there was no question this woman was a ball of fire. Her short auburn hair accentuated her light blue eyes and creamy white skin. The sleeves of her blue and charcoal plaid shirt were rolled up above her wrists, exposing the knit, long-john top she had on underneath. She also wore hiking boots and tight new blue jeans that underscored her slim figure.

Grant hadn't had much time to date while working on his master's degree. In fact, he hadn't ever been seriously involved with a woman in his whole life. Even though he had never meet this woman, there was something about her that did strange things to his insides. Things he had never felt before.

"Just who do you think you are, Billy Jack Boone," the feisty woman said in a low raspy voice. Her cheeks were flushed with anger, and her eyes seemed to slice through him like a knife. "Coming in here like a cocky banty rooster, shoving old men around, and picking on little kids. We've had enough of your bully tactics." The wiry woman stood right in front of Billy Jack, practically in his face.

Billy Jack just laughed at the woman and said, "Are you done? Now can I have my coffee and longjohn?"

"I'm not joking! I've about had it with your attitude here this morning!" she growled, shoving a finger toward his face.

Billy Jack caught it and began to twist her arm. "I don't think you better do that again."

"Take your hands off of her," Grant demanded, as he grabbed the man's arm. A quick flash went through his mind. Why in the world he was getting involved in all this?

The next thing he knew he'd been hurled across the room and was banging into several tables and chairs and a few of the customers. He sat sprawled on the floor, partly dazed, staring up at the man with the black beard, who was towering over him.

The man said, "And you are?"

Before Grant could get to his feet and respond to the brute, another man in a tan uniform stepped between the two of them and said, "That's enough, Billy Jack. Go sit down with your clients and behave yourself like a normal human being. I'll bring your coffee and longjohn to you."

"Fine. That's all I asked for," Billy Jack said with irritation. As he started to strut away he turned his head. "Sheriff, you moonlighting now, waiting tables?" Then he walked by Grant and stopped for a moment. "I'll see you again, Wonder Boy. We'll get to know each other up close and personal." Then he continued on his way, weaving between tables and chairs, to the young couple seated by the north wall.

A small feminine hand appeared in front of Grant's face. "Hi. I'm Charlie Sanford, the owner of this place. Let me give you a hand."

He looked up in surprise to see the woman who had sent flutters through his stomach. She was also, he just now realized, his landlady. How embarrassing, he thought. Her lips were curved in a gentle, sincere smile, and her face was even more beautiful close up. He sat there for a second, consumed by her gorgeous eyes. They twinkled with the morning sunlight, which glinted off the large plate glass window in the front of the building.

"Hey Pal, you all right?" she asked, bending over and looking more closely into his eyes.

"Yeah. . . . I'm okay. Thanks," he said and grasped the woman's hand. He was immediately struck by the strength of her grip and the ease with which she pulled him to his feet. More than that, though, her hand felt warm and gentle. It was not particularly soft, however, just warm and gentle, like the way his grandmother's hand felt. He stood there, just staring in her eyes.

Charlie cocked her head and propped her hands on her hips. "Well, do you have a name or not?"

"Oh, sure. I'm sorry. Grant Rawlings, your new tenant," he said. "You know, the cabin."

"Mr. Rawlings, the student Dr. Barlow called me about," she said, extending her hand. "Pleased to meet you." Her eyes were locked on him now, but not in an uncomfortable way. "Thanks for you help. I'm sorry we had to meet like this."

Before he could say anything, the sheriff stuck out his hand and said, "And I'm Frank Kicklighter, the peacekeeper in this area. Pleased to make your acquaintance, Mr. Rawlings. Yeah, I'm sorry too, about this little incident. Usually, it's pretty quiet around here."

"Yeah, that's what Victor told me," Grant said.

"Look, I have to get back to work," Charlie said. She turned to walk away, then looked back at him and held out her right hand, wiggling her fingers. "We'll talk later. Is it okay to call you Grant?"

"Uh . . . yeah, sure. That's what everyone calls me," he said, distracted by Charlie's beauty. She laughed as she walked toward the cash register to take care of a customer. She must have noticed his clumsiness and obvious fascination with her

Frank smiled and followed her. "Charlie, I'll get that coffee and longjohn for Billy Jack."

"Come on, Lover Boy. Let's go sit down," someone said, grabbing his arm. It was Victor.

"Thanks, Sam," Charlie said after giving the customer his change and closing the register drawer. "I'm pretty sure we have that many snare traps. Check with Butch next door at the general store."

"Thanks, Charlie, I'll do that. Oh, by the way. Tell Edith the waffles were great this morning." Sam turned and head for the front door.

"I will," Charlie said. "Edith always likes to hear that her cooking is good." Charlie's eyes were fixed on the young man with Victor, as she spoke. The two men were sitting at the table in the far corner.

"Charlie, I'm sorry about the dishes," Jonah said, looking up at her. He was holding a dish tray half full of broken plates, cups, and glasses.

"That's okay, Honey," she said, laying her hand on the boy's shoulder. "Dump the tray in the trash out back."

This was the first year Jonah had worked part-time for her. He had just turned twelve in March, and that's when his mother said it would be okay for him to work a few hours a day at the Trading Post, as long as it didn't interfere with his school work. They agreed he could go in for a while, before and after school. Charlie told Jonah she agreed with his mother, and in fact, she wanted to see his report card too, to be sure the job wasn't affecting his grades.

"These broken dishes aren't going to come out of my pay are they?" the boy asked. "It really was Billy Jack's fault."

"No, it's not going to come out of your pay, silly. And yes, I know it was Billy Jack's fault," she said, comforting the boy. She leaned over and kissed him on the top of his head. "Now come on. Let's go back in the kitchen and see what we can do to help your mother."

Before she followed Jonah through the two swinging doors leading to the kitchen, she glanced back at Grant. The young man was staring at her. She smiled at him, looked away, and hustled on into the kitchen.

"I haven't seen that sparkle in your eyes since that guy you dated a few years ago," Edith Irick said as Charlie entered the kitchen. "What was his name? Hank something or other? You remember, that helicopter mechanic stationed at Fort Greely. The one that disappeared in the middle of the night."

"Please don't remind me of him," Charlie said, avoiding eye contact with the cook as she opened the large refrigerator door. "And I don't know what you're talking about . . . sparkle in my eyes. It was the sunlight from the windows."

Edith had been the Trading Post's cook for as long as she could remember. She was here when Charlie bought the place seven years ago, and Edith was here when she used to come in as a customer, before she'd even dreamt of buying the place. They had struggled through some pretty hard times together with the business. As a result, a close bond between them had developed. Edith was in her early fifties and a very special person in her life. Sometimes she was like a mother, with her wisdom and advice about almost everything. Sometimes she was like an older sister, consoling her and boosting her spirits when they needed it. And sometimes she was just a good friend, someone she could sit down and drink a beer with and have a nice conversation.

"Sun, my eye," Edith said with a noticeable grunt. "What do you take me for? I know that look. I've had it myself a time or two. It's been a while, but I still remember that look." Edith was a large woman, close to two hundred pounds. Her back was to Charlie, as she stood in front of the grill, cooking. The sound and smell of sizzling bacon and sausage filled the air.

Charlie turned around and looked at her friend. "Can you really see a different look in my eye?"

"Absolutely, and so does everyone else around here. That young man has the same look in his eyes, too," Edith said without looking up from the grill.

"Really? He is good looking. A little on the thin side though," she said. It had been a long time since she'd felt this way. This was silly though. She hardly knew the man. "Too bad I'm too old for him. If I were only five or six years younger, I'd send out some signals."

This time Edith looked away from the grill at Charlie and said, "Honey, I hate to tell you, but you've already sent out the signals. And that young man has read your messages loud and clear. Believe me, he understood every single word of your message, too. And that's pure horse manure about being too old. I don't want to hear that kind of talk. Besides, what are your choices around here . . . Billy Jack?"

"Edith Irick, bite your tongue. Anyway, what would people say? I was robbing the cradle?"

"Look Charlie, there's not much to pick from way up here on top of the world, and you're not sweet sixteen and never been kissed anymore, either. Excuse my unladylike manners for a moment, but who gives a damn what other people think?"

"Think about what," Jonah asked, coming into the kitchen from the back door.

"Nothing," Charlie and Edith answered in unison.

It was a little past eight. Grant and Victor were still at the Trading Post. They had just finished breakfast and were sipping their third cup of coffee. It had taken Grant almost an hour to calm down from the skirmish with Billy Jack, if that's what the one-sided affair could be called. He certainly didn't do much skirmishing, other than slide across the floor on his rear end in front of the woman he was trying to help and impress. What a bonehead he must have looked like to her.

Grant started telling Victor about the silver-blue wolf he'd seen earlier that morning across Denning Fork, when his new boss, Linsey Hogan, showed up. She had told him at their meeting yesterday in Fairbanks, that she would meet them here this morning. Grant never saw her and kept on talking. "I tell you, Victor, I'm sure, at least, I think I'm sure I saw that silver-blue wolf across the stream this morning."

"Sh-h-h-h. I told you to hold it down about that silver-blue wolf stuff," Victor warned, holding his right index finger to his lips.

"Why?"

"I'll tell you why," a female voice answered.

They both looked up in surprise. Grant jumped from his chair and said, "Miss Hogan. Good morning. We didn't see you come in. Sorry. Victor and I were talking about a silver-blue wolf I saw this morning." He noticed that Victor remained in his chair sipping his coffee and was now looking down at the floor, as if Miss Hogan was not there at all. Victor never even said good morning to the woman. Grant thought that seemed pretty rude.

"Correction. You said you thought you saw the silver-blue wolf in the fog," she said very matter-of-factly. She sat down at the table, across from Victor. "Most likely you saw a gray wolf with tiny mist droplets on its pelt that made it appear to be silver-blue. Grant, the silver-blue wolf is a myth that some of the Indian tribes in the area pass along in their folklore fairy tales. Sorry, Victor, I hope that doesn't offend you."

"No offense taken," Victor said, his voice lacking emotion. He continued to glare at the wooden floor. "White men have their ways, and red men have theirs. Sorry, Miss Hogan, I hope that doesn't offend you by not making the gender politically correct."

Linsey stared coldly for a moment at the top of Victor's lowered head, then broke the silence. "I need some coffee." She raised her right hand and began to snap her fingers at Charlie, who was standing by the cash register talking to a customer. "Waitress . . . Waitress! I need some coffee over here as soon as you can. Black, if you have it," she barked.

Victor glanced up at Grant and grinned, then looked back at the floor before Miss Hogan could see him. The tension around the table was thick and felt like high humidity on a sultry day. It was obvious these two people didn't like one another very much. To try to ease the situation a bit, Grant said, "You're probably right, Miss Hogan, and I was mistaken. It was the fog that gave the animal the silver-blue look. Maybe we should talk about the wolf study project."

Charlie brought Linsey's coffee. She set the cup and saucer onto the table a little harder than necessary, spilling some of it. She strode away without a word or a smile.

Staring at Charlie who was already across the room, she grumbled, "The service you get these days. It's a wonder this place is still in business." She said it loud enough so Charlie and several customers could hear her. Then Linsey turned her head back to the table and continued with what she was saying. "Now, Grant. Item number one," she said, pointing her index finger at him and flashing a phony smile, "You call me Linsey." She then pointed her finger and stared at Victor. The smile dropped from her round face and an expression appeared as if she had just tasted something bad. "He calls me, Miss Hogan. Number two, you made the right decision to agree with me on the silver-blue wolf issue. I like that. It shows promise. Before we get into the study project and what I expect from you two, let me finish what I was saying earlier about the silver-blue wolf. I do believe that down through the ages, there have been a few of these lovely animals. But they are very, very rare. Would you agree with that, Victor?"

The lanky Indian raised his head and looked at Linsey Hogan with the same silly smile he had on his face a moment ago. "That's correct, *Miss Hogan*," he said with emphasis. "They are like what your people might call angels."

"Yes, ma'am . . . Linsey," Grant rushed in to say, trying to change the subject. "I just have one question before we discuss the project, if you don't mind of course." She nodded her head with an aristocratic smile as if she were royalty. He had waited six months to ask this question. "The videotape on TV last fall, of the wolves in the snare traps here in Alaska . . . the last wolf shown on the tape—the adult wolf—was it killed? They didn't show that part on the station I watched."

Linsey clasped her hands together and laid her elbows on the table, resting her chin on top of her hands. "You think it was a silver-blue, don't you, Grant?"

He shook his head.

"So does every person in Alaska that saw that damn tape. Alaskans understand the significance of that animal, too. The Fish and Game people were flooded with thousands of phone calls and letters, not only about the inhumane way the animals were killed, but also about the silver-blue wolf. They were asking the same question you just asked me. Because of this, they have refused to release the information outside of the department. Those involved in that fiasco, are sworn to secrecy. They have been threatened with termination if it leaks out. So that probably means the wolf is dead."

Grant's eyes dropped to the table in an effort to hide his disappointment. "I was afraid of that," he said solemnly.

"Okay, let's get down to business before we all get teary-eyed here," Linsey said sarcastically. "First of all, I want to cover some background information on the so-called big picture, before we get down to what your actual assignment is on this project. Some of this information you may already know, so bear with me."

"That sounds like a good idea. The more facts I have up front, the better it is for me," Grant said enthusiastically.

"Good. That okay with you, Victor?" Linsey asked, more as a dig than an actual inquiry.

Most of the time Linsey had been talking, Victor looked down at the floor as if not paying attention and fiddled with his braided hair. He didn't even bother to look up when he answered with a less than exuberant, yeah.

"Good to have your support, Trnavsky," she said coolly. "All right. Let's get started. In June of 1993, the state voted for a three-year wolf control program in the Tanana Flats, and the foothills of the Alaska Range. As you might know, and probably should know, this is southwest of Fairbanks. What you might not know, is that it is designated as Game Management Unit 20A. Gentlemen, this is less than one percent of the state of Alaska. Of course, the land adjacent to Denali National Park, and the military lands in the 20A area, are excluded from the plan." She threw up her hands as a display of exasperation. "Why the public, worldwide, has gotten so upset over all this wolf control stuff, I don't know. But they have." She took a sip of coffee then continued. "That means that ninety-nine percent of the wolf population in the state will retain the classification of 'game and furbearing animal.' This will keep the wolf subject to regular hunting and trapping rules during regulated seasons, and to full protection during the rest of the year. Historically, about one thousand wolves are harvested by hunters and trappers annually in Alaska."

Grant straightened up in his chair and asked, "But that program has been abandoned since they showed the videotape I just mentioned. And supposedly the newly elected governor has ordered a new study in that area, right?" Victor remained silent, still looking down at the floor and messing with the beads in his braids.

"That's absolutely correct," Linsey said in a huff. "And I might add that I'm not particularly in agreement with the new governor's point of view, either. We are still faced with a declining population of caribou in that area. The Delta caribou have diminished from a population of eleven thousand in 1989, to less than twenty-five hundred this spring."

"What are the suspected causes for their decline?" Grant asked, already knowing that the wolf would be listed as one of them.

"We have had three harsh winters in a row, which certainly could be some of the cause. But I believe wolf predation is the primary cause of the caribou's decline," Linsey said. "The department biologists believe the control program would have allowed the herd to recover to six thousand to eight thousand animals in three to five years. There are 150 to 200 wolves in this area, which is around eighteen packs, and the control program would have reduced that number, by fifty to seventy-five percent. If you do the math it's pretty simple to see the problem. A pack of wolves will kill a caribou on the average of every two days. That's about 180 animals per pack. If you take that number and multiply by eighteen, you have over three thousand caribou, just to feed the present population of wolves in that one area alone. And three thousand caribou just happens to be the entire Delta population."

Linsey coldly spit out the information as if the wolves were non-living creatures, and they had no important role in nature's plans. Grant shuddered at the thought of her insensitivity toward another living creature. He was beginning to see just what a callous person Linsey Hogan was.

"Is there still hunting allowed in Unit 20A?" he asked, hoping to find something that indicated the wolf was not the total problem.

"No. Not since 1991. And the herds' numbers are dropping. That's the real problem. You can't believe the pressure the department gets from hunters, because there are not enough caribou for them to hunt. Some of these people are very influential, too."

"Has a wolf control program been tried in this area before?" Grant asked, again trying to find something in the wolf's favor.

"Yes," Linsey fired back proudly. "From 1976 to 1982. And at that time, the caribou herd's numbers increased significantly as a result. By the early 1990s, the wolf population had fully recovered. It doesn't take long when the alpha pair in a pack has five pups a year. Of course that's five pups times eighteen packs. See what I mean, Grant, about it getting out of control?"

Her enthusiastic answer made Grant feel worse. It was obvious to him from Linsey's background presentation, and how she answered his questions, that she had slanted all the facts to disfavor the wolf. There was no question in his mind that Linsey was not an animal lover by any stretch of the imagination. He was having second thoughts about this job and if his conscience would let him perform the required tasks. Of course, at this point, he really didn't know just what those tasks were.

"So how do you think my research is going to help your department solve the problem of the declining Delta herd?"

"Excellent question, Grant. Right to the point. I like that. You're going to do well in this department," Linsey said, sipping a little more coffee. "It's my belief that your study will reveal the true menace of the wolf in this area. By doing so, it will slap on a scientific seal of approval for another wolf control program. The governor will have to accept it, and the public won't be able to deny it. They're born killers, and they were eradicated in the lower forty-eight states by the mid 1800s. There's no reason they shouldn't be in Alaska as well. The sooner the better, I say."

Chapter 5

Billy Jack had just checked the stern rotor blade of his helicopter for what seemed like the hundredth time and was just rounding the tail section, when Nancy Peterson poked her head out the sliding door of the aircraft. "It's after nine o'clock, Mr. Boone. Aren't you through inspecting the plane yet?" There was a definite edge to her voice.

He'd been piddling around, waiting for Victor and the new guy to show up, because there were a couple of things he wanted to tell that guy. So to kill time, he pretended to be doing a routine inspection of the helicopter. He just made sure he moved at a glacier's pace while doing it. Then he walked to the airplane hangar as if he needed something.

During all of this, the Peterson woman was growing more impatient. He could hear her sighing and grumbling, and once when he looked in the cabin, she was squirming in her seat as if she were about to deliver a full term moose calf. Her husband appeared immune to things, immersed in the latest issue of *Psychology Today*.

Billy Jack looked at Mrs. Peterson, drew in a breath, and answered slowly. "Helicopter, Mrs. Peterson. You're in a helicopter, not a plane. And yes, I know it's after nine. I'm just about finished. Please calm yourself."

As he was speaking, Victor's muddy Suburban pulled up next to the hangar and stopped. Billy Jack looked toward the Suburban, then back to Mrs. Peterson. "I need to speak to those two state agents for a minute," he said. "Then we can leave, and you can shoot all the wildlife you want." He headed straight for the hangar, knowing they would have to sign in and file a flight plan before leaving.

Billy Jack was leaning against the door jam chewing on a dry weed and scraping dirt from under his fingernails with his hunting knife, when Victor and Grant walked in. Extending his hand to Grant, he said, "Say, I want to apologize for what happened at the Trading Post this morning"

Before Grant could accept, Victor reached over, held him back, and said, "What do you want Billy Jack? We've got a lot of air space to cover today. We don't have time for games."

"Victor, Victor," he said, ignoring the Indian and continuing to hold his hand out to Grant. "My name is Billy Jack. I don't believe I caught yours."

"It's all right, Victor," Grant replied, shaking Billy Jack's hand. He noticed the power in it. "I'm Grant Rawlings. I'm sorry too. Maybe we can start fresh?"

"Sounds good to me," Billy Jack said. "Did I hear you say something about a silver-blue wolf this morning?"

"I thought I saw one behind my cabin," Grant said, "but I guess I was wrong. I hear they're very rare. It was foggy earlier, and the mist probably made the wolf look silver-blue."

It sounded like bull, Billy Jack thought. He's lying. To Grant, he said, "Well, maybe. But you never know. If you ever see it again, I sure would like to know where—"

"What for, so you can kill it? Skin the thing and sell its pelt?" Victor asked.

"Victor, I've told you a hundred times. All I shoot now is a camera," Billy Jack said, displaying a toothy smile.

"Huh. That's what you say, but I know better. I can feel it." Victor was calm, but his deep voice resonated through the open hangar.

Billy Jack avoided Victor's glare and directed his attention to Grant. "The other thing I wanted to mention to you, Grant, is that I—and everyone else in the Trading Post this morning—saw the way you ogled Charlie." Billy Jack could feel the heat rising in his face as the blood rushed through the tiny vessels in his cheeks. He took a deep breath and stepped closer to Grant, staring him right in his pretty-boy hazel eyes. He was impressed to see that Grant never wavered, not even a blink. But that didn't stop him. "Listen to me, Cheechako," Billy Jack snarled, "because I'm not going to repeat myself. Charlie is off limits. Got it? Stay away from her!"

"I'm not sure ogle is the word I'd use. But you're right. I was admiring Miss Sanford," Grant said, meeting Billy Jack's stare. "And why not. She's a very attractive woman. Besides, I didn't see a wedding ring on her finger or a BJ brand on her forehead."

A burst of anger shot through Billy Jack. Who did this jerkwater punk think he was talking to, anyway? His massive right hand swooped up, latched onto Grant's crotch, and squeezed the young man's testicles. Grant doubled over, his face distorted in pain. He grabbed at Billy Jack's hand. At the same time, Victor lurched forward and tried to free his friend.

"I wouldn't do that, Chief," Billy Jack said. He squeezed tighter.

"It's all right, Victor," Grant groaned. "Please!"

Victor stepped back.

"That's better," Billy Jack said. "Now, Pretty Boy. I'll tell you 'why not.' Because *I* said so. And that's all you need to know." He squeezed hard one last time, then walked out. Grant dropped to the floor and gagged.

Nancy Peterson was out of the helicopter, with hands on her hips. "Mr. Boone! We didn't pay all this money—"

"We're leaving," Billy Jack said. "Get in the chopper!"

In the hangar, Victor leaned over his friend and asked, "You all right?"

"Yeah," Grant said, struggling to stand. "Just give me a minute. What was that name he called me? Cheechako?"

"Cheechako is a Indian word here in Alaska. It means tenderfoot, or greenhorn," Victor chuckled. "Which is exactly what you are."

Still trying to get up, Grant heard voices outside and glanced in that direction. Linsey Hogan was hollering and waving to Billy Jack. She had just driven up in Grant's Suburban, parking next to Victor's mud-spattered one, and was walking toward Billy Jack. They stood talking in the lot between the hangar and Billy Jack's helicopter. Grant couldn't hear what was being said, but both were very animated, waving their hands and arms. "Wonder what they're talking about," he said without looking at Victor.

"I don't know, but I wouldn't trust either one of them any more than I'd trust a den full of wolverines," Victor said in a disgusted tone.

Grant guessed Linsey was around thirty. To him she was only mildly attractive. She looked like a dwarf standing next to the muscle-bound Billy Jack, and she puffed constantly on a cigarette, spewing smoke from her mouth as she talked. Linsey couldn't have been over five feet tall, and her black skirt, which was substantially above her knees, seemed to draw his eyes even more to her short legs. The lady in the helicopter was out again. From the way she was storming toward Billy Jack, it was obvious she was furious.

"Just what kind of clients does Billy Jack have, anyway?" Grant asked, as he carefully stood on his rubbery legs.

"He wants everyone around here to think he only takes photographers and photo-journalists out," Victor replied. "That may be, but I wouldn't bet on it. Even if his clients are what he says they are, they're shooting more than their cameras."

"How do you know that? Do you have any evidence?" Grant asked. "I'm not passing judgment here. But my scientific training taught me to look at only facts."

"Well, Mister Scientist, I don't have any hard-core facts you can roll around in your hands and look at," Victor replied. "But I do have this gut feeling that the man is up to no good. Something, you probably don't understand."

"Well, like I said. I deal better with facts. But even if his clients are shooting more than their cameras, isn't that legal? Aren't most of the game animals in season right now?"

"No, not all. Besides, I believe Billy Jack and his clients are poaching wolves in areas where hunting's not allowed. They're also probably using illegal methods as well as taking more than the daily limits," Victor said. "Why do you think Billy Jack wanted information about the silver-blue wolf?"

"He said he wanted pictures," Grant said.

"Pictures, my rosy-red butt," Victor said sarcastically. "Do you have any idea what the pelt of a silver-blue wolf is worth, Cheechako?"

"Well, an ordinary wolf's pelt ranges from two to three hundred dollars, maybe as high as five hundred. Since the silver-blue is rare, its pelt might go for a thousand, maybe even two thousand dollars," Grant said matter-of-factly, ignoring the "tenderfoot" dig.

"Try fifty thousand."

Grant sucked in a deep breath of disbelief. Before he could respond though, he noticed Billy Jack and Linsey had finished talking. Billy Jack was headed toward his storming client, while Linsey was now headed toward Frank Kicklighter, the sheriff. He had just driven up and parked near Grant's truck. Grant watched the two of them talking.

"Close your mouth before the mosquitoes set up squatter's rights on your tongue," Victor said to Grant. "Come on. Let's go inside and file a flight plan so we can get in the air. I want to show you the territory we'll be investigating."

"Yeah, okay," Grant said, following Victor. "I wonder what Miss Hogan and the sheriff are talking about?"

Victor stopped at the hangar door, turned around and said, "Who knows. Linsey's the type who likes to keep her bases covered. Frank's a good man though. Strictly by the book. You know—crosses all the t's and dots all the i's. He knows exactly what she's up to, and you can bet your last dollar he'll keep a close eye on her." He motioned with his hand and headed toward the hangar door. "Come on, let's get to work."

Twenty minutes later they were 250 feet in the air. Speaking through his headset, Victor started the tour. "All this," he said, making a sweeping motion with his right hand, "is Denali National Park. On the left is the Alaska Range. Mount McKinley's there in the distance. It's real name is Denali. That's where the park got its name. Denali is an Athabascan Indian word that means High One. That's what I am." Victor leaned the controls to the left, and the helicopter shot off in that direction.

Grant glanced at Victor, not knowing if he was joking or not.

"Why are you looking at me like that?" Victor asked.

"You're a High One?"

"What a cheechako," Victor laughed. "No, I meant I'm an Athabascan Indian. We all have red hair." Victor's eyes swung back to the front as he piloted the aircraft eastward. His face was somber, lacking the jester's expression.

"Oh, I didn't know that." Grant had never heard of a native tribe of Indians, anywhere, where the entire tribe had red hair.

They had just flown over the small town of Two Forks. Grant glanced back at the tiny community through the side window of the helicopter.

"There's the Trading Post up ahead," Victor said. With that, he pushed the controls to the right, then down. The helicopter shifted direction, then dropped like a giant monolith.

Grant gripped the armrests of his seat and dug his fingernails into the leather. "What in the world are you doing?" he asked, as the ground came rushing up toward him. His earlier doubts about Victor's ability to fly a helicopter, returned. He was convinced the man was a lunatic.

"You didn't laugh at my joke," Victor said calmly, eyes straight ahead.

"What joke?!" Grant yelled, as the they dropped closer to the roof of the Trading Post. "What in God's name are you talking about?" He pressed his feet against the floorboard as hard as he could, as if that would push him farther away from the rapidly approaching building.

"That bit about all Athabascan Indians having red hair. It was a joke and you didn't laugh," Victor said, very composed. He was scanning the gauges in front of him on the dash.

"I'm sorry!" Grant yelled.

"Too late for that now," Victor said, momentarily glancing over at Grant. "The joke's lost its effect. I had to tell you it was a funny."

"Victor, you're going to kill us!" Grant screamed. His chest heaved up and down as the Trading Post screamed closer. They were seconds from crashing.

"Kill us?" Victor asked, as he pulled back on the controls. The helicopter quickly zoomed upwards. "Do you think I'm crazy or something? I've got a wife to take care of and kids to raise. I was just buzzing Charlie's place. She likes it, so I do it."

Grant peeked out the window at the runners of the helicopter, which were twenty-five feet above the building's roof. He swallowed hard and quickly looked away. As the aircraft leveled off, he took a deep breath and settled back into his seat, loosening his death grip on the armrest, though not completely. Once he calmed down a little, he felt his anger rising. This nut could have killed them both pulling a stunt like that. He didn't have to put up with this kind of treatment.

"Victor, I'm not much of a prankster, which I'm sure you've already figured out. It's just not in my nature. If we're going to work together, we need to get a few things straight right now. First of all, if you're ever going to pull a trick like that again, tell me ahead of time so I can plan on being somewhere else. I think I almost had a heart attack."

"No problem," Victor responded, cheerfully. "What are the other things you want to get straight?"

Grant thought for a moment, then said, "I don't know exactly. I'll let you know as I think of them."

"Good plan. Glad we got that settled."

Grant couldn't tell if Victor was serious or just patronizing him.

"Now," Victor said, "let me explain about the red hair. My hair and name come from my Russian heritage. Russian trappers were the first white men to settle in Alaska. The old ones say it was nearly two hundred winters ago when the Russians first discovered the Koyukon region, which was the prime area for hunting beavers. Not long after that, they set up trading posts along the Yukon River. I guess some of those mountain men must've met up with some of the Indian maidens, because viola, here I am."

"I was wondering where you got that hair and name from," Grant said.

Victor chuckled. Pointing out the window, he said, "That's Crooked Creek in front of us. And the stream off to the right is Denning Fork."

"Is that my cabin?"

"Yup. And the other cabin up from your place, is Charlie's."

Grant leaned toward Victor, straining to see. He could clearly see where the dirt road leading to his cabin had ended. The last mile or so was no more than an overgrown logging trail. Charlie's cabin was about one and a half times the size of his and also located on Denning Fork, but it was about three-quarters of a mile off the dirt road, nestled in a stand of spruce. That's why he didn't see it yesterday on the way to his cabin.

For the next fifteen minutes, neither of them spoke. There was just the dull roar of the helicopter engine and the whipping sound of the blades. The time went quickly, as Grant was engrossed in watching the terrain beneath him. He was amazed at the number of run-off streams that carved their way down steep slopes and fed into larger creeks and rivers. He was also fascinated with the hills and mountains that pressed toward the sky, and the way the taiga terrain gave way to the treeless tundra and snow-crested peaks. This beautiful place would be his home and office for the next two or three years, maybe longer—maybe even forever—and he liked what he saw. It felt right. It felt like home.

Victor brought the helicopter to a stop and hovered in place. "This is the heart of Unit 20A, the one Miss Hogan told you about this morning," Victor said. "Over there on the right, way off in the distance, are the Clearwater Mountains. It's a glacier field. Hunting caribou is not allowed anywhere in this unit. On the other hand, hunting wolves is, except for three places—one's Fort Greely, which is straight ahead, the second is Fort Wainwright, over there on the left, and the third is Denali National Park, which we just passed. When you're on the ground you'll have no trouble identifying the boundaries of the two army bases. They're well marked. Only the northern half of Denali is in Unit 20A. I guess I don't have to point out to a wildlife biologist, that a wolf pack establishes its own territorial boundary lines, and they may or may not coincide with the ones we humans have set up."

Grant nodded, then asked, "What's the territorial range of a wolf pack in this area?"

"Their basic home range is about two hundred miles," Victor answered, as he leaned the controls to the left. The helicopter spun around and headed for home. "This means you'll have wolves moving into Unit 20A from other units, they'll stay for a while, and then they'll move out. Trying to keep up with them and study them, will keep the job challenging, to say the least."

"Yeah, I know that," Grant said. "What are the hunting limits on wolves in Unit 20A?"

"Five per hunter per season, and the season is open from August 10 to April 30."

"So they're out of season now," Grant said, more to himself than to Victor. "What's the bag limit for trapping?"

"No limit, and the season is from November 1 to April 30."

"So, no activity until August 10," he said, speaking to himself again. "That's good. It will give the alpha pair of each pack, time to den. Their pups will be about four months old by the time the season starts. That'll also give me a chance to get used to the lay of the land before I have to worry about some crazy hunter taking pot-shots at me."

"Well my friend, don't be too sure there'll be no wolf hunting or trapping until August 10," Victor muttered.

"Billy Jack. Right?"

"And others."

"Let's table this discussion to another time," Grant said bluntly. "Right now I'd like to ask you about that silver-blue wolf I saw this morning."

"You thought you saw," Victor said. "Mostly likely, even though I hate to admit it, Linsey was right. What you saw was a gray wolf in the fog, and it looked like a silver-blue wolf."

"Well, maybe. But what if I really did see a silver-blue wolf?"

"That is highly unlikely," Victor answered. "Let me explain a few things. The wolf is one of the greatest hunters. It has a lot of prowess and its endurance is amazing. My people believe the wolf is a celestial animal—a great long-distant traveler—and a guide to those seeking the spirit world. It's a messenger. When the wolf howls, it is speaking with the spirits. The silver-blue wolf is a very special animal in our beliefs, and it has special powers. It only allows itself to be seen by a few chosen people and for very specific reasons. You are a cheechako, and a white man, so I doubt very seriously that you would be one of the chosen few."

"Probably not, but what if I were?"

Victor glanced over at him, then looked away. "In my culture, it is of the highest honor to be selected by the silver-blue wolf," Victor said reverently. "It has been said by our shamans, that those who lay eyes on the silver-blue wolf in this world, will be great chiefs in the afterworld."

Feeling a little silly and uncomfortable, Grant figured it was about time to change the subject. "Yeah, I guess maybe you and Linsey are right. I must've been seeing things. Now, I'd like to know how you feel about Miss Hogan. From your look this morning, I take it you don't agree with her . . . on anything."

"How could you say such a thing, Master Grant? Cut me right to the quick." Victor's serious mood changed instantly, and here he was, jesting again. "Just think about the things she had to say. She's part of the 'me' generation, Grant. It's obvious she doesn't give a hoot about any animal, other than herself, of course. And beyond that, all she cares about are the hunters, especially rich, powerful ones with political connections. She said it herself—the wolf should be eradicated from the state."

"Yeah, that did bother me, too," Grant said. "But everything else she had to say was pretty convincing for a wolf control program."

"All those numbers she threw at you this morning, were nothing more than a smoke screen. She's trying to overwhelm you and get you to believe the wolf is overpopulated and wiping out the caribou. The fact is, and you know it too, the mortality rate in wolf pups is greater than fifty percent. And that's not counting what the hunters, trappers, and poachers take each year. It's not the wolf, at least by itself, that's killing off the caribou."

"What else do you think it could be, then?" Grant asked.

"I'm not sure," Victor said evenly. "I was hoping a smart college boy like you could figure that one out."

"Hey, what's the name of that little lake down there?" Grant asked. He was looking out the side window to his right, at a deep blue teardrop-shaped lake.

"Broken Eye Lake."

"Really. I was just thinking it looked like a teardrop. Hey, look over there!" Grant called out suddenly, pointing to the lake. "Down by those willows!"

Victor looked, then swung the craft down.

Thirty minutes later, after landing a half-mile from the lake and hiking back to it, Grant and Victor approached a moose cow caught in a wire snare. Grant's heart felt sick. The animal was exhausted and breathing heavily, but was still very much alive. She tossed her head and kicked her hind legs at them. The wire noose had cut deep into her muzzle. Blood was everywhere. A red froth bubbled from her mouth and nose. The harder she strained, the tighter the wire squeezed. He knew the moose's agony was only made worse each time she tried to free herself. The snare's locking device tightened with each movement, and it would not release its tension, even if she ceased straining.

"I thought the Fish and Game people picked up all their wolf control snares after the Governor's ban," Grant yelled, angry at the incompetence.

"That's not a Fish and Game snare," Victor replied. "It looks like the type Charlie sells at the Trading Post. She told me a couple of weeks ago, that she's had a real run on these over the past couple of months. This is not a small game snare, either. And trapping large game, other than the wolf, is illegal."

"Look at the way the willows are all beaten down. I'll bet this poor animal has been here for a while," Grant said.

The moose tugged furiously on the snare, trying to get away from them. Victor knelt down and picked up one of the broken willow branches. Then he ran his fingers over the fresh soil in the circular trench that had been made by the moose's powerful hooves, during its attempts to get free. "Three days. She has been here for three days. No food. No water."

"God," Grant said his voice cracking slightly. "This poor creature has to be scared to death. We've got to free it. This is a horrible way to die."

"Come here, quick. I want to show you something," Victor said as he swung the backpack from his shoulder. "When you go out into the wild, there are two things a good wildlife biologist never leaves camp without." He pulled a polished wooden box from his backpack and opened it. It was about the size that silverware would fit in and contained a dart gun and wire cutters. "Notice there's two different sized darts," Victor said. "One's for large animals like moose and bear, and the other's for animals the size of a wolf. I don't think I have to explain the wire cutters. There's an extra set of each in the helicopter. Remind me to get them out for you when we get back to Two Forks. You can use them until you get your own."

"That's great, Victor," Grant said, looking relieved. He watched the animal continue to struggle and snort, then studied Victor as he prepared the dart gun. "How long will it take for the sedative to work?"

"About ten to fifteen minutes—"

Before Victor could finish his sentence, the snare broke loose from its anchor. The hurt and frightened animal spun away from the two men and shot through the thick brush surrounding them.

"We've got to stop her!" Victor yelled. He ran after the animal, holding the dart gun in front of him, trying to get a steady aim.

Grant followed close behind.

"Her mouth is still wired shut," Victor said as he ran. "If we don't get that off of her, she'll die."

They had run maybe twenty feet, when they came to another trampled down area of willows. The object on the ground caught their eyes. Victor slowed for a moment, then continued on, trying to shoot the moose with the dart gun before it got away.

Grant came to a complete stop. His right hand rose to his mouth, covering it, and he turned away. It was all he could do not to throw up. Finally, he looked back. A week-old moose calf had gotten caught in the snare. Like its mother, the young animal's mouth was bloody and wired shut. Two inches of its tongue had been bitten off, and it lay there near its head, in a dark pool of dried blood. Unlike its mother, the young calf had not had the strength to break free, so it died a slow death from starvation and dehydration.

Linsey Hogan's feet were propped on her desk as she took the long-distance call. Her head was cocked to one side, firmly cradling the receiver between her ear and shoulder. A cigarette rested between the middle fingers of her right hand, and she was doodling on a yellow notepad with her left.

"Like I said," she told the man on the other end of the line, "the new grad student is in place. I went down to Two Forks earlier this morning to get him started. I guarantee, that boy doesn't know crap from Shinola about what's going on."

"Are you sure he's not going to be a problem?" the man asked.

"Absolutely. He's too fresh to know anything yet. Besides, he doesn't have enough time to find out anything before our business is conducted," Linsey said.

For a moment, she wondered if Grant's native companion might muddy the water for her. But she wasn't going to mention that concern to her friend on the phone. What he didn't know wouldn't hurt him.

"Good. That makes me feel a little better," the man said. "My colleagues and I will arrive in Anchorage late Saturday evening. We'll be ready to start our business Monday morning and can be there the rest of the week. Will you be ready for us?"

She took a deep drag from the cigarette and tried to blow smoke rings. "You bet we'll be ready," she said. "I spoke with my contact in the field this morning. He's got everything organized and under control. We're right on schedule."

"It sounds like you're on top of things, Miss Hogan. I think this is going to be a lucrative endeavor for both of us."

She swung her feet down to the carpeted floor and straightened up in the chair. Dashing out the cigarette in an odd-shaped lava ashtray on her desk, she said, "I agree. Tell me again how much you said you would pay for a silver-blue pelt?"

"In Japan, a silver-blue wolf pelt in excellent condition, would bring close to seventy-five thousands dollars on the blackmarket. I would be willing to pay you fifty thousand." Linsey leaned back in the chair and smiled.

It was late afternoon by the time Grant and Victor had gotten back to Two Forks Airport. The moose cow was stronger than both had thought, and it was an hour of hard running before Victor had been able to get a clear shot at her with the dart gun. Also, his prediction of how fast the sedative would work, was a little off. It took another three miles at a pretty fast clip before the sedative began to do its stuff, and the large animal's legs buckled. Luckily, she went down in a clearing where there was level ground, and she wasn't injured any more than she'd already been. After removing the snare from her muzzle with the wire cutters, they hung around until she shakily lifted herself up on her feet and wandered off into the woods. Once certain of the animal's safety, they started their long journey back to the helicopter.

When Grant and Victor finally reached the spot where the moose had been caught in the snare, Victor suggested they examine the surrounding area for any evidence of foul play. To Grant's surprise they found that a quartered section of a moose had been laid out in strategic places to attract predators, most likely wolves. It appeared that Victor had been right all along. Poachers had obviously baited the area and put up a curtain of wire snares over a span of at least a hundred feet.

In the course of their investigation, they found other unfortunate animals that had met the same fate in the wire snares. There were two wolves, a coyote, and three martens. All had been caught by the neck, and they choked to death. Victor said the wolves and coyote had been dead for at least a week, maybe longer. He wasn't sure about the martens.

Grant couldn't believe the lack of respect some humans showed toward animals. This was killing out of control, killing for the thrill of killing. There was no concern for life or ecology, no interest in conservation and the preservation of wildlife. He was appalled and literally heartsick over what he had witnessed in the field today. His first day on the job had been full of unexpected surprises, and he would have plenty to write about tonight in his personal diary and research notes.

He and Victor had been so busy, they didn't even notice the time slipping by and had completely forgotten about lunch. After spending a few minutes with Victor at the airport to arrange the next day's schedule, Grant decided he was too exhausted mentally and physically to take on the challenge of grocery shopping. Instead, he stopped by the Trading Post for an early dinner.

He had two cheeseburgers with fries, a Pepsi, and a piece of Edith's chocolate pie. The pie was good and reminded him of his mother's cooking. He almost ordered a second piece to take home with him for later in the evening, but decided against it. Even though Charlie wasn't busy, and acted as though she wanted to chat with him, he wasn't in the mood for conversation. He was still mulling over the tragedy he had seen today. Even though Charlie went out of her way to have a conversation with him, his responses were no more than brief answers like yes, no, I don't know, maybe, or just a shrug of his shoulders.

A light breeze blew through the open back door of Grant's cabin and played with the hair on his legs. He stood leaning against the door jamb in a long-sleeved shirt, his underwear and woolen socks. There had been only one thing good about the day—the temperature had risen to fifty-nine, which was above the average maximum of fifty-three for this time of year.

Grant popped the top on a can of beer and gazed out at the rambling stream behind the cabin. After leaving the Trading Post, he had mustered enough energy to drive back to the market in Two Fork and buy a six-pack of beer. As he drank his beer and listened to the gurgling water, his thoughts were on the silver-blue wolf he had seen this morning and on what Victor had said about the Indian beliefs toward the wolf. Linsey may have been right about the fog and the morning light casting a silver-blue appearance on a gray wolf. But now that he'd had more time to think about it, he really didn't think so.

He took a long draw off the beer and glanced at his watch as he lowered his wrist. It was 5:42 and the sun was high in the western sky. Plenty of daylight left yet. He felt a little better since he'd eaten, and his thoughts now drifted to Charlie and how he'd acted toward her at the Trading Post. "I was really rude," he scolded himself. "She'll probably never speak to me again."

At that moment, a lady's voice rang across the room from the front door. "Hello, is anyone home? You left the front door open. Is it all right to come in?"

It was Charlie. Good. He could apologize to her for the way he acted this afternoon. Grant swung around to greet her and said, "Come in, Charlie. I didn't hear you drive up. I'm glad you dropped by. I wanted to apologize for my mood earlier."

Charlie stood just inside the door. Her arms were behind her back as if she were hiding something, and she had an odd look on her face that turned into a silly grin. There seemed to be a touch of embarrassment to her expression. He also noticed that Charlie had gone home and changed since he'd seen her at the Trading Post earlier. She now wore a white and blue floral print blouse, a tight pair of blue jeans, and a white pair of lady's tennis shoes instead of her hiking boots.

"Maybe I should come back later," she said with some hesitation.

"No, no, it's really okay. Come on in," he insisted. "Would you like a beer?"

"But you don't have any pants on."

Grant looked down at his hairy legs, and his face instantly flushed to a deep pink. Sure enough, there he stood in his underwear. He'd been so glad to see Charlie that he'd completely forgotten he wasn't wearing any pants. "Oh man, this is so embarrassing," he mumbled. He dashed over to the sofa with his head down, avoiding eye contact with her, grabbed his gray sweatpants from the armrest, and quickly jumped into them. When he looked up, she was standing with her back to him. Her hands were now in front of her.

"All right," he said. "You can turn around now. I have pants on."

When Charlie turned to face him, she had a smirk on her face and was holding a piece of Edith's chocolate pie in her right hand.

"I'm really sorry about that, Charlie. I hope I didn't offend you."

"It's nothing. Don't worry about it," she said. "Besides, I'm the one who came to offer a peace offering. Here." She held out the pie.

"What's this for?"

She came walking toward him. "Well, the way you were acting this afternoon at the Trading Post, I thought maybe your mood was from what happened out at the airport between you and Billy Jack this morning. One of my customers told me about it. Or is it just your nature? Not to be very talkative, I mean."

"No. No, it's not," he said as he moved toward her to receive the pie. "What I mean is, I'm not normally moody, and what happened with Billy Jack had nothing to do with it either. I just had a bad day, that's all."

"Oh."

He took the pie and said, "This is awful nice of you. You really didn't have to do this, though it is great pie."

"Well, I wanted to. So what was bad about your day?" Charlie asked. "Mind if I sit down?"

"No. Please do." He gestured with his hand. "How about that beer?"

"Yeah, okay. That sounds good."

Grant walked over to the counter, pulled another beer from the plastic holder and gave it to Charlie. He began to tell her the terrible saga of the moose cow and its newly born calf, caught in the wire snare traps. By the time he finished, they had drunk two beers apiece.

They sat in silence for a moment, then Grant said, "When Victor and I found the curtain of snares baited with pieces of quartered moose, it was pretty obvious to me that he was right about the poachers. Do you know anything about any of this?"

"No, not really. Not anything about poaching." Charlie answered. "But now that you mention it, I have noticed in the past few months that the sales of wire snares has almost tripled. In fact I had a customer just this morning who asked if I had four dozen of the locking type in stock. The kind you said you saw today."

"Victor had mentioned that they looked like the type you sold."

"Yeah, he asked a few weeks ago about the volume of wire snares I was selling."

Grant took a sip of beer and set the can on the end table, he turned back to Charlie and asked, "Would you mind giving me the name of the customer that bought those snare traps this morning?" He didn't want to offend her, but he really wanted to know the man's name.

"Let me think about it," she answered. She squirmed a bit, as if unsure what to do. "Lets change the subject for a minute and talk about the cabin."

"Okay."

"First of all, lets get the business out of the way. Did Dale Barlow tell you how much the rent was?"

"Three hundred dollars a month," Grant said.

"That's not too much, is it?"

"No. It's worth every penny."

"Good. If there's anything you need let me know. I take it you found the blankets, the extra pair of clean sheets, and the cooking and eating utensils?"

"Yes, and it's all just fine."

"I'm having two cords of wood delivered tomorrow. And you can wash your clothes and bedding at my place any time you want," she offered. "The door to my cabin is always unlocked. Well, I guess that's about it."

"Thanks, Charlie, I appreciate that," Grant said. There was a pause as they stared at each other for a few moments. She would smile then look away, then look back at him. He did the same with her. Finally, he broke the silence. "Is that all the business?"

"Huh?"

"You said 'lets get the business out of the way first' when you asked to change the subject a minute ago. So what do you want to do now?"

"Excuse me?" Charlie's face was red.

"I'm sorry. That came out wrong. What I meant was, is there anything else you wanted to talk about?" Grant said, trying to explain.

"No, I guess not." Standing up, she smiled and headed for the front door. "Well, I better get back to the Trading Post."

"Thanks for dropping by, Charlie. Stop by any time. I'll try to have my pants on the next time," Grant said with a smile.

With a devilish grin, Charlie stopped in the doorway for a moment and said, "Oh, that's okay. I kind of enjoyed the view. Say, I close the Trading Post early on Wednesdays. How about supper at my place tomorrow night? Say about seven?"

Grant's heart pumped double for a second. Smiling broadly, he replied, "Yeah, that would be great! I would really like that. Seven? I'll be there. Thanks." He stuck out his hand for some dumb reason and Charlie quickly reached out and shook it. Her hand was very warm, but not quite as soft as he had expected.

"Tomorrow night then," she said, turning and heading toward her Jeep Cherokee.

CHAPTER 6

THE TEMPERATURE IN THE CABIN WAS twenty-eight degrees, a six degree improvement over yesterday. Considerably more organized this morning, Grant had already fired up the cook stove, had water heating for his coffee and he was now headed out the back door with the pitcher, to get water from the stream for another spit-and-saucer bath.

There was no fog hovering over Denning Fork. He paused in the doorway and carefully scanned the perimeter and the other side of the stream before stepping out. No wolf in sight. He was disappointed. If he'd had a dream of the silver-blue wolf last night, there were no memories of it rattling around his brain this morning.

He headed toward the stream. Learning from yesterday's cold temperatures, he opted for jeans and a heavy green nylon jacket for today's water run, instead of the woolen blanket he'd wrapped in yesterday. He hurried to get his water because Victor was to meet him at the cabin this morning. They were going to hike along Denning Fork and look for signs of wolves.

As he approached the stream, he noticed tracks in the damp soil near the water's edge. They were wolf tracks, fresh ones, and lots of them. His first thought was of the silver-blue wolf. There were so many tracks that Grant knew they must have been made by a pack, maybe eight to ten animals. He wondered if it could be the silver-blue's pack. At least, he hoped it was. He knelt down and carefully examined the prints, then rushed in to get ready. He couldn't wait for Victor to get there and see these.

By the time Victor wheeled up to the cabin at 6:45, Grant had already bathed, drank three cups of coffee, and eaten the chocolate pie Edith had made. Eager to get out in the woods and show Victor the tracks, he greeted his companion at the door. Victor's backpack was draped over his left shoulder and he carried a small white paper sack in the his right hand.

Victor lifted the sack and said, "Here. My wife made us up a little something to eat before we hit the trail—eggs and moose sausage wrapped in homemade biscuits. I think there's a half a dozen for each of us. I stopped by in Two Forks and got us some milk too."

He wasn't that hungry, but it sure sounded good, and he didn't want to hurt Victor's feelings. Besides, a piece of chocolate pie wasn't going to carry him very far out on the trail.

"Your wife is going to spoil me, Victor. But I'm not complaining," Grant said with a smile of gratitude. "What's your wife's name, anyway?"

"I call her Squaw Woman, but everyone else calls her Mary Margaret. That'd probably be the safest thing for you to call her ... or she might scalp you," Victor said in his usual playful manner.

Grant laughed and took the paper sack from his friend. Setting it on the counter, he said, "Before we dig into this, I want to show you something really interesting out back."

Outside, next to the stream, Grant proudly showed Victor the tracks in the moist soil. "See, look at all the wolf tracks," he said excitedly.

"Those aren't wolf tracks," Victor said firmly. "They're feral dog tracks."

"How do you know that?" Grant asked.

"A white man's eyes are like a skunk's, partly blind. An Indian's eyes are like an eagle's. He can tell by sight these are not wolf tracks. Since you wouldn't believe me if I didn't measure them, I'll use this." Pulling a tape measure out of his pocket, he knelt down and started to measure the width and length of one of the tracks. "From pad to pad, an adult wolf's paw is normally two inches wide and two inches long. A feral dog's is about an inch and a half wide and long. This track is a fraction less than that, and none of the others here are any larger. Also, look closely at the track where the claws on the paw go into the soil. The wolf claw would be deeper and better defined than these are."

"Are you sure?" Grant asked, disappointed.

Victor stood up. "Yup. It would be extremely rare for a pack of wolves to come up to your cabin, anyway. However, a pack of feral dogs wouldn't be so unusual. You need to keep a sharp eye out for these devils. Feral dogs have a high incidence of rabies."

"Where in the world would a pack of feral dogs come from, way out here in the boonies?" Grant asked.

"That's a good question," Victor said. "A lot of people around here don't realize it, but there a few individuals who've been experimenting with mixing wolves with different breeds of domestic dogs. They're trying to develop an improved species for sled racing. Aside from the Iditerod, there are several other races in the state each year. Like everything else, it's become big money. So any animals that haven't proven out as good sled dogs, are turned loose in the woods, or shot and thrown in a ravine somewhere."

"You're kidding," Grant said in disbelief.

"Lets go back to the cabin," Victor said. On the way he continued to tell Grant more about the feral dogs. "In addition to the sled dog breeders, there are those that mix wolves and dogs to sell as domestic pets. When the half-breed doesn't work out for the client, and they rarely do, they bring the animals back to the breeder. Again, many times these creatures are just turned loose in the woods and wind up joining a feral dog pack. Sometimes the clients take the animals to the dog pound. But the pound always puts those animals down right away. That's why most people bring them back to the breeder, and let them worry about it."

Grant hurried up the back steps and into the cabin. "Man, I didn't realize that these kinds of things were going on."

"Well, unfortunately they are," Victor said, following him into the cabin. "Of course, the feral dogs always seem to find one another. Then they run and hunt and scavenge together. More times than not, the wolf gets blamed for the damage these packs of feral dogs will do. They'll do stuff like kill cats and dogs, get into trash cans, and generally make a real mess, stuff like that. And since we've had three pretty tough winters, most people believe it's drawing the wolves down out of the mountains for food. I think it's the feral dogs."

Grant opened a cabinet door and lifted out two plates, while Victor pulled their breakfast out of the sack. "Have there been any cases where these feral dogs have harmed humans?" Grant asked him.

"No, not recently. But it's only a matter of time," Victor said. He pulled out a couple of the biscuits filled with scrambled eggs and moose sausage. Each was wrapped in a paper towel. "Several years ago, we had two or three bad winters in a row like this. A pack of feral dogs killed a couple of children and maimed a few others. I was a kid myself at the time." Victor seemed to get a sad, distant look in his eyes for a brief second, then he continued. "Obviously, the community was outraged. They formed groups and hunted down the pack of killer animals. Unfortunately, however, many wolves were killed during the massacre as well."

Neither man said much after that as they ate.

Every time the bell over the Trading Post's front door rang, signaling a customer was entering or leaving, Charlie's eyes darted toward the door. She looked at the clock hanging on the wall up over the coffee maker. It was a little after nine. She was disappointed that Victor and Grant, mainly Grant, hadn't come in this morning for breakfast. Not because of the business so much, but because she'd wanted to see Grant's handsome face. She also needed to talk with him, because she'd forgotten to ask what he would like for supper tonight.

Her thoughts drifted back to late yesterday afternoon, and the look Grant had given her while they were sitting on the sofa, talking. His eyes had flecks of gold in them, and they sparkled in the late day sunlight. There had been an awkward moment where each had run out of things to say, and they just sat there and stared at one another. Her heart had fluttered and she felt her face flush with embarrassment, as if she were sixteen again. She couldn't believe she had said such a stupid thing about enjoying the view, when Grant was standing there in his underwear. He probably thought she was awful. But the truth of it was, she did like the view of his stocky muscular legs. Their handshake, when she left, seemed kind of awkward and dumb, like they'd just negotiated a deal or something. But she had to admit, she'd enjoyed the warmth and manly strength of it.

Charlie was wiping off the counter when the bell rang again. Her eyes shot toward the front of the room, hoping it would be Grant. Instead, it was the sheriff, Frank Kicklighter, coming in. His face was long and solemn. He headed toward her, carrying his usual plastic bottle of Alaska Sparkle bottled water in his right hand. She could tell something was wrong by the way he carried himself, and the sick expression on his face. His lumbering stride sent out signals of depression.

Frank plopped down on one of the stools across from her. He had a dazed look, as if he hadn't had any sleep for several nights, and there were large dark circles under his eyes.

"What's up, Frank. You don't look so good. Can I get you some coffee?"

He motioned with the hand holding the bottle of water, then just kind of dropped it down on the counter as if he didn't have the energy to hold on to it. "Nah, better drink this stuff. Kidneys you know," he muttered, looking up at her. "Charlie, I need to ask a big favor of you."

"Sure, Frank, anything."

"I need the payment on this place."

"Now?" she asked, stunned, her voice elevating slightly.

Frank held the second mortgage on the Trading Post. Business had been slow the last couple of years, because of the recent hard winters and the tourist boycott over the wolf control controversy. Many had chosen not to vacation in Denali National Park because of it. By the end of last year's tourist season, she had been completely broke and in hock up to her eyeballs. She'd had two choices, close the place down, or try to borrow more money to carry her through the next year.

She didn't want to put the cabins and the two hundred acres she owned, up as collateral. Her father had worked so hard all his life to pay them off. And besides, if the Trading Post failed, at least she would have a place to live. With what she currently owed, there was no banking institution in the state that would have loaned her a dime on the business.

Frank Kicklighter had been a long-time friend of both her and her father, and he knew of her financial predicament. Not wanting to see Charlie lose the place, especially a place that he felt was good for the community, Frank stepped forward and loaned her twenty thousand dollars. That, combined with whatever she would make the next year, would provide enough cash to keep the Trading Post afloat for another year or more. With the wolf control program now shut down by the governor's ban, everyone expected business to pick up for the entire state. Frank and Charlie, expecting a banner year for tourism, had agreed on an annual payment, due the first of October, after the tourist season was over.

"You're not kidding are you, Frank?" she asked, stunned at the thought of coming up with the payment at this time.

"No, I'm afraid I'm not."

"But why? The payment's not due for another six months," she said.

Frank unscrewed the lid from the plastic water bottle and took a swig. He laid the cap on the counter. "I'm really sorry about this, Charlie. I don't have any choice. My daughter has bone cancer." His words trailed off and his lower lip began to tremble.

"Oh my God. I'm so sorry. I didn't know," she said, raising her hand up to her mouth.

Frank's eyes glistened. He blew heavily through his mouth, trying to compose himself. "I haven't told anyone about this, Charlie. You're the first one. My daughter wanted it that way. Her chemotherapy has been very expensive." He looked down at the floor for a moment. "And this past year, it has financially drained me. I've borrowed on all my insurance policies, on my retirement funds, and on my 401K with the state. None of the treatments have worked, and now the doctors want to do a bone transplant. I know this is going to put you in a bind, but there's no other way."

Charlie reached down to the counter and laid her hand over the top of Frank's cold, clammy hand. "When do you need it, Frank?"

"As soon as you can get it, I'm afraid. They want to operate in about three weeks or less." His voice quivered.

"Do you need all the money I owe you, or just this year's payment?"

"Just this year's, at least for now," Frank said, sniffling. "The doctors want half down before they will perform the operation. It's amazing how little insurance pays these days. I have a few other sources I'm tapping into, and along with your payment, that should be enough."

"Are you sure? I'll get the whole amount if you want," she said, not knowing how in the world she would do that. But somehow she would have to.

Frank capped the bottle of water, stood up, looked at her with his sad eyes and said, "Yeah, I'm sure. Thanks Charlie. Look, I've got to go." He walked slowly to the door.

After Frank left, she headed back toward the kitchen. She was really depressed. Poor Frank. And his daughter. His wife had died four years ago of cancer and now the dreadful disease was trying to snatch another loved one from him.

She went through the two swinging doors into the kitchen. Edith was standing right there. "Oh, Edith, I nearly ran into you," Charlie said.

"I'm sorry," her friend answered

"That's okay."

"No, I mean I'm sorry for eavesdropping. I overheard what Frank said about his daughter. It's terrible, but God has his reasons," Edith said, wringing her hands.

"Yes, it is terrible."

"I also overheard about the money," Edith said, gazing to the floor as if ashamed for hearing something that was none of her business. "I have a little nest-egg saved up for Jonah's college. You are welcome to it if you need it, Charlie."

"Absolutely not," Charlie said, thankful for the offer but hoping she wouldn't have to take her good friend up on it. "I'll get the money somehow. In fact, I'm going to call this banker I know in Fairbanks and set up an appointment." Without hesitation she strode toward the general store next door. "I'll be back in a couple of minutes. Watch things for me."

Ten minutes later she came walking back into the kitchen. Edith was standing at the grill frying a couple of eggs, sunny-side-up. She wasn't smiling like her usual self. Charlie knew her well. Edith was a sensitive person and was obviously upset about Frank's daughter.

"Eleven o'clock Thursday morning. I'll get someone to help out front." She walked up to Edith and put her arm over her friend's shoulders. "It'll work out, Edith. I'll get the money. All we can do for Frank and his daughter now is pray."

"I know. I've already started."

"Good," she said with a little more cheer in her voice. "Now let's talk about what I'm going to fix for supper for Mr. Grant Rawlings."

Edith turned her head, her sad face replaced with a large grin. "You little devil," she said, chuckling. "I knew it. I could see it in your eyes and the way you were bouncing around here yesterday. That boy's got your heart."

"Now don't get any funny ideas," Charlie said. But deep down, she knew Edith was right. "It's not what you think. I'm just being neighborly. Besides, I am his landlady, and we have business to discuss."

"Business, my eye." This time Edith laughed out loud. Her large belly and sagging breasts gyrated, like a bowl of JELL-O. "Yeah . . . I know what kind of business you want to have with that good-looking young man. Funny-business is what you've got on your mind."

"Edith, shame on you," she scolded. She tried to keep a serious expression on her face, but after a few moments she broke out laughing.

At 1:30, Grant and Victor were several miles from the cabin, trekking up a steep slope, toward the top of a high ridge. The day turned out to be another beautiful one—sunny, a few white clouds lumbering by, and temperatures that would probably reach the high fifties or maybe even low sixties.

At noon, they had stopped to eat lunch and rest on two large flat rocks near Denning Fork, before moving on. They each had a can of cold pork and beans, and a can of deviled ham, spread over two slices of bread. Mary Margaret had packed the lunch for both of them in Victor's backpack. She was even thoughtful enough to add an apple for each, to help clean the food from between their teeth. Grant thought, Victor is a lucky man to have a wife to take care of him as well as she does. One day soon he would have to meet this woman and express his appreciation for her kindness to him.

Grant followed Victor, who was leading the way to the top of the ridge. The incline was steep and littered with loose rock that made the going rather tough. "I've been thinking a lot about that moose we found yesterday, and all those snare traps that were set out," Grant said.

"Yeah?"

"You know. Today, with the widespread sympathy there seems to be for animals in general, especially animals that have been persecuted through the ages as much as the wolf has, there's absolutely no reason to kill a wolf, other than the fact that someone just feels like doing it."

"Hunting is an ingrained activity, Grant, especially for men," Victor said, his breathing labored as he made his way up the slope. "But most people never question their own role as predators, nor their right to kill another animals, like the wolf. There's something deep-seated that makes them want to conquer the outdoors, as if something in the wild were challenging them to do it. Killing a wolf represents a victory over that challenge. So they do it. No regard for the creature or its life, and no regard for the effects it may have on the whole scheme of things."

"I guess. But that doesn't make it right," Grant said. He knew that his views about the wolf were in conflict with Linsey Hogan's, and that the two of them would possibly lock horns over it someday, too. That's why it was important for him to solve the puzzle of why the Delta caribou herd's population continued to decline.

"I agree with you, but a lot of people don't," Victor said. "Just the other day, I was reading this article about three ranchers in Montana, near Yellowstone National Park, and it really showed the terrible meanness someone could have in their spirit. They were on horseback and chased down this female wolf. I guess she gripped the lasso with her teeth so it wouldn't close around her neck. Anyway, they dragged her around the prairie until all her teeth broke and fell out. But that wasn't enough for them. While two of them stretched her between their horses with ropes, a third rancher beat her to death with a hammer. After that the wolf was taken around to the local honky-tonks to be shown off. Later they threw her body in a roadside ditch somewhere."

"That makes me sick just to hear it," Grant said as his stomach got queasy.

When they reached the top of the ridge, Victor quickly knelt down and held his right hand up for Grant to be silent. Grant acknowledged the sign and bent down beside his lanky companion. There, twenty yards in front of them was a dead animal that looked to him like a wolf. A raven was perched on the ribs and pecking like a chicken at the decaying meat. The animal looked to have been dead for a couple of weeks.

"Is that a wolf?" Grant asked.

"No." Victor stood up. "It's a feral dog. Must have gotten too close to the wolves' den, and they killed it."

"How do you know that? I haven't seen any wolves, much less any signs of a den."

Victor pointed to a mountainside across the ridge from where they standing. It was a good distance away, but he saw a gray wolf darting in a zigzag fashion toward an outcropping of large boulders. When the wolf reached the face of the rocks, it stopped for a brief moment, cocked its head, and glanced back in their direction. Then the agile animal climbed through an opening in the boulders and was gone.

"It looks as though she's had her pups, or is going to very soon," Victor said with confidence. "Her belly's extended, and the hair around the mammaries is shed. I'd say the den is up there in those rocks."

"It looks like a good place for a den, but what makes you think it's up there?" Grant asked.

"You must not have seen the sparrow up by the rocks," Victor said. "It flitted in and out pretty quickly. It was gathering some wolf hairs for its nest."

Grant stood there, amazed at how Victor had accumulated all that information about the wolf and the bird in less that fifteen-seconds. He'd seen the wolf for a very short time, and at that distance, he couldn't be sure about the animal's extended belly or the condition of her mammaries. He hadn't even seen the bird. Maybe there was some truth about the red man's eyes being sharp like an eagle's.

They walked over to the dead feral dog. The raven took flight when they came closer. Victor circled around the animal, bending over to inspect various locations on its body. "Yup. It was a fight that killed it, all right. Three or four wolves I'd guess. Like I said, it's probably because of the den. Could've been because it wandered into this pack's territory, too." He knelt down and pointed. "Look at how the throat is torn out, and all the bite marks on its hind legs and sides. The way this dog was bitten, shows the precision of a wolf's incisors—trademarks of that fabulous predator."

The rotting dog smelled. It was a male that weighed around eighty-five to ninety pounds. It looked a lot like a German Shepherd, but had a larger head, like a wolf. Standing seven to eight feet away to avoid the rank odor, Grant was jotting some notes on a pad, while Victor was talking.

"I see," Grant said. "But most of the time, at least with the wolf kills I've seen, there's not been much left. They pretty much eat everything. They even lick up the blood from the ground."

"Exactly. They're one efficient animal. But they won't eat their own kind. Not unless they're absolutely starving to death." Victor said, standing up and facing Grant.

Looking back at the dog, Victor said, "One of the major difference between the wolf and the feral dog, is that the dog doesn't eat all of its kill. It doesn't have the raw power in its jaws to crush and chew large bones like the wolf does. That's why a pack of feral dogs will rarely kill a caribou or a moose. They'll eat smaller animals and scavenge like a coyote or a bear. Speaking of bears, they're out of hibernation now. I've found through experience, that it isn't wise to go looking for wolf kills this time of year. Bears are opportunists, and many times they'll run wolves off from a caribou or moose they've just killed. If you're around, they'll come after you too. So if you see a wolf kill this time of year, stay away from it. Wait until winter time. We'd better get moving."

"Just finishing my notes," Grant said as he followed Victor toward the point of the ridge. "Thanks for the tip on the bears. I didn't know that."

Pointing to the ground on his left, Victor said, "A wolf trail. They have a certain look to them. A certain width and depth. See, they are just light little trails, not like caribou trails that are all chopped up."

Grant looked down at the ground, stopping his note-taking for a moment. He hadn't noticed the trail before, but now that Victor had pointed it out, he could see it. His companion continued toward the end of the ridge, which narrowed down to only ten feet across.

"Now there's one for a postcard," Victor said.

Grant reached back and slipped the notepad in the side pocket of his backpack. He walked carefully along the narrow spur that shot out twenty-five to thirty feet from the end of the ridge. Growing at the point of the ridge, was a small lone spruce, slanting off toward the heavens at a forty-five degree angle. When he came up beside Victor, he cautiously leaned forward and peeked over the edge. The end, and both sides of the spur, fell off to shear rock walls that plummeted several hundred feet below them. At the bottom, was the shimmering crystal clear stream of Denning Fork, carving its way through the belly of the deep narrow gorge. From this height, the stream looked like a silver thread snaking across a vast carpet of dark green felt. Victor was right. It was a beautiful sight indeed. He wished he'd brought a camera so he could take some pictures to send back to his folks. His father would love this place.

This time Victor pointed in the distance and said, "That's where we're going today. Broken Eye Lake. It's about two miles from here. Then we'll head back. The caribou water there quite often. I think you should see it up close."

It had taken them a little over two hours to get to the lake, as they had to maneuver over some pretty rough terrain. Grant had almost fallen at one place, where they'd had to hug the face of the rocks along a narrow ledge, to get to the side that would lead them down to the lake. Halfway across the ledge, Grant had lost his footing. If Victor hadn't broken his fall, he would have plummeted several hundred feet into the ravine, and to a sure death.

As they walked, Grant studied the rivers and streams that fed the lake. Denning Fork was the largest one. Here it was more of a river than a stream, at least four times wider than it was behind his cabin. As they made their way along the trail, Grant took mental notes of the numerous feeder streams that emptied into Denning Fork. His best estimate was that he'd seen thirty or forty of these smaller tributaries.

Broken Eye wasn't a large lake, as far as natural lakes go. It was maybe a hundred acres or so, give or take twenty acres. It was certainly a beautiful body of water, gin-clear, with mesmerizing, steep sloping mountains surrounding it on all sides.

They were at the northwest end of the lake, which was fairly shallow. "There's a natural spillway on the right side of the southeast end," Victor said softly, pointing to the far end of the lake.

They were hiding a little way from the water's edge, in a stand of willows. Directly in front of them, standing in the shallows, was a large bull moose dipping his head under water. A few moments later, when it lifted its dripping head to the surface, it was chewing on a mouth full of succulent water grass. To their right, across Denning Fork, was a small herd of fifteen to twenty caribou, drinking from the stream. "Man, I wish I'd brought my camera," Grant whispered.

"There'll be plenty of time for that," Victor said. "See how small the herd is? Just a few years ago, it would have been three times that size. I don't think they're having as many calves as they used to."

"Why not?"

"I'm not sure. But it just doesn't seem like there's as many calves running with the herds, as there should be."

Grant glanced at his watch. It was nearly four o'clock. "It's getting late. I'd like to get some water samples from different locations around the lake, before we head back."

"What for?"

"Scientific deduction, my friend. What you can't rule out, is where your problem lies. My major professor at MU, used to say that all the time. His name's Johnny Boy Jackson. He said it's one of the first rules of problem solving," Grant said proudly. "I'm sure the water's fine, but let's check it out anyway. I'll have the samples analyzed at the AWMC Fairbanks Lab, when I go up to give my first report to Dr. Barlow and Linsey Hogan in a few weeks."

"It doesn't get dark until around eleven this time of year. What's your hurry?" Victor asked.

"I just have something I need to do."

"Like what? You haven't been here long enough to meet any women, so I know it's not that," Victor said.

"It's just something," Grant answered again. He was embarrassed to tell Victor about his dinner date with Charlie.

He slouched his right shoulder and slipped off his backpack. Unzipping it, he pulled out a plastic sack that contained ten polyethylene bottles, each one able to hold up to one hundred milliliters of liquid. "How about going up that side of the lake about a hundred yards and collect five water samples along the way?" he asked Victor. Giving him a marking pen, he said, "Label them so that you know where you collected them. If there's a problem, we'll know where to come back to."

"I can do that," Victor said, taking the bottles and pen.

"While you're getting those, I'll get some samples from the stream and a few spots along the lake's edge."

Grant was getting anxious. His first date with Charlie was tonight, and he was going to be late for supper if he and Victor ran into any trouble on the way back. "Hurry it up, okay Victor?" Grant called as he hurried off. "I need to be somewhere at seven."

It was 7:25 when Grant pulled up to Charlie's cabin. Apparently she'd heard the Suburban coming down the road, because she was standing in the doorway waiting for him with her hands on her hips and a sour expression on her face.

Grant learned very quickly that Charlie was not the type of person to hold back her feelings, at least not about anything that upset her. And there was no doubt that she was upset. The moment he stepped from the truck, he was informed in a firm and sharp voice, that it was rude and inconsiderate to be late. She further let him know that she'd spent all afternoon fixing a special supper for him, and that it was probably ruined now because he was late. After Charlie finished venting, that was it. The subject was closed, and it was never mentioned again. But she'd had an effect. He'd felt bad about being late before he'd even gotten there. After she got through, he had the guilts big time. He'd never let that happen again.

The meal wasn't ruined by any stretch of the imagination, at least not as far as he was concerned. Everything was delicious. Charlie had prepared smoked salmon with some type of cream sauce that he'd never had before, fresh steamed green beans, and fresh mushrooms sautéed in butter. To accompany the meal, she had a dry white wine.

Even though the sun was waning, it was still daylight. Charlie achieved a romantic ambiance by closing the curtains and lighting candles. She had on a one-piece shiny black pants outfit and a single string of pearls. The outfit looked like silk, but he wasn't sure, and it molded to her body like a well-fitting leather glove. It was cut low in the front, displaying a sizable cleavage, and he was having a difficult time keeping his eyes from darting down the deep valley. He suspected that was Charlie's intention, because when she caught him looking, she smiled sweetly as if she enjoyed it. He found himself speculating on whether or not she wore a bra.

After dinner, they moved to the sofa in front of the fireplace. It was lit, roaring, and romantic. They were both slowly sipping their wine.

Her cabin was designed a lot like his, except it was much larger. The main room where they were, had the fireplace at one end and the kitchen at the other. A small round oak dining table sat in the corner just off the kitchen, next to a large window that overlooked Denning Fork. Beyond the kitchen, were the bedroom, a bathroom with a shower, and a utility room for the washer and dryer. These would be nice additions to his cabin, along with running water and electricity, he thought.

Above the fireplace, he noticed she had a beautiful Indian blanket, like the one at his cabin. It had bilateral symmetrical patterns that were woven with black, white, yellow, and blue yarns. "Is there a family history that goes with these blankets?" he asked. "I noticed a similar one over my fireplace."

"As a matter of fact there is," Charlie said. "They are Chilkat ceremonial dancing blankets that a tribe gave to my father many years ago. The yarn for the blankets is spun primarily from the wool of the mountain goat. My father was a great champion of the Indians and had a very close bond with the Chilkats in particular."

"That's neat. Victor sure had some very nice things to say about him," Grant said.

"Thanks. Dad was pretty well thought of in these parts." Charlie gazed at the flickering flames, and for a moment, she seemed lost in a memory.

Grant set his wine glass on the end table next to the sofa. "Did you buy this lamp locally?"

"No, my father made it," she answered, coming out of her daze.

"Really. The wood has a very unusual grain. Victor wears a wooden pendant that has the same pattern. Did your father make the lamp in my cabin, too?"

"Yes, as a matter of fact he did. It's called diamond willow wood. My father found a tree of it right here on Denning Fork, somewhere close to Broken Eye Lake. The design in the wood is caused by a particular fungi."

"That's really interesting. I like stuff like that," he said. For a moment, he wondered if she thought that sounded dumb.

They continued to talk for a couple of hours, telling each other about themselves. He sat at one end of the sofa, she was at the other, and there were a few throw pillows in between. He was beginning to feel very comfortable around this woman. She was easy to talk to and certainly easy to look at. For some reason, he'd always found it difficult to talk to and share things with other women. Not that they were getting into anything really deep or heavy this evening—mostly childhood stuff and things life that—but it was just so nice to talk with her.

Charlie got up and stoked the embers, then threw another log on the fire. "You ready for dessert yet?" she asked.

"What do you have?"

"It's a surprise. You'll like it."

"Sure." He started to get up from the sofa. "Can I help?"

"Nah, I'll get it. Tonight is my treat," she said, walking over to the kitchen area and opening the refrigerator. A few moments later she came back carrying a white rose-patterned china bowl in each hand. "Here." She handed him one of the bowls. "I bet you've never had Eskimo ice cream before." Charlie moved the throw pillows to the end of the sofa and sat down beside him.

He looked at it suspiciously, afraid of what its ingredients might be. It was frothy like soapsuds and didn't look like homemade ice cream, or the ice cream he had made from snow when he was a kid. He glanced over at Charlie and asked, "What's in it?"

"Taste it first, then I'll tell you. I promise. It's a native delicacy, popular all over this state." She smiled and took a bite of hers.

He picked up a small glob of the frothy stuff with his spoon and dabbed his tongue with it. It was sweet, but had a slightly bitter aftertaste. Finally, Grant licked the remaining Eskimo ice cream from the spoon. "Not too bad. Now, tell me what's in it."

"Whipped berries, seal oil, and snow." Charlie said, beginning to laugh.

"Seal oil?!"

"Yup."

"What kind of berries are in here? I don't recognize the taste."

"Soapberries." She continued to chuckle.

"Soapberries! Really. I've never heard of a soapberry before."

"Well, that's what gives the ice cream its sudsy look. They're a local berry. I don't know if they grow in the lower forty-eight or not," she said.

They chuckled together and finished their Eskimo ice cream. It really wasn't too bad, but he wouldn't go out of his way for another bowl of it.

Then Charlie asked him how his day had been. She turned to face him and scooted a little closer. She was an attractive woman, and he was happy they were hitting it off so well. He began to tell her about his day, starting with the feral dog tracks at his cabin. Then he mentioned the dead feral dog they had found on the trail, as well as the denning wolf they'd seen. Of course he praised Victor's phenomenal tracking abilities and told her in great detail about the sparrow that was gathering wolf hair in its beak for its nest.

"Has Victor mentioned anything to you about the pack of feral dogs that killed a couple of children several years ago?" Charlie asked.

He told her what Victor had told him.

Charlie looked thoughtful, then said, "What he didn't tell you, was that one of the children who died, was his little sister. She was four and Victor was ten when the tragedy happened. It was in the winter, and he was watching his sister that day. He took her with him to check a few of his marten traps close to their home. It had been a hard winter, and all the animals were having a difficult time surviving. They were attacked by a pack of feral dogs on their way home. He tried his best to fight them off and protect his sister, but he was too small. His efforts were in vain. Her poor little body was dragged several hundred yards. It was ripped and torn to shreds by the time they found her. In the process, Victor was badly maimed himself. That's where that long scar down the length of his face came from. Luckily, one of the neighbor men was in the area and heard the ruckus. He came to Victor's rescue just in time. Victor was in the hospital for weeks."

"God, that's awful," Grant said. "No, he never told me any of that. Especially about his sister."

"That doesn't surprise me. The old-timers say Victor never did get over it. He blames himself for his sister's death. To this day, he believes it should have been him that died, instead of her."

Now Grant understood why Victor knew so much about feral dogs, and how different people in the area had experimented with breeding dogs crossed with wolves. He felt terrible.

While they were on the subject of Victor, he mentioned to Charlie what Victor had said about the decline in the caribou population and the reduced number of calves. Grant also mentioned that he didn't believe wolves were the only culprits for the waning herd. "Do you have any theories?" he asked Charlie.

"Well, I don't know any reason why there would be less calves born each year, unless the herd has some kind of disease," Charlie replied. "And I haven't heard anyone else mention it. Most people around here, and I guess I include myself in that, believe the caribou numbers are declining because of the three harsh winters we've had, and the wolves."

"Yeah, that's what my new boss, Linsey Hogan, said, too. How do you feel about a wolf control program?" Grant asked

"I really don't have an opinion on that, to tell you the truth," Charlie answered. "I would like to think that nature can take care of itself without man's help. But man has interfered in her business so much, I'm not really sure it'll work with the caribou and wolves. The Delta herd has dwindled to a pretty low number in the last five or six years."

"Well, I don't know what's causing the decline, but I intend to find out," Grant said. "I'm going to check everything. Victor and I even collected water samples from Broken Eye Lake, to rule out the possibility that it's contaminated with something.

I'll run them up to the lab in Fairbanks for analysis, the first chance I get."

"Say, I've got to go to Fairbanks tomorrow on business. Would you like me to drop them off at the lab for you?" Charlie asked.

"You sure it wouldn't be too much trouble?"

"No, I'd be glad to."

"Okay, great," he said, happy to get the samples analyzed quicker. "I'll bring them by in the morning when I come in for breakfast." He looked down at his watch. It was 11:25. He had to get up in about six and a half hours, but he hated to leave because he was having such a good time.

Before Grant could say anything, Charlie must have read his mind and said it for him. "Time flies when you're having fun, doesn't it? I know . . . we both have to get up early in the morning, and you need to go home."

"Yes, but I don't really want to," Grant said. "It has been a great evening and dinner was wonderful. I really enjoyed it, and I especially enjoyed talking with you, Charlie. Thanks for inviting me." They both stood up. "Maybe next time we can do this at my place."

"You're on. Just let me know when," she answered, quickly.

It was a little awkward for a moment as they stood there staring and smiling at one another. He wasn't sure whether he should kiss her or not. He decided not to.

As he started toward the front door, he spotted a watercolor painting he'd not noticed before. It was the scene he had viewed up on the ridge that afternoon with Victor. He stopped for a closer inspection. "I was there today," he said in amazement. He didn't see the artist's signature on the painting. "Who did this? It's really good."

"You won't believe it when I tell you," Charlie said. "Billy Jack Boone. He did this for me when we were in high school. We had kind of a thing back then. But that's ancient history."

"It is hard to believe," Grant said, shaking his head. "It sure doesn't fit his personality. This is good though. Does he still paint?"

"No, I don't think so," Charlie said. "His daddy died right after he graduated from high school, and he's had to take care of himself ever since. His mother died when he was born. Probably hasn't had much time to paint."

"That's too bad. He has talent," Grant said. "His situation might explain his disposition though. He seems to be mad at the whole world. Not that it gives him the right to bully people."

"Well, that's Billy Jack. You peel away the crust, and deep down, he's got a heart as big as the Northwest. He's really a pretty good guy," Charlie said.

They were at the front door. Another awkward moment. "Let me break the ice," Charlie said quietly. She stood on her tiptoes and kissed him flush on the lips. Not a long passionate kiss, just a short sweet one.

He stood there like a dead tree, in shock. Charlie opened the door and pushed him out. "I'll see you tomorrow," she said, chuckling.

Grant was thinking about his evening with Charlie as he drove slowly along the old logging trail to his cabin. Just as the white beam of the Suburban's headlights peeked around the corner of a stand of spruce trees, he saw it. He slammed his foot on the brake pedal and stopped the vehicle so fast, he lunged forward.

The silver-blue wolf was standing in the middle of the trail. Staring directly into the lights, the animal's eyes looked green and eerie. There was no fog, no mist, no rain, nothing to give the illusion that a gray wolf's fur appeared to be silver-blue. If only he had a video camera, he could prove to everyone that he really was seeing this incredible animal.

He gently pulled on the handle and opened the door, easing himself out of the truck. He wasn't exactly sure why he was doing it, but he felt he had to. But before he could get completely out, the wolf calmly trotted off into the woods, disappearing like a ghost in the night.

There was no doubt in his mind this time that he'd really seen the silver-blue wolf. He recalled what Victor had said yesterday, in the helicopter, "You are a cheechako, a white man, and I doubt very seriously that you would be one of the chosen few." Of course, he realized that everything Victor had said was Indian folklore, and he didn't put a great deal of stock in it. But whatever the facts, he knew for sure now, that he'd seen the silver-blue wolf. If there was any truth to the Indian legends, then he'd been chosen by this special, spiritual animal for something.

As soon as the Suburban's lights flashed across the front of the cabin, he knew something was wrong. The front door was wide open. He was positive that he'd closed it. He turned the engine off, but left the lights on. Digging out the emergency flashlight from the glove compartment, he turned it on and cautiously stepped from the truck. He scanned in all directions for the slightest movement. It could have been a grizzly that raided his cabin. He didn't see anything lurking about though.

As he moved toward the cabin, he saw that one of the woolen blankets and a pillow had been dragged from the house and left in the front yard. Both were ripped and torn. Grant continued toward cabin cautiously, swinging the light from side to side, not sure if something was going to leap out at him from the shadows. An icy chill of fear ran down his back, and he shuddered. Moving closer to the cabin, he saw a fresh pile of scat on the front stoop. It appeared to be no more than an hour old.

"What in the world is going on here?" he asked out loud. Stepping around the excrement, he poked his head through the doorway and peeked into the cabin. At first glance, everything looked normal. He shined the light over toward the bed, just to his right. As he expected, the blanket and pillow were gone. To his surprise, there was another pile of scat in the middle of the bed. That was strange. Why would a wolf do something like that? They're usually timid and elusive animals around humans and human habitats.

He stepped in the cabin. Bringing the beam toward the center of the room, he saw the clothes he had worn on the hike today, sitting in the middle of the floor. His jeans appeared to have a large wet spot on the legs.

Grant eased over to the pile of clothes, still watching all the shadows as he moved. Kneeling down, he lifted the pants and sniffed the dampened area. The strong caustic smell of ammonia immediately burned at his nasal passages and throat, bringing tears to his eyes. He jerked his head away, dropped the jeans, and stumbled outside for fresh air.

Why would a wolf mark its territory on his clothes? And defecate on his bed and front stoop of the cabin? He just couldn't figure it out.

He had just seen the silver-blue wolf a short distance from here. Had it done this?

Grant recalled something else Victor had said to him: "In my culture, the Indian way, it is of the highest honor to be selected by the silver-blue wolf."

He didn't see how any of this could be an honorable gesture. For the time being, he would keep this to himself.

Chapter 7

Grant peeked out the kitchen window and yawned, as he wiped the sleep from his eyes. It was Wednesday morning. To his disappointment, there was no fog, and no silver-blue wolf sitting across Denning Fork. After what he'd found last night when he got home, he was surprised that he hadn't had any bad or strange dreams about the wolf. At least he couldn't remember any. The only thing he could remember, was the tender kiss Charlie planted on his lips when he left last night. Not a bad memory.

Grant opened the back door, yawned again, and bounced down the steps toward the stream. He was feeling really chipper this morning. Not even the chill in the air seemed to affect his mood.

His evening with Charlie had gone well. She was a nice person, and a darn good cook, too. He wished he'd had a little more experience with women though. There was a couple of times where he felt clumsy and kind of stupid, not sure what to say or do. But everything worked out just fine. One thing was certain. Of any woman he'd ever been on a date with, Charlie was the easiest one to talk to. He was definitely interested in this high-spirited gal. And after last night, he was pretty sure she was interested in him, too.

As he came up to the stream, Grant's eyes were drawn to the damp soil along the water's edge. "Man, the wolves must've had a convention here last night. There's tracks everywhere." He gazed at the ground up and down the stream, then bent down on his haunches and looked at a few of the prints more closely. "Or are these feral dog tracks?" He wasn't sure, and not experienced enough to tell the difference, yet. He'd mention it to Victor later today and see what he thought.

Leaning over the rippling creek, Grant cupped his hands and splashed some of the frigid water on his face. His cheek muscles instantly tensed, and it nearly took his breath away, but it felt good, clean, and refreshing. Water ran down his face, dripping from his chin, as he glanced over to the other side of Denning Fork. Thinking of the other day, he was now convinced he saw a silver-blue wolf and not an illusion caused by the fog.

Grant had only been here three days but was already beginning to take a real liking to this state. This place felt like where he belonged. He splashed another handful of water on his face. "Br-r-r-r, that feels good," he said, shivering.

He heard a noise. Someone, or something, was coming up behind him. Just as Grant turned his head to see what was there, something powerful grabbed the back of his head and shoved it down into the cold water. His eyes were open, and the side of his face was pressed against the gravely bottom of the stream. The cold smooth rocks felt like ice cubes pressing against his right cheek. He pushed back with all his strength, his fingers clawing into the damp soil as he tried to pop his head above water for a gasp of air. But the creature holding him in this fluid tomb, was much stronger than him.

Grant struggled to blink as the icy water rushed over his eyes. But his eyelids seemed to be numb and frozen. His long hair wiggled back and forth in the stream in front of his face. He felt the freezing water rapidly draining the life from him, as the strength seeped from the muscles in his arms and legs. His efforts to push his head from of the water, were failing. He needed air, or he was going to die.

The iron-vise clamped to the back of his head, eased somewhat, then clenched into a fist, gripped his hair tightly, and painfully pulled at the roots. A moment later his head was yanked from the water.

The first gulp of air felt like liquid fire surging down into his lungs. His heart banged against his rib like a jackhammer. He thought it was going to burst out of his chest at any moment. His vision was blurry from the cold water dripping from his wet hair. Plopping backwards, Grant stared up at the large figure.

"Being a cheechako is no excuse for not paying attention," Billy Jack said, resting his heavy boot on Grant's chest.

"What's the matter with you?!" Grant screamed, choking and gasping for air. "You nearly drowned me."

"Next time I will," Billy Jack said.

"Are you crazy or something?"

"Some think so."

"And what do you mean, next time?" Grant asked. He jerked Billy Jack's boot off his chest with both hands and scooted backwards across the ground, away from the lunatic.

"It's pretty simple, Farm Boy," Billy Jack said sarcastically. "I told you to stay away from Charlie. And what does the numb-brained hayseed do? You go to her house and have dinner with her last night. Then to rub it in my face like salt in a wound, you stay late, leaving after eleven o'clock. And you kiss her."

"I don't believe it. You were spying on me," Grant said, shocked and appalled. "Just who do you think you are?" Besides, he thought to himself, she kissed me, not the other way around. But Billy Jack wouldn't have made that distinction.

"Wrong, Cheechako," Billy Jack said, pulling the hunting knife from its leather sheath on his belt. "Just who do you think you are? Coming in here all high and mighty, Mr. Graduate Student."

Grant was still on the ground, still scooting backwards on his butt and pushing with his hands and feet as fast as he could to get away from this nut. Billy Jack came at him with the knife, waving it in front of his own face. It looked at least a foot long and six inches wide, more like a meat cleaver than a hunting knife. Sunlight caught the cold chrome-steel blade and glinted off of it into Grant's wide, frightened eyes.

"Some of us don't have rich parents like you do, to put us through college, Cheechako." Billy Jack was still coming at him at a steady pace. "You think that gives you the right to come in here and take advantage of our women? Well it doesn't."

"What are you talking about? Have you gone completely out of your mind?" Grant cried.

Billy Jack lunged forward, catching the left pant leg of Grant's jeans and dragging him back. Using his free foot, Grant kicked with all his strength, trying to knock the hunting knife from Billy Jack's hand. But he couldn't do it. His heart was really pounding now. He shook all over, but not because of the cold temperatures.

Billy Jack jabbed the long-bladed knife toward the fly of Grant's jeans. But the gleaming sharp point failed to penetrate the denim material. He instantly stopped kicking his free leg at Billy Jack.

"I only give one warning. You had yours," Billy Jack said in a deep voice. "Now, I'm going to do some damage to you, boy."

"I only give one warning, too," a familiar voice said from behind Billy Jack. "And if you don't drop that toad-sticker and let my friend go, I'm going to do some serious damage to you—like blow your brains all over the ground."

Billy Jack dropped the knife, let go of Grant's leg, stepped to the side with his hands in the air, and eased his head around to see who was behind him.

Victor stood tall, with a slight grin on his face and a shotgun tightly gripped in his hands. The double barrels were aimed at Billy Jack's face.

The man lifted the phone receiver from its cradle very carefully. It was the second time he'd done so in the past sixty seconds. He stared at the receiver for a long time, as if it were a foreign object, and tried to decide whether to make the call or not. Finally, with a shaking hand, he pushed the appropriate buttons on the keypad, then punched in his PIN number from his phone card. The receiver felt cold and unfriendly against his ear. Was this the right thing to do?

After three rings he lowered the receiver and gawked at it as if were a poisonous snake squirming in his hand. The phone was still ringing. Maybe he should hang up and not make the call after all. Let this whole mess he'd gotten himself into, unravel on its own. Take his punishment like a man. What he was doing was wrong. He knew that, but what else could he do.

Someone finally answered. "Linsey Hogan. . . . Hello. . . ."

He was still looking at the receiver. His hand quivered worse than before, and his brain screamed at him. Hang up for God's sake, he thought to himself. Stop this madness now, before it gets completely out of control.

"Hello," Linsey repeated.

"It's me," the man finally said, talking low and cupping his hand over the side of the receiver so no one would hear what he was saying. His eyes darted in every direction like a common criminal. "I thought you'd like to know that your new boy is sending lake samples to the lab for analysis."

"I told you to not call me on this line! Call the other number," Linsey said.

"It was busy, and I needed to talk to you," the man explained.

"I don't care. Wait until it's not busy," she snapped. "It's 8:30 for crying-out-loud. Samples from what lake?"

"You know what lake," the man replied.

"Yeah, yeah. When?"

"Today. Charlie Sanford is bringing them. I overheard her and that Rawlings boy talking about it."

"Good," she said, pulling a cigarette from the pack on her desk. "I'll be here all day, so I can greet her. Thanks for calling."

"I tried to tell you something like this was going to happen. I want out before it gets any messier."

"Shut up and listen to me," Linsey said abruptly. "Your not getting out of anything or doing anything except what I tell you to do. Let me refresh your memory. I have enough on your ass to have you thrown into the slammer for twenty years. Maybe even longer."

There was a pause on both ends of the line, while Linsey lit her cigarette. He heard the scratching sound of the lighter, her deep inhaling of the cigarette, and then her blowing the smoke back out over the mouthpiece. She was an evil woman. How could he have gotten mixed up with her?

"Look, it's going to be all right. Trust me. After our deal in Anchorage comes through, we'll both have more money than we'll know what to do with," Linsey said in a calmer tone. "Don't call this number again, okay. Keep me posted on the progress of our project."

"Okay, I guess you're right. I'm just nervous that someone's going to figure it out. When I find out anything I'll let you know." Billy Jack hung up the phone. "God, I hope this lady knows what she's doing," he said to himself, as he walked out of the hangar office. "If she doesn't, she'll ruin everything."

"It's about time," Whitie Saylor said. "Other people want to use the phone too, ya know." He had stopped his pacing in front of the office door and glared at Billy Jack. "What's all the secrecy, huh? Closing the door and everything. You aren't doing something illegal are ya, Billy Jack? Boy, I'd love to know about it if you were, just so I could personally burn your butt."

"Shut up, you old drunk, and get out of my way." He shoved Whitie to the side and stomped off toward the open hangar doors where his clients for the day were waiting for him.

"You got your gear all loaded?" he asked as he came up to them.

"You bet, and we're ready to get going," one of the three men said, standing in the doorway.

He couldn't remember any of the men's names. His mind was on next week in Anchorage. Well at least he wouldn't have that pesky woman client from the other day to put up with.

Motioning toward the helicopter, he said, " Well then, let's rock and roll. You guys will get some good shots in today."

Charlie closed the cash register and headed for the kitchen doors. Frank Kicklighter ambled around the corner, coming from the hallway where the rest rooms and phone booth were. His face was long and weary. As usual, he had his bottled water clutched in his right hand.

She stopped at the kitchen, turned, and walked behind the counter toward Frank. "Sheriff, can I get you anything?"

"Nope, I don't think so. Thanks anyway." The sheriff uncapped the bottle of water and took a swig, then capped it.

"Frank, come over here and sit down for a minute. I'd like to talk to you," she said. "You look terrible. If you don't stop worrying and get some sleep you're going to be the one sick and in the hospital. Then who's going to be there for your daughter."

"I know, but it's hard, Charlie," Frank said listlessly. He sat down on a stool across the counter from her.

She leaned over with her elbows on the counter and cradled her chin in her cupped hands. "Look, I'm going to the bank in Fairbanks this morning," she said. "I should have your money for you before the weekend, or early next week. Okay?"

"Yeah, that'll be swell. I really appreciate it, Charlie."

"I mean it about getting some sleep," she said with a bit of force. "You know if there is anything I can do, all you have to do is ask."

"Thanks, Charlie," Frank said as he got up from the stool. "Look, I've got to go. I've got some people I need to meet." The sheriff turned and headed for the door, walking like an old man.

CHAPTER 8

CHARLIE WAS THE ONLY PERSON IN THE STATE of Alaska that she knew of, who could take on Billy Jack without getting her face broken. And that's exactly what she intended to do, after Victor told her what had happened at Grant's cabin that morning. She was so angry she could have spit roofing nails. Of course, Grant was unaware that his Indian companion had spoken to her about the issue. So as not to embarrass him, Charlie waited until Grant and Victor had left for Two Forks Airport for their chopper run. Unfortunately, Billy Jack had left about the same time, so she didn't get a chance to chew him out.

A few minutes after Charlie had talked with Frank Kicklighter, she got a phone call from the bank, saying they would have to postpone her appointment until 1:00. That was fine with her. Maybe she could catch Billy Jack at the airport before he took off with his new clients.

As Charlie walked up to the helicopter, she noticed three gentlemen sitting inside with their seat belts secured. Billy Jack was outside and had part of the engine cover pulled off, apparently working on some kind of a problem. She walked up behind him and asked, coolly, "Got a problem?"

Billy Jack turned around with a surprised look on his face. Smiling, he said, "Charlie, it's good to see your pretty face. Yeah, a darn fuel leak. What brings you out here? You want to go up with me today?"

Charlie stood there with her hands on her hips, controlled rage seeping through her voice. "No, I don't want to go up with you today or any other day," she said, slowly emphasizing each word. "And I'll tell you what brings me out here. Trouble. Big time trouble. Like you've never seen before." With that, she twisted his left ear as hard as she could and dragged him behind the helicopter.

"Ouch! Charlie, that hurts! Let go! What's this all about?" Billy Jack yelled. He could see one of the men in the helicopter peeking out to see what the commotion was.

Still hanging onto his ear, Charlie let him have it. "I heard what you pulled out at the cabin this morning," she hollered, sparks flying. "I'm so angry at you! This is the last time, Billy Jack. No more! You understand?" Her voice stomped out the words.

"Yeah. Now will you let go of my ear? It hurts."

All three men in the helicopter were now peeking their heads out the side door to see what was going on at the back of the aircraft.

Charlie twisted Billy Jack's ear even harder. "No, I won't let go. Not until I'm done talking to you."

"Ouch! Not so hard. It hurts," Billy Jack cried.

"Good, maybe this conversation will stick in that thick skull of yours for more than thirty seconds," she barked. "I am not your woman, your girl friend, your sister, your mother, or your grandmother. So it's not your responsibility to protect me. Got it?"

"Yeah," Billy Jack said, his face wrinkled up in pain.

"Billy Jack, you have run off every male friend I've ever had since high school," she said. "And it's going to stop. Right here, right now! Is that clear?"

"Yes. Now will you let me go?"

"No. I'm not through yet, and I'm not convinced you're sincere," she fired back.

"I am, I am, I promise," Billy Jack whined. "I just don't want to see you get hurt, that's all."

For some reason the whole scene suddenly struck her funny. Here was Billy Jack, twice her size, bent over, red-faced, crying like a little boy, while she told him what he was going to do. Holding her laughter in check, she said, "I'm a big girl now, Billy Jack. I'm not going to get hurt. And I can take care of myself." She gave his ear one last twist for emphasis. Billy Jack's face curled up even more but he didn't say anything. "I happen to like Grant Rawlings. You leave him alone. Understand?"

"Yes."

"Yes, what?"

"Yes, I understand."

"Understand what?" She grabbed his ear again.

Trying to dodge her hand, Billy Jack muttered, "To leave Grant Rawlings alone. Now let my ear go."

"Promise?"

"Promise."

Charlie jerked her hand away, turned around, and strode forcefully toward her vehicle. As she walked by the helicopter, she barked at the three men peering out the bay opening, "What are you looking at?!"

The grins dropped from their faces, and they jerked their heads back into the chopper. Looking back over her shoulder, she said, "I've never known you to break a promise, Billy Jack, so I'm holding you to it." She stopped as she climbed into the car and said, "Oh, and by the way, have a nice day." The car door slammed shut.

This time of year, Highway 3 to Fairbanks was a pleasant drive. It was almost 11:30 when Charlie pulled into the Alaska Wildlife Management Commission's parking lot. There were only about ten cars there. The two story building was yellow brick and appeared to be just a little larger than the Trading Post.

She grabbed the paper bag with the water samples, off the front seat of her car and walked toward the building. As she headed in, she thought to herself that the day seemed to be working out just fine. She'd had time to straighten out Billy Jack, she would have time to drop off these samples, and she might even have time for a quick bite to eat before meeting with the bank to see about getting money for Frank. Charlie decided to not put the cabins up for collateral. She felt confident the bank would loan her the money.

Just inside the front door was a pretty young receptionist, typing and answering the phone. Charlie explained who she was, and why she was there. The young woman was very helpful and gave her directions to the lab. It was at the back of the building, and she was told that the forth door on the right was the office of Allen Colbert, the chemist in charge. He would help her.

Allen Colbert's nameplate was on the wall outside his office. The door was open. Charlie peeked in and knocked lightly. In front of her, was a short thin man about her age, with crewcut blond hair and thick black-rimmed glasses. Wearing a white lab coat, he sat behind a cluttered desk, looking down at a stack of papers with numbers on them.

"Excuse me," Charlie said to him. "The lady at the front desk said that you might be able to help me."

The skinny man looked up. Seeing Charlie standing there, he quickly stood up, smiled slightly, and stuck out his hand. "Hi. I'm Allen Colbert. Pleased to meet you. How may I help you?"

As she did with the receptionist, Charlie explained who she was, and why she was there. Then she handed the chemist the note Grant had sent with her.

Allen quickly read the note, then gazed up at the ceiling and scratched the side of his head, as if trying to remember something. "Broken Eye Lake," he finally said. "Seems to me we ran some analyses on water from that lake, or somewhere near there . . . maybe about a year ago."

She found that to be unusual and quite interesting. "Really? For whom?"

"I'm not sure," he said, still scratching the side of his head. "The name doesn't seem to click right at the moment. It was an unusual name though. I do remember that. I'll look it up later and let you know."

"Yes, please do. I'm sure Grant would like to know that. It may be of some use to him," she said. "You still can analyze these samples, can't you?"

"Certainly," Allen said. He looked down at Grant's note, then back up at her. "There's only ten samples so it shouldn't take too long to do them. Any of the organic EPA priority-pollutants, would be detected on a machine called a gas chromatograph/mass spectrometer. The guy that runs it, can do them on Friday. The biochemical oxygen demands for bacterial activity take twenty-four hours, so I'll start those myself, right after lunch. For those two analyses, we'll have the results sometime Friday. But the ICP-MS for heavy metals is a different story. That instrument is backlogged for the rest of the week. I run that instrument and I'll be going on vacation for three weeks starting Monday, so I'm not sure when they'll get analyzed."

"Oh gosh. I don't know," she said, batting her eyes at the chemist. Turning on the charm while she tried to figure out a way to get him to run the samples, Charlie said, "I'm so dumb about these things. What did you say that last thing was?"

"ICP-MS? Inductive Coupled Plasma Mass Spectrometry," Allen said with pride. "It's the real workhorse around here."

Charlie batted her eyes again and smiled. She was not above using feminine wiles if something was important, and this was important. Grant had asked her to see if the samples could be analyzed as soon as possible. He said they would provide him with some good information for his first monthly report to his professor, Dale Barlow, and his boss, Linsey Hogan. Charlie did not intend to fail him.

"Isn't there any way you can work these in? Like you said, there's only ten samples. That's not very many, is it?" She flashed her eyes again and gave Allen Colbert the "poor little me" look, hoping that would persuade him to run the samples.

"Well, I don't know," Allen said. "I'll be working until noon on Saturday. Maybe I could work them in then."

"That would be great," she said with a large smile on her face. "I know Grant Rawlings would appreciate it. It would help him out a lot with his research for Miss Hogan."

"Miss Hogan? These samples are for Miss Hogan?" Allen questioned. He seemed suddenly nervous and started shuffling papers on his desk. "You didn't tell me that."

"Yes, Grant just starting working for the AWMC this week, and his immediate supervisor is Linsey Hogan," Charlie said, noticing the change in the man when she mentioned Linsey's name.

"Well, on second thought, I think we can work these in without too much difficulty," Allen said. "Do you have a fax machine where I can send the results?"

"Yes, as a matter of fact I do," she said happily. "Let me have Grant's note and I'll write the number on there." Allen handed Charlie the piece of paper. She set the bag of samples down on the messy desk, then wrote both the fax and regular phone numbers for the Trading Post on the back of the note. "If you need to call me for any reason, I gave you my business number, too."

"Good," Allen said, taking the note back from her and stuffing it in the breast pocket of his lab coat. "I'll fax you the results for everything some time late Saturday morning, before I leave for vacation."

"Well, Miss Sanford, what brings you to the big city," Linsey Hogan said, coming down a flight of stairs from the second floor. She held out her hand. "It's good to see you again."

"Likewise, Miss Hogan," Charlie said with a forced smile. She didn't like this woman. Something about her rubbed Charlie the wrong way. Linsey was wearing a leather coat with a beautiful gray and white wolf pelt collar. Charlie wondered what Grant would think about his new boss if he knew what she had around her neck. "I brought some water samples to be analyzed for Grant."

"Oh, really. So it's *Grant*, huh? How sweet that you're on first name basis," Linsey said as she cinched the waist tie of her leather coat and stared at Charlie. "From where?"

"Broken Eye Lake," Charlie said. She continued to give the catty, plump woman a little more information about *Grant* to rub it in. "He and Victor collected them on their first day out in the field."

"I like that boy," Linsey said, digging a pack of Salem cigarettes from her coat pocket. Lighting one, she added, "I'm glad we could work something out so he could work for us."

"He is, too," Charlie said.

"For a couple of women with a little maturity, like ourselves, it's good to see a *young* person with such enthusiasm and energy," Linsey said with a smirk on her face. She blew smoke out from the side of her mouth. "Isn't it?"

Charlie was sensitive about that topic—the age difference between her and Grant—and she took Linsey's comment as an intentional dig. "Yes it is," she said coolly. She would have loved to sling a dig right back at this woman, but instead, she gritted her teeth and checked her anger.

"I knew you'd feel that way," Linsey said, blowing out more smoke. "Allen will take good care of you. Won't you, Allen?"

Until now, Allen hadn't said a word. He just looked down at his desk like an animal that had been beaten into submission. "Yes, ma'am." His stare never left from the top of his desk.

"I'm sure there's nothing in the water," Linsey said. "But I always say it's good to not leave any stone unturned when it comes to protecting the environment and wildlife."

"I agree," Charlie said, thinking what a line of bull this lady was spreading.

"It's been nice chatting with you, Miss Sanford, but I have a lunching engagement with Senator Markson." Linsey began to walk off. "Ciao."

Charlie turned the engine off and dropped the keys into her purse. It was five minutes before her appointment. She was nervous, worrying about her chances of getting a loan to pay Frank Kicklighter the money he needed for his daughter's operation. The parking lot of the bank was jammed full. She'd had to wait several minutes for someone to leave before she could find a parking space.

She leaned over and looked in the rearview mirror. Her hair was an absolute disaster. Coming out of the restaurant after lunch, her hair had been blown apart by a stiff northerly breeze. She quickly tried to brush it back into place. She put on fresh lipstick and dabbed a bit more mascara onto her lashes.

During her lunch, Charlie repeatedly rehearsed in her mind, what she was going to say to the loan manager at the bank. When they rescheduled her appointment, they had also changed who she was going to see. She was now to meet with a manager named Peter Worley. She hoped it wasn't the same Peter Worley she had gone to high school with. He was a real jackass. If it was the same guy, she might be in trouble with the loan.

Charlie crammed the cosmetics back in her purse, got out of the car, and hurried toward the entrance of the First National Bank of Fairbanks. It was one of those modern buildings with an abundance of glass.

Inside, the whole place was busy. Several people were standing in line at the teller windows, while others were conducting business in a row of glass-walled offices to her right. The last office at the end of the row, belonged to the bank president. It was the largest.

Standing there in the large open area, Charlie was freezing. She pulled her light jacket together in front. Either the building was having a problem with its heating unit, or they just didn't like to give their customers any heat.

Just inside the front door was a middle-aged lady with dark hair, sitting at an L-shaped desk. Her fingers were flying over a computer keyboard. The woman was wearing a peach colored sweater, buttoned most of the way up.

Charlie walked up to her and said, "Hello, my name is Charlotte Sanford, and I have a 1:00 appointment with Mr. Worley."

"He's running a little late," the receptionist said coldly. She pointed to a row of chairs with a large stone planter behind them. "You can sit over there in the waiting area. I'll call you when he's ready." There was no smile or acknowledgment that Charlie was even there. The lady's eyes never left the computer screen, and her fingers never stop pecking at the keyboard, the whole time she was talking to Charlie.

"Thank you," Charlie said. "Would you know how long that might be?"

The woman stopped typing for a moment, let out an exasperated sigh, and said, "five, fifteen, thirty minutes, maybe an hour. Who knows. Certainly not me. Like I said, I will call you when Mr. Worley is ready for you. Please have a seat." She went back to typing. Never once did her eyes leave the computer screen.

Charlie sat down. Her first impression of this place wasn't very good. They sure didn't seem to have the same level of commitment to the customer, if they had any at all, as they did the last time she was here. But then the bank had been bought out by a large financial conglomerate a year ago.

Forty-five minutes later, almost grudgingly, the stone-faced receptionist called her name and told Charlie she could go in now. The moment Charlie walked into Mr. Worley's office, she knew she was in trouble. The man sat behind an obscenely large walnut desk with his back to her, typing on a computer. It was the same jerk she'd gone to high school with. Back then he was known as "Short Peter."

A thick lump rose in her throat. She swallowed. At the moment, she didn't feel real good about this. She almost turned around and walked out. But she was here, and it had been a long drive. Maybe it would be all right. Maybe he'd forgotten that she was the one who gave him the nickname.

"Excuse me, Mr. Worley—"

"Come in and close the door," he said, never turning around. "Have a seat. I'll be with you in a moment."

Charlie sat down, crossed her legs, and rested her hands on the purse in her lap. She had worn a black pantsuit with a white silk blouse, one of the few nice outfits she had. Most of the time she wore jeans, a blouse, and hiking boots. Running the Trading Post, she didn't need much else.

She glanced around Peter's office. Everything was orderly and in its place. There were no pictures of children, or a wife, or of anyone for that matter. The hair on top of Peter's head was thinning in the back. He was still short and skinny as always. The jacket of his dark blue pin-stripped suit, was neatly draped on a hanger behind the door. She could tell he took his white shirts to the cleaners, by the heavy starch in his collar.

Peter twirled around in his chair and scooted up to the large walnut desk. "Now Miss Sanford, how can I help you today?" he asked. Then he looked up at her. "Charlotte. Charlotte Sanford. I remember you. Aren't you the one that tagged me with that dreadful nickname in high school?"

Charlie could feel the heat rise in her face as it flushed. She couldn't believe he brought that up at a time like this. After all these years. What a jerk. "That's in the past, Peter. A long time ago. Besides, we were all crazy kids back then. All forgotten."

"Uh-huh. Maybe for some of you," he said, staring at her from behind his desk with beady little eyes and a mean grin. "Back to my original question. How may I help you?" This time his tone seemed to be a little cooler.

God, he has never forgotten that stupid nickname, she thought. I'll bet he's going to hold that against me for this loan. Charlie cleared her throat and straightened up in the chair. "I need to borrow five thousand dollars," she said.

Without altering the cold expression on his face, Peter leaned over and lifted a few sheets of papers from the printer tray. He looked at them for a moment, then peeked up at her from behind the papers and said, "Really. Do you have anything as collateral?"

A cold chill ran down her back. She squirmed in the chair and swallowed again. "Well, yes. I have a business—"

"The Trading Post in Two Forks."

"Yes, and—"

"Accord to this credit report," he tossed the papers on his desk, "you already have a first and second mortgage on it. I'm afraid that won't do. Not at all."

"You've already done a credit report on me?" she asked. Her voice was rising.

"I always do a credit report on prospective clients," he said smugly. "Many times that will save both of us a lot of valuable time. In your case, I think that may be the situation. You are already overextended. And quite frankly, I don't know how you are making your current obligations."

His statements knocked the wind right out of her sails. She slumped down in the chair. Charlie took a deep breath and said, "Peter, I desperately need this money." Then she proceeded to tell him what the money was for. As much as she hated to admit it, she was begging.

"That's a very touching story, Miss Sanford," Peter said tersely. "But I have to make decisions based on facts. And the facts present you as a credit risk. The bank can't loan you the money under the current circumstances."

"Okay, okay, so I owe a little money. What would it take for you to loan me the money?" she asked.

"A credible cosigner would be nice," Peter said. "Do you have anyone that could do that?"

Charlie dropped her head and looked at the plush carpet at her feet. She shuffled them, racking her brain for anyone that might be a possible cosigner. There was just no one she could think of. This whole ordeal was turning into a humiliating experience. "I guess not," she said sadly. She got up from her chair.

Just as her hand touched the doorknob, Peter said, "Maybe there is a way we can work something out."

Her spirits lifted. She turned back to Peter with a hopeful smile on her face and said, "Really? What? I'll do anything to help Frank out."

Peter had a devilish smile on his face. He leaned forward and rested his elbows on the desk, clasping his hands together. "That's a good way to put it, Charlotte. We all have needs." That's when she noticed the wedding band on his finger. "Maybe we could have dinner tonight and talk about it. If you know what I mean."

What a jerk, she thought. WHAT A JERK! Charlie could feel the steam building up inside of her. The blood vessels in her neck began to bulge and pulse with each beat of her heart. She grabbed the doorknob again and jerked the door open. It was best to not say anything, she told herself. Just leave. Just get out of here before you slap his face. Red-faced, she marched out of the office, her anger very apparent.

Halfway across the lobby Charlie stopped, turned around, and headed straight back to Peter Worley's office. No, she wasn't going to let that slime-bucket get away with this. Without closing his door to keep it private, Charlie said loudly for everyone to hear, "Short Peter, let me tell you something. I wouldn't go to bed with a snake like you if my life depended on it. And you can take your money and stick it where the sun doesn't shine."

She spun around, banged into the door jamb, and headed back across the lobby. A bald-headed man with a shocked looked on his face, poked his head out from the president's office. Charlie kept marching, while pointing a finger at the president. "And you, sir, will hear from my attorney about sexual harassment charges against this piece of crap you have working for you."

The man's eyes grew big and wide. His bald head twisted toward Peter Worley's office. As she went by the receptionist's desk, the lady with the stone face now wore a huge smile. In a low voice, she said, "Way to go. This place needs someone to put them on their ear."

Charlie blasted through the front entranceway and on out to her car, never looking back. She sat in her Cherokee in the bank parking lot for several minutes, venting her anger on the steering wheel, hammering it with her fist. She was furious that

Short Peter had propositioned her. No, extortion was the proper term for what that slug had done. She not only felt violated, but angry and hopeless. She had promised Frank the money by early next week at the latest. What was she going to do now?

Distraught, and feeling very low at the moment, Charlie lightly dabbed her eyes with a tissue from her purse. She was an emotionally strong woman and didn't cry every time she didn't get her way. But this was different. She had made a promise to help a good friend, and now, she might not be able to keep that promise.

Charlie positioned the rearview mirror so she could see the damage her crying had done to her face. She blotted the puffiness under her red eyes once more and wiped away the mascara that had streaked down from the corners of her eyes. She felt childish and silly, sitting here crying. She would figure something out. She always had before.

Just as Charlie reached up to adjust the rearview mirror back to its position for driving, she caught a glimpse of Linsey Hogan. Surprised, she turned around to get a better view. There was a man walking with Linsey on her other side. His face was blocked from Charlie's view, but from what she could see, it looked like Frank Kicklighter. The two of them went into the bank, crossed the lobby, and walked straight over to Peter Worley's office. He jumped up from his seat to greet them, a big smile on his face. They all shook hands, then sat down. Linsey and the man with her had their backs to Charlie.

She recalled what Frank had said about borrowing on his insurance policies and his retirement, and how expensive his daughter's treatments had become. Maybe Frank was getting a second mortgage on his house to pay the balance of the bone transplant. But why would Linsey Hogan be with him at the bank? They weren't friends, at least, she didn't think so. Maybe there was some other reason why they were at the bank together.

And maybe I'm letting my imagination drift up into the ozone layer, she thought. She didn't even know for sure that it was Frank Kicklighter in there with Linsey.

"This has been a bad day," she said to herself. "I've got to get out of here." Charlie started the Jeep, backed out from her parking slot, and headed for Two Forks.

It had been a wasted trip as far as the loan went, but she had another idea for getting the money. Her thin lips arched into a tiny smile, and she reached over and turned on the radio, cranking the volume up so loud the speakers vibrated.

It was turning out to be a good day after all. So far during their chopper run, they had seen two loner wolves and two separate wolf packs, with eight to ten animals each. If it hadn't been for Victor saving him from Billy Jack this morning, he wouldn't be here at all. It was now around two o'clock, and Grant noticed that the subject of what happened that morning, hadn't been mentioned even once that day. It was as if it had never happened.

Victor's wife, Mary Margaret, had packed them a wonderful lunch again. About noon, they landed Flutter Butt near a small lake in the northwestern section of Denali National Park. Because of the abundance of lakes in the area, this particular one didn't have a name. The sky was clear, blue, and tranquil, allowing bright sunlight to bring the temperatures up into the high fifties. They sat on a small knoll eating their lunch and watched three moose cows lumber along, eating and drinking near the water's edge.

At one point, a bull moose came sauntering up to the water and waded right in. He was only in the cold lake for a few seconds, when he came plodding back up on the bank and shuddered vigorously to shake the water off. Amazingly, as the animal shook, a cloud of glistening red mist exploded from the creature's body, surrounding it like a crimson aura.

"Did you see that? What was that red stuff coming off that bull moose?" Grant asked Victor.

Victor took a bite of the apple Mary Margaret had packed in his lunch and calmly said, "Blood." Then he chomped down on the apple as though nothing out of the ordinary had happened.

"Blood?" Grant asked, as he reached into his backpack and dug out his binoculars. "From what?"

"Well, that old bull is probably eaten up with winter ticks, I'd guess," Victor told him, tossing his apple core to the side. "Probably several hundred of them, maybe thousands."

Grant focused the binoculars on the moose as it wobbled over toward the three cows. The water dripping from its belly was bright red.

"That old guy will be prime prey for a wolf pack in the very near future. Out here, the injured, the old, and the diseased animals are the main victims of the wolf." Victor said.

"Yeah, I knew that," Grant agreed. "But I wasn't aware that parasitic infections like ticks played a role in the scheme of things too."

"Yup. Winter ticks can bleed an animal practically to death," Victor said. "He looks pretty weak."

Shortly after that, Grant finished his apple and lunch was complete. They sat there on the knoll a few more minutes, enjoying the scenery and saying little to each other. Then they gathered up their litter, went back to the helicopter, and took off to continue their work.

Grant leaned over to look out the side window of the chopper, wondering about a few things Victor had said at lunch. He spoke into the mouthpiece of his headset. "Victor, what do you think happens to the members of a wolf pack when they become too old to be in the hunt? Do they just go off and die in the woods somewhere?"

"Maybe . . . sometimes," Victor answered. "But our people believe that the elders in a wolf pack are useful to its survival in some way, and so an old wolf is fed and protected by the other members. It's not banished from the pack because it's no longer a strong hunter and warrior."

"If a wolf can't hunt, then what use is it to the pack?" he asked.

"Knowledge, wisdom, and experience," Victor replied quickly. "For example, an older wolf may have the unique or best ability in the pack, to track or smell out a herd of caribou, moose, or sheep. But its old muscles have been stretched too many times and have lost the endurance for the long chase. Or its worn teeth are now nubs, not sharp enough to inflict the slashing killing bites to bring down a caribou. So the older wolf tracks the herd, but the chase and kill are done by the younger wolves."

"I never thought about it that way before."

"That's why you were assigned to me, my boy," Victor chuckled. "Wolves don't have old folks homes like humans do, where the children can shuffle their parents to when they're no longer useful to them in a material way. Indians are a lot like wolves in that respect. They take advantage of their elders' knowledge and wisdom and use it to mold and guide their societies, something the white man has yet to learn."

The last image Grant had of his parents, flickered through his mind. They were standing in the Springfield, Missouri airport, his father's arm around his mother's waist, squeezing her tightly. Both were trying their best to smile as they waved at him. Grant looked over his shoulder as he walked toward the plane, and there were tears in his mother's eyes. That had only been four days ago. It seemed like years.

His parents would never go to a retirement home. Like the wolf, he would protect and care for them until they met their Maker once again. The thought of that, sent a sharp pang to his heart. He missed them already and decided to call them from the Trading Post that evening.

The chopper passed over a tundra ridge. On the other side, in the ravine, Grant spotted something unusual on the ground. "Wait a minute. I see something down there," he said. "Can you bring the chopper closer?"

"You bet." Victor swung the helicopter around and headed down into the ravine. As they neared the location, Victor said, "Looks like some kind of carcasses."

A few moments later, they landed close by and walked up to the site. There, piled together, were four skinned animals.

"Are those wolf carcasses?" Grant asked, alarmed.

"Those heartless, cold-blooded poachers! Yes, those are wolf carcasses," Victor said with sadness and disgust in his voice. In frustration, his companion kicked a rock, the size of a baseball, down the slope of the ravine. The Indian knelt down next to the bloody, fleshy bodies. "This was done sometime yesterday. No more than thirty hours ago." With great care, he pulled the bodies apart to examine them closer. "Just as I thought. They've been shot. From a helicopter, I suspect."

"How do you know that?" Grant said.

"I saw the marks of a chopper's runners in the soft soil where we landed," Victor said.

"But this is a national preserve. They can't do that. It's illegal to hunt or trap in here," Grant cried, outraged.

"For the poacher, any land is hunting land," Victor said. "That's a fact that you're going to have to accept, whether you like it or not."

"But why are so many wolves being poached right now?"

"I can't answer that," Victor said. "But something big is up. I can tell you that much for sure."

"I know you think Billy Jack is involved in this in some way," he said. "But how? When he comes in from taking his clients out, do you see any wolf pelts in his helicopter?"

"No, I haven't seen that," Victor admitted. "A smart man wouldn't do that though. A smart man, after killing and skinning the wolf, would stash the hides somewhere safe, before coming back to the airport. Then in a few days, or weeks, when a fur buyer is in the area, they'd collect the pelts and sell them."

"Well, I'm not convinced, yet, that Billy Jack is involved in this poaching business," Grant said as Victor stood up from the carcasses. "Even though he tried to gut me this morning. But I do know one thing for sure, my friend. We have to pull out all the stops to catch those responsible for this, before there are no more wolves in Alaska to study."

It was 6:20 when Grant walked up the steps to the Trading Post. He had felt low all afternoon, after he and Victor had found the skinned wolf carcasses. But his appetite was strong, and his stomach growled for food.

Grant could hardly wait to tell Charlie what he'd seen and ask her if she might have any ideas as to who might be killing these wolves. They only found four today. How many dead wolves had they not found? He would never know the answer to that, and based on the massive number of wire snare traps he and Victor had seen the other day when they released the moose cow, it could be in the hundreds.

But why? That concerned him even more after Victor said that something big was up. He wasn't exactly sure what that meant, and didn't ask, and Victor never offered to elaborate. Maybe Charlie could shed some light on all of this.

The bell rang as he opened the door and stepped in. After last night, he was anxious to see Charlie again to set up another date. He would just take his chances with Billy Jack. Maybe once the man realized that he had no intention of hurting or taking advantage of Charlie, the two of them could reach a truce. Who knows, maybe they could even become friends. The truth of the matter was, Charlie seemed to be the kind of a woman that could take care of herself.

Grant's eyes immediately caught Charlie's figure in the corner. There were only a couple of other people in the place. She was leaning over a table with her back to him, talking to a big man. She had one foot on the floor while the knee of her other leg rested on a chair. Across the table from her, was Billy Jack Boone. They were talking in low voices.

When the bell rang over the door, Charlie glanced over her shoulder to see who had come in. He immediately noticed her eyes were red, puffy, and wet. She looked as if she'd been crying. She turned back toward Billy Jack, without acknowledging Grant.

That hurt him. All of the sudden, he wasn't hungry anymore. He didn't understand what was going on and wondered if the morning's events with Billy Jack had anything to do with her cold-shoulder treatment, now

Charlie pulled a tissue from a napkin holder on the table, dabbed her eyes, and then blew her nose. Billy Jack's face was somber, and he clasped one of her hands between his and spoke to her. He seemed to be consoling her.

A knot twisted tightly in Grant's stomach. He looked away from the two of them, walked toward the counter, and sat down on the stool closest to the cash register. Whitie Saylor was sitting at the other end of the counter, next to the wall, slumped over with his head resting on his arm. He was apparently sleeping off another drunk.

While sitting there, he debated about just going to the cabin and making a peanut butter and jelly sandwich. He liked PBJs. That's what he had survived on in college. Maybe Billy Jack was right. Maybe he should stay away from Charlie. Keep his distance, at least for a while.

He had planned on going to her place later tonight, after work, just to talk. She was so easy to talk to. But not now. He wasn't sure what had changed, but something was different.

The bell over the front door rang. Someone was coming into the Trading Post. He wasn't really interested in who, either. He was more interested in feeling sorry for himself and getting out of here.

"Hi, Grant. What can I get you," Edith asked, in a cheerful tone.

The woman's voice surprised Grant. He jerked, then raised his head up. "Oh. Hi Edith. Gee, I don't know. I guess a cheeseburger, fries, and a cherry Coke."

"Have it out in a jiffy," she said. "What's the long face for? You really look down in the dumps."

"Just a rough day," he said, not wanting to tell her the truth. "Where's Jonah?"

"At the house. Got homework to do," she replied. "He's having a heck of a time with his math. I guess he's going to get through it, though. Let me get this burger on the griddle for you." The chunky woman turned, pushed through the double doors, and went into the kitchen.

"How's it going," Frank Kicklighter said to Grant, as he sat down next to him. He set his half-full bottle of water on the counter.

"Hi, Sheriff," Grant said, looking over at Frank. "Oh, I guess I'm doing all right."

"That doesn't sound very convincing. What's wrong, have a bad day at the office?"

From the other end of the counter, Whitie lifted his wobbly head and grumbled, "Give me some more coffee," then dropped it back down onto his crusty hands.

Both Grant and Frank looked down at the old man, then chuckled a bit.

Grant figured the sheriff would be a good person to talk to, about what he and Victor had discovered today. As he finished telling him the story, Grant asked, "You wouldn't know of anyone that would do such a terrible thing, do you, Sheriff?"

Frank chuckled, then said, "I know plenty of guys that would poach game animals in a heartbeat, young man. Some of them would even sell their own mother for a hot cup of coffee on a warm day. Trouble is, I don't have any evidence on a single one of them."

"Did I hear something about poaching wolves," Billy Jack said from behind Frank and Grant.

Charlie slipped around to the back of the counter and into the kitchen. She never even looked in Grant's direction. Another knife jabbed into his heart. Just what was going on with this woman.

"That's right," he said, looking over his shoulder at Billy Jack with a cold stare.

"Either of ya got any ideas who's doing it?" Billy Jack asked, his eyes darting toward the sheriff and away from Grant's steady glare.

"Nope," Frank said.

"No, do you?" Grant asked, in an accusatory tone.

Billy Jack's eyebrows raised, and his forehead wrinkled before he answered. "How should I know?"

"Where'd you take your clients yesterday?" Grant asked, being persistent.

"Everyone knows that," Billy Jack answered, quickly. "We went up to the northwestern corner of Denali National Preserve. They wanted to get some good pictures of the caribou herds. Why do you ask?"

Grant looked over at the sheriff. He had just told Frank where they had found the carcasses. Maybe Victor was right, Billy Jack was involved in all of this. He turned his head and looked back up at the large man. "That's where Victor and I found four dead wolves. Shot from a helicopter, then skinned."

"Wait a minute—"

"I can tell you who the scoundrel is-s-s-s," Whitie mumbled, lifting his head again for just a second before it plopped back down onto the counter with a thud.

Charlie came through the kitchen doors, one hand holding a plate with Grant's cheeseburger and fries, and the other hand holding his cherry Coke. "Billy Jack wouldn't do anything like that and you know it Frank," she said harshly, slamming the plate down on the counter with a bang. She set the cup down roughly also, spilling some of the cherry Coke. "And Grant, I'm surprised at you, accusing a man you've only know for a few days. For that matter, how do any of us know that you're not the one behind all this wolf poaching?"

He was shocked that Charlie said such a thing to him. Before he could respond, she shot out from behind the counter and marched back to the corner where she'd been earlier. Billy Jack trailed behind her like a robot, with a permanent smile plastered on his face.

Frank got up from his stool and said, "With that, I'd better get on home. It's getting late and my daughter will be wondering where I'm at." He turned and headed for the front door.

Grant was all alone again, except for Whitie, and he was asleep in a drunken stupor. He wolfed his cheeseburger and fries down, wanting to get out of this place as quickly as he could. When he finished, he dug a five dollar bill out of his wallet, laid it on the counter, and headed out. It had been a big mistake to come here this evening.

Just as he reached the door, he glanced back to the corner. Charlie was facing him this time, and Billy Jack had his back to him. She was smiling and gazing into Billy Jack eyes, unaware that Grant was leaving. Then she leaned over the table and kissed Billy Jack on the cheek. Grant watched her thin beautiful lips move and heard her say, "Thank you, Billy Jack. You'll never know how much this means to me."

He felt another cold slash to his heart. The cheeseburger and fries churned in his stomach. Grant opened the door and left.

Chapter 9

THE SUN DROPPED LOWER IN THE CLEAR WESTERN SKIES. It was nearly nine-thirty. Grant sat on the back steps sipping his fourth beer and moping about what had happened earlier that evening at the Trading Post. After leaving the Trading Post, his spirits were lower than they'd ever been before, so he went back to Two Forks and bought a twelve-pack of beer, a bag of pretzels, and several beef jerky sticks.

Grant had never been one to drink much alcohol. When the other guys were out partying on the weekends, he was usually home or at the library, studying, or rewriting his class notes from the day. But this evening was different. He wasn't looking to get drunk, but the whole episode at the diner had left him in a bad mood. He just wanted to feel good. He was halfway through the current beer and was beginning to feel a little woozy.

His eyes looked across the backyard and on out toward Denning Fork. The water tumbled and swirled on its way to Broken Eye Lake. As he stared at the rushing water, all the things that had happened to him since he came to Alaska, were dancing around in his head. One of the first things Victor had said to him when he arrived, was that this area was a sleepy peaceful community, and that nothing exciting ever really happened here. So far it didn't seem that sleepy to him.

And then there was Charlie. He tried to forget the things she had said to him earlier in the evening. And the way she acted, compared to last night. It was like she was another woman. He was confused about everything. Maybe it would be best if he just cooled it with Charlie for a while and concentrated on his work. Let her make the next move. If she ever did.

Grant lifted the brown bottle to his lips, tilted his head, and took a long pull. When he lowered the bottle, his eyes fell on the small building on stilts, to the left of the cabin. A cache, Victor had called it. He wondered just what was stored up there. After finishing off the beer, Grant went inside, opened another, and took it with him as he made his way toward the cache.

As he plodded along, his thoughts strayed to the silver-blue wolf. There was no question in his mind now, that last night he had truly seen that magnificent animal. Since then, he kept thinking about what Victor had said when they were in the chopper. The tall Indian's words swirled in his head: "Wolves travel in the spiritual world, carrying messages back and forth." That particular phrase seemed to hang in his mind like a catchy jingle. Just the thought of someone killing and skinning that beautiful creature, sickened him to his core.

Grant set the bottle of beer next to a spruce near the storage building. He lifted the ladder that lay on the ground next to the cache and carefully propped it against the platform that extended three feet beyond the front door of the structure. Even though he was feeling the numbing effect of the beer's buzz, it did not shield him from the brisk chill in the air, brought on by the rapidly fading daylight. He rubbed his arms with his hands to warm them. Grant had left his jacket inside the cabin. He decided it would be a good idea to get it, before climbing the ladder to see what was stashed in the storage building.

As he was checking the ladder to insure it was securely in place before he headed to the cabin, he heard a growl. His first thought was that the silver-blue wolf had decided to show itself again. So as not to spook the animal, Grant very slowly turned his head and tried not to not move any more of his body than was absolutely necessary. Then he just as slowly peeked over his left shoulder to see what was behind him.

Standing in a semicircle between him and the cabin, were four large feral dogs. All had their lips curled, to reveal sharp teeth that glistened in the waning sunlight. They had markings very similar to wolves, but he could tell the difference because of the shape of their heads. The angry dogs were fairly close together, with a larger one, a male, and most likely the leader of the pack, out in front.

His eyes rose to the back door of the cabin. It was a good thirty-five to forty feet away from him. The feral dogs were about halfway between. There was no way these animals were going to just let him casually walk by them and go into the cabin, without trying to rip his face off.

Grant remained as still as a granite statue, trying to not provoke them. He stared at the four wild dogs, trying to figure a way out of this mess. They began to inch closer, growling and snarling, with their heads hung low, and white stringy saliva dripping from their mouths. When he saw this he instantly thought of rabies.

He could dash up the ladder to the safety of the cache. Surely the dogs couldn't climb the ladder. The only problem with that plan, was that now that the sun was going down, the temperature would drop quickly and be in the twenties within an hour or so. If he stayed in out there for very long, he would suffer from hypothermia, and maybe even die.

The dogs continued to creep closer. They were about ten feet away now.

His only chance was to run around them and sprint as fast as he could to the front of the cabin. Maybe he could get in the door before the dogs got to him, hopefully before they did to much damage to him. That plan wasn't much better than the one of climbing up the ladder, but at least he wouldn't freeze to death. If he made it to the cabin, that is. But his options were pretty limited at this point, and running for it seemed like the best of the two.

As he slowly turned to face the ferocious animals, he thought of the time he watched a pack of wolves bring down a caribou. They charged alongside it, biting, slashing at its sides, neck, and head, and tearing large chunks of flesh from the caribou's hams with their sharp teeth and powerful jaws. Blood gushed and streamed everywhere.

He glanced back at the ladder and swallowed hard, questioning his plan to run for it. Gingerly, Grant stepped once to his right, inching toward the cabin. The lead dog's mouth opened slightly, baring even more teeth. Its ears fell back. Grant knew this was a display of more aggression, maybe even a little fear. He took another step toward the cabin, keeping his eyes on the four dogs.

The dogs pressed closer and began to fan out, matching his moves toward the cabin. There was still a small open gap for him to get by the animals, but if he was going to run, he had to do it now.

A fifth feral dog, a female, and smaller than the rest, stepped out from the cabin and onto the back stoop. Grant stopped cold. That animal had been in his cabin. Were there more dogs in there? He didn't know. Precious seconds ticked by as he hesitated, trying to decide what to do.

He had to take the chance that there were no more wild dogs in the cabin. Grant took another step in that direction and was now next to the spruce where he had set his beer down. Scooting over behind the tree to block the dogs' view of him, he very slowly slid down against the trunk and picked up the bottle. He could use it as a weapon if he needed it.

Gripping the neck of the bottle so tightly in his right hand that the knuckles went pale, he took a deep breath of the cool evening air and prepared to run for it. Before lunging out from behind the tree, he peeked around the trunk to see where the enemy was and what they were doing. If necessary he would make a final adjustment in his plan before putting it into motion, because there was no turning back once he started.

The smaller fifth dog had joined the pack. All were slightly hunkered down, wild-eyed, and continuing to slink forward. Every single one of them had a mean hungry look on their face, as if they were ready to tear him into shreds.

Grant slipped around to the side of the tree closest to the cabin and scanned the pack one last time. He braced himself against the trunk of the spruce, planning to use it as a springboard. It may not help much, he thought, but he needed every small advantage he could get to avoid being chewed into hamburger.

Just as he was ready to burst across the yard to the front of the cabin, a sixth feral dog came from that direction and charged right at him. It was an enormous animal. Its fangs were drawn, its ears were back, and its demon eyes were locked on him.

Out of pure instinct, and perhaps a good bit of fear, Grant spun away from the tree and the oncoming dogs, and bolted toward the ladder. It was a short distance. He might make it. He wasn't sure.

It had only taken him four long strides until his left hand gripped an upper rung and his right foot hammered a bottom one. He felt a little more secure and glanced back to see where his attackers were.

The lead dog had already left the ground and was almost on top of him. Grant caught a flash of jagged teeth in the wide open mouth. Flaming eyes bulged from its head. The sixth dog that had come from the front of the cabin, was in full stride and was just steps away from him. Its menacing jaws were spread wide, displaying a set of frightening fangs, dripping with saliva.

As Grant scurried up the ladder, he swung his right arm around, bottle of beer in hand, and caught the flying dog square in the face. The bottle smashed across the bridge of the dog's snout, shattering the glass bottle into a hundred pieces. He dropped what remained of it, to the ground. The pale yellow liquid flung everywhere.

The dog yelped, and there was enough force in Grant's blow to divert the animal. He looked down as he continued to scurry up the ladder. There was a long wide gash across the beast's snout where the bottle had struck it, and it was bleeding profusely.

The building was at least ten feet off the ground, and Grant was almost to the platform. Almost to safety. As his right hand grabbed the last rung, the entire ladder vibrated with a tremendous shudder. He jerked his head around to see the sixth dog climbing up behind him. Paw after paw wrapped around the rungs as it pulled itself up with amazing speed. It drew closer, snapping at his heels and snarling ferociously.

Grant was moving as fast as he could and was almost there. But not quite. The determined monstrous dog lunged upward and sank its savage fangs into the lower muscle of Grant's left thigh. Grant screamed in agony, fiery pain shot up his leg. His cry echoed through the cold night as blood spewed and flesh tore.

When he fell onto the platform, Grant gathered all his strength and mule-kicked the beast in the side of head with his free foot. The animal finally jarred loose on the third kick, sending the creature to the ground with a loud thud.

Grant pushed the ladder away from the platform and watched it tumbled to ground. All six dogs were gathered around the building, staring up at him and snarling. He leaned back against the storage building, holding onto his leg to try and stop the flow of blood from the gaping wound, safe for the moment.

Linsey Hogan kicked off her shoes, merrily sauntered over to her plush white sofa, and flopped down, curling her legs up under her. She was as happy as a fat cat. Everything was going her way. She took a long pleasurable drag on her cigarette, sucked the smoke deep into her lungs and blew it out in a narrow stream. She followed that with a sip of expensive chardonnay from a fine crystal wine glass.

She was only thirty and had been the director of the newly formed Alaska Wildlife Management Commission for a year. Her salary from the state was a cool hundred grand, more than any of her male counterparts. But that was only the taxable income. What the IRS didn't see, were the fat kickbacks from multiple vendors and businessmen that made her salary from the state look like pocket change. And now that the sleazy banker, Peter Worley, had agreed to invest in her latest scheme, she would become richer than she ever dreamed.

Yes, she'd done all right for a gal from white trash who was abandoned by her parents when she was eleven. There had been scores of foster homes, all of them bad. In several of them she'd been sexually abused, and not always just by the man of the house. It seemed like such a long time ago, and she tried to forget it. But it had left her bitter and determined never to be at anyone's mercy again. She learned to use anything, including her feminine wiles, to get what she wanted. Now she was the director of the AWMC, someone with power and authority, who commanded dozens of people with the snap of her fingers, and who could make or break careers with a simple scribble of her pen.

Linsey took another deep pull on the cigarette and exhaled it slowly, letting the gray smoke drift from her mouth and snake up her face. She leaned over from the sofa toward a glass topped coffee table and crushed out the butt in an ashtray. She immediately lit another, then leaned back on the rich sofa and sipped some more wine.

Men were stupid and helpless when it came to a cunning woman like herself, and they were so predictable. Linsey had learned early that she could manipulate men to do just about anything. It was so simple. Just smile, bat your eyes at the appropriate moment, and show a little leg. Not too much, of course. Just enough to entice them. And the best trick of all was to leave a few blouse buttons undone and bend over in front of an eager man, displaying her voluptuous cleavage. She had always been slightly on the heavy side, but that never seemed to matter for that the stunt. It worked on every man she'd ever tried it on. And she only used it on ones that could benefit her.

Thank God for Affirmative Action, she thought to herself, especially in government where the regulation was followed to the letter. There were a hundred men in the state who could have gotten the job, but she got it. Of course, her quick advancement into the management ranks had a little assistance from her cunning ingenuity. She was an opportunist, and proud of it, and she took advantage of every situation that promised some kind of payoff for her.

Before becoming director for the AWMC, she was a secretary for Alaska's attorney general. Intentionally, she had crafted a web of deception to trap her boss and put him in a vulnerable situation. She'd had no plans of staying a nonexempt girl-Friday for very long for a buffoon like him. He was the perfect mark just waiting to be had.

Linsey smiled at how she'd lied, deceived, and cheated her way up through the clerical pool, to finally become the attorney general's secretary. After being in that position for six months, she put her scheme into action. It didn't take long before the poor slob had his hands all over her.

On one particular day, the governor was scheduled to visit the attorney general's office. Of course she failed to inform the attorney general of this, and the governor, who always had the habit of walking in unannounced like some sort of grand ruler, burst into the office to see her sitting on the attorney general's lap with a torn blouse and her large upturned breast, bared. She was whimpering in a helpless voice, "No, no, please don't do this to me. I beg of you," which was what the fool had asked her to say. Meanwhile, he'd had his face buried between her two mounds.

The attorney general had a notorious reputation as a womanizer, and had been charged numerous times by other women, for sexual harassment. But this was the first time he had ever been caught red-handed, and by the governor no less.

Linsey ran her hand across the expensive silky material covering her right breast and gently stroked the nipple until it became hard. She laughed wickedly at the memory. That maneuver with the attorney general had gotten her the director's job. Linsey leaned forward again and stamped out another butt just as the phone rang.

Picking up the portable unit that was on the coffee table, she heard the familiar man's voice say, "It's me again."

"For crying-out-loud, what is it now? It's 9:30," she snapped.

"That boy you hired is becoming a real problem. He and Victor found a few of the skinned wolf carcasses today," the man said with a trace of frustration. "I don't need this trouble right now."

"Well I don't either," she barked. "Where the hell did they find them?"

"Somewhere over the northwest section of Denali Preserve, while they were flying around in the chopper."

"What in God's name were they doing way over there?" she asked, as she finished the remaining wine in one gulp and lit up another cigarette.

"I think Victor was showing Grant some more of the area, and they just happened to spot the wolves' bodies."

"Well what were the bodies doing out in the open, for God's sake? Who left them out for everybody to see, anyway?" she asked. "Your people are going to have to be more careful in the future."

"I can't keep track of every trapper we have on the payroll like he was in the first grade. You know that. I'll speak to them though and tell them what you said."

"Good. And that damn Indian. If it wasn't for the quota system, I'd fire his red butt in a heartbeat," she said. "I'd better explain to both of them again, what their job assignment is, and just where their territory is."

"I hope so, because everything's on schedule. But you're going to have to keep those two out of the way for a few days. I have the meeting set up with your Oriental friends next week.

The buy will go down if they like what they see, and if they don't suspect any problems," the man said firmly.

"Fine. I'll take care of Grant and Victor. I'll keep them both so busy with bureaucratic crap, they won't have time to wipe their aggravating butts, much less get in your hair. What about that silver-blue wolf? Have you heard anymore about it?"

"Not a thing."

"I want that wolf. Do you understand? I don't care if you have to go out and track it down yourself. I want that silver-blue wolf. I might even keep it for myself. If not, it will bring a tidy sum from our Asian friends. Remember, you have more to lose over this deal than I do, so don't screw things up. Got it?"

"Yes, I think I can grasp the concept," the man said sarcastically.

"You'd better," she snapped, and hung up the phone.

A strong cold front had swept into the Two Forks area and set down like an iron slab. By 10:30, the temperature had plummeted into the teens—a guaranteed death warrant for those who ventured out unprepared.

Grant's fingers were numb and stiff, and even though he had stuffed them in his pants pockets, it hadn't helped much. His breathing had created a lot of moisture in his nostrils, and it was mostly frozen now. The wound on his leg had finally stopped bleeding, and the once wet blood was now hard and crusty, frozen to his leg and shredded jeans.

At first he was more worried about rabies or some kind of infection from the bite, but now it was the deadening cold that occupied his mind. His metabolism had slowed considerably. His eyelids had become extremely heavy. He fought their closure with all his strength, because he knew if his eyes slipped shut for more than a couple of seconds, he would never wake up again. The simple task of keeping his eyes open, had become the most difficult thing he had ever encountered in his life.

The door on the storage building was locked. He had pried and jerked and tugged on the lock and hasp, until his fingers were raw and bleeding. If only he could've gotten inside, there might have been a blanket, or old coat, or something to help keep him warm. Even if there hadn't have been anything in the building to warm him, he would have at least had the protection of the building to shield him from the cold. The Swiss army knife his father had given him at age eleven, when he was a Boy Scout, could have been used to loosen the screws to the hasp's hinges. But the knife was in his backpack in the cabin, and there was nothing in his pockets but lint.

Grant sat scrunched up, leaning against the small building, shivering uncontrollably. His teeth had chattered hard for so long, that his gums and jaws ached relentlessly. He knew he was going to die if he didn't warm his body soon.

All the feral dogs were still meandering around beneath him, glancing up at him on occasion, as if waiting for their meal to come down. Once, five of the dogs had wandered to Denning Fork for a drink from the stream. But the largest one remained, the one that had bitten him and tasted his blood, and there was an evil glare in its eyes.

The lone dog watching him, reminded Grant of a humorous folktale Victor had told him, about an Indian beaver trapper that had been chased up a tree by a pack of wolves. The wolves hung around below the tree all night long, waiting for the man to come down, but he didn't. Then early in the morning, all the wolves left except for one, who constantly stared up at the trapper with a grin of satisfaction and anticipation on its face. A short while later the rest of the pack came back with a beaver they had released from the Indian's trap. As a favor to the wolves for freeing him, the beaver chopped the tree down.

He had laughed at the time Victor told the story, but now there was no laughter within him. Now his mind was consumed with the freezing cold, and the struggle to keep his eyes open. If only he could see the sunrise one more time.

He looked around. Though it was dark, his squinting eyes had adjusted reasonably well to the dim light. He noted the clear sky and the silvery radiance of the half moon. Scooting to the edge of the platform, he peeked down at the ground.

There were no dogs. He immediately became more alert, and his shaking limbs and chattering teeth stopped for a moment. The shaking returned a moment later, this time with greater intensity. He poked his head out over the platform and wiped his eyes to be sure he wasn't imagining things. He had to be certain that the dogs' absence wasn't just a wishful dream he had conjured up. It had been a while since he'd checked their whereabouts. He wasn't sure how long. Where had they gone? Had they finally given up or was this just a sneaky ploy? He wondered if they were hiding in the shadows somewhere, waiting for him to leap to the ground so they could attack and kill him.

There wasn't time to ponder the question. It he stayed on the platform much longer, he would freeze to death. This was his only opportunity to make a run for the safety of the cabin. He was on his hands and knees. With an enormous amount of difficulty, he stood up and began to rub some warmth and life into his arms, hands, and legs. They were bitter cold and shook like a flag on a pole in an arctic gale. Like an old man, Grant hobbled to each end of the platform and scanned the area for signs of the feral dogs. There were none. There was no movement anywhere.

Grant jogged in place for a few seconds, preparing himself for the forty foot dash to the cabin. It wasn't a great distance under normal circumstances, but these weren't normal circumstances by any stretch of the imagination. At that moment, the forty feet seemed like miles to him.

His eyes probed the perimeter one last time. Finally, he stepped to the edge of the platform and leaped off without a second thought. The ten foot descent seemed like minutes, instead of the few seconds it took him to reach the ground. He hit hard. The ankle on the injured leg gave way and turned, badly spraining it. "Ouch!" he groaned, trying to muffled his cry of pain so as not to alert the wild dogs.

With a great deal of effort Grant lifted himself up. He was hunched over and shaking from the cold, as well as the excruciating pain in his thigh and ankle. Holding the wounded leg, he began to limp as fast as he could toward the cabin. The foot of his lame leg dragged in the dirt.

Before he had taken two steps, he heard panting, and the pounding of large paws against hard soil. There was a rushing movement in the shadows behind him. He was too frightened to look back. Sluggishly, he struggled to move faster toward the cabin.

On the third step he was slammed to the ground. It knocked the air from his lungs. The sixth feral dog, the largest one, had lunged from the darkness, onto his back. The vicious beast immediately sank its large fangs into Grant's neck and right shoulder, ripping and slashing his flesh. A tremendous pain, like nothing he'd ever experienced, seared down his back, across his right arm, and toward his head, like molten steel. The creature's hot steamy breath poured out of its nostrils in tremulous puffs and spilled across Grant's face, like toxic gases from hell.

Grant was completely helpless and gasping for air. In the creature's frenzy to rip him apart, it whipped Grant's head from side to side. Unrecognizable objects flashed in front of Grant. For just a second, he saw the open back door of the cabin. There were two feral dogs on the stoop, sitting on their haunches, watching the slaughter like spectators at a championship fight. Their long pink tongues dangled from their mouths.

As sprays of his own blood splashed across his face, onto the ground, and into his mouth and eyes, Grant grew weaker. He thought of the nobility of death. Victor had told him that in the animal world, death was a spiritual event. There was dignity and honor in the death of the prey, because it provided the predator with nourishment, replenishing its body and allowing it to hunt another day.

Grant's eyes closed, as the ruthless beast mercilessly pounded his head into the granite-hard earth. Somehow, he had managed to open his lids for a moment, just in time to see a silver-blue streak flash by. It rammed the feral dog that was on top of him, knocking the huge animal end over end.

Grant tilted his weary head up out of the dirt. Dazed, he saw the blurry images of the two dogs on the stoop, as they leaped to the ground and dashed into the darkened forest, their tails between their legs. He heard the yelping, vicious growling, and clashing of heads behind him—two warriors deep in battle—but he didn't have the strength to look back. All he could think of now, was saving his own life.

To his right, in front of the cabin, was the Suburban. The keys to the truck were in his jacket pocket, which was inside the cabin. But there was a spare key above the visor in case of an emergency, another bit of good information Victor had given him.

Blood spewed from the ragged gashes in his neck and shoulder. There wasn't enough strength left in him to get to his feet. He was so cold, and every part of him was numb. Each second ticked by in slow motion, and he sensed his life force was growing dimmer and dimmer. His vision became even more blurred.

Grant's right arm was useless. Although nearly unconscious, the pain in his neck and shoulder was still almost too much to bear. His strong will to live was all that remained now. But he wasn't sure how much longer that would last.

His left arm was too heavy to lift. He slid it over the ground and pushed it out in front of him. Digging his raw and bleeding fingers into the frozen soil, he began to drag himself toward the vehicle. Dirt and small pebbles ground into the left side of his face as he pulled himself along. It was too much. Grant's eyelids slowly closed. The last thing he heard before his mind went black, was the howl of a wolf.

Business had been unusually heavy for a Thursday night, Charlie thought to herself, as she drove her Jeep Cherokee over the old wooden bridge crossing Crooked Creek. Lord knows, she wasn't complaining, though. The business was certainly welcome. She needed the extra money, especially now that Frank Kicklighter wanted an early payment on the Trading Post's second mortgage.

For some reason several of the local trappers had come in late this evening, delaying her closing time to around eleven-thirty, about an hour later than normal. The rugged looking crew had gathered in the back corner, around three tables they pushed together. They talked in hushed voices. Most of the men smoked, and a gray haze hung over them like an evil cloud. There was definitely something big going on, something secretive and odd, and that something, she was certain, was illegal.

Every time Charlie came around to warm up their coffee, they stopped talking and squirmed in their seats, as if a nest of winter ticks had settled in their shorts. They looked up at her, with big innocent grins that spelled trouble, and eyes filled with guilt. None of the men even flirted with her, or tried to slap or pinch her butt, which for that testosterone-loaded bunch, was a real oddity. The curiosity of not knowing what they were up to, was about to drive her crazy. Only one thing slipped past their sealed lips about whatever was going on—it was taking place in Anchorage early next week.

The digital clock on the dash blinked 11:50. She stopped the Cherokee at the turn off to her place. Edith had caught her earlier and lectured her about how she had wrongly treated Grant Rawlings that evening. Charlie wasn't quite sure why she'd acted that way, except that Billy Jack had been her friend for over twenty years, and she was just defending him. There was no question that Billy Jack could be arrogant and obnoxious, but he'd always been there for her when she needed someone, and she sure needed someone now. But after Edith's "make-you feel-bad" sermon, she felt about as low as pond scum.

Charlie pondered whether to go on down now to Grant's cabin, so she could apologize to him. But he was probably already in bed. She took her foot off the brake, turned the steering wheel toward her place, and started to gently roll down the dirt road. Before the vehicle moved the length of itself, Charlie slammed her right foot on the brake, backed up, and headed toward Grant's cabin. Edith had said in her usual knowing way, "Never wait 'till tomorrow, to say what needs to be said today. Tomorrow may never come for one of you."

The memory of the day her father died, seeped into her mind. If only she'd had another day, or another hour with him, to say the things that needed to be said. There was little talk between the two of them. They rarely said how much how much they loved each other. Like most folks, she supposed, that was just the way it was. But it didn't make her feel any better right now. A single tear trickled from her eye and ran down her cheek. She wiped it a way with the back of her hand. Pressing her left foot on the gas pedal, she moved the Jeep a little faster.

She didn't care if Grant had already gone to bed or not. She'd just wake him up and get this off her chest, once and for all. If she didn't apologize now, she wouldn't sleep a wink tonight worrying about it.

When the Cherokee's headlights washed across the front of the small cabin, Charlie knew something was horribly wrong. The door was wide open, and all the lights were out. The first thing that popped into her mind, was a grizzly. The next thing, was the temperature it had gotten down to tonight. Grant might be the outdoors type, but leaving his front door open so he could sleep in fresh air on a freezing cold night like tonight, was absolutely ridiculous.

Charlie pulled the Cherokee past Grant's Suburban and drove as close to the front door as she could. Because of a scattered stand of spruce, she could only get about thirty feet away. She left the lights on and the engine running. From where she sat, she could see nothing moving inside. Her eyes slowly scanned the area for anything unusual, or for signs of movement in the shadows around the cabin. Everything seemed in order, other than the front door being wide open.

She turned around and lifted her daddy's Winchester .30/30 from the window rifle rack. The rifle was a vintage lever-action model, with a five-shell clip. A single shot might not down a full grown grizzly, but it would sure get his attention. Charlie laid the rifle on the front seat, opened the glove box, and dug out a fully loaded clip. She carefully pushed it into the slot on the underside of the rifle, until she heard the familiar click indicating it was locked into place. She engaged the lever, which set the first shell into the chamber. For now, Charlie left the safety on.

She pulled an emergency flashlight from the driver's door pocket and shined it down toward the floor to see if it worked. Luckily, Whitie Saylor had replaced the batteries a week ago, when he detailed the vehicle for her, to pick up a few extra dollars. Most likely for another bottle of cheap rot-gut whiskey, she thought.

Charlie stepped out from the driver's side as quietly as she could, leaving the car door open in case she needed to make a fast exit. Cautiously, she moved toward the cabin's front door, holding the rifle barrel out in front of her. The Winchester and the flashlight were shaking in her hands.

She didn't like this. Not one bit. Even with the headlights shining on the cabin, it seemed unusually dark inside, and way too quiet. It was spooky.

As the weight of her body came down on her right foot, the stoop's old cedar boards creaked, ringing loudly across the crisp, frigid air. The hair on the back of her neck immediately prickled. An icy shiver galloped down her spine, and she shuddered. With her eyes wide open, and her fingers trembling, she clicked off the rifle's safety.

Charlie cautiously stepped the rest of the way up onto the stoop and stabbed at the darkness inside, with the beam of her flashlight. The white light sliced straight through to the other side of the room. She could see the open back door. Another bad sign.

"Hello. Grant. Are you here?" she said quietly. There was a slight quiver in her voice. She repeated herself, hoping her friend was inside, asleep. But deep down, she was afraid that wasn't the case.

Finally convinced it was safe to go in, she eased through the doorway of the cabin and swung the flashlight from side to side. She immediately flashed the light over to the right, to where the bed was located. No Grant. One of the pillows had been shredded by some animal. Feathers were everywhere—on the floor, the bed, the washstand, everywhere. She began to bite her lower lip, as her Adam's apple jerkily slid up and down her throat when she swallowed. The colorful woolen blanket that one of the Indian tribes had given her father was gone, and the sheets were rumpled in a pile on the bed.

There was a large dark wet spot on the mattress. At first she thought it might be blood and moved closer to examine it. Three feet away from the bed, it wasn't necessary to get any closer. She knew what the stain was. The strong caustic odor of urine hung over the bed like a heavy fog. She jerked her head away and began to cough, as the corroding vapors burned the insides of her nose. A wolf had left its scent and marked the bed.

"Oh Grant, what's happened to you?" she asked herself in a whisper, feeling even more guilty now about the way she acted toward him earlier.

Charlie moved slowly through the cabin, piercing all the shadowy corners with light. The entire room was in disarray. One of the sofa cushions had been chewed and shredded, while the other had wolf scat on it. The end table had been knocked over, and the diamond-wood lamp was lying on the floor, its lampshade gone and its bulb shattered. She had seen the lampshade's ripped and torn remains, jammed up in the far corner. Many of Grant's clothes were strewn across the room, most of which had large holes chewed in them.

Maybe she should go back to her place and call for help. Phone Victor and Frank. Billy Jack would be good in a situation like this, too. There was no telling what had happened to Grant. Before leaving to get help, Charlie decided to check behind the cabin. She walked to the back door and shined the light around the yard. There was nothing to the right of the cabin, or out toward Denning Fork.

Thinking she'd heard something behind her, Charlie looked back for a moment. She was really getting anxious and wanted to leave this place in the worst way. The bright headlights shining through the front door briefly blinded her, and it took a minute to focus. When she could see again, it was evident that the only thing behind her, was the chaotic room.

She was relieved that no living creatures were sneaking up on her, but where was Grant? She was ready to form a search party for him. In this temperate, he would die of hypothermia before morning.

Directing her attention out back again, Charlie hurriedly swung the narrow beam of light toward the storage building. She was about to give up, when the light shone across a woolen blanket lying on the cold ground, between the cache and cabin. She almost ignored it and went on, assuming the wolves had dragged it out there. But that's when something caught her eye and made her look back at the blanket. Squinting in the darkness, she suddenly realized what it was—a boot. There was the sole of a boot sticking out from the blanket.

"Oh my God. Grant!" she yelled, as she charged down the back steps, light and rifle still in hand. Coming closer, Charlie could see there was definitely something under the blanket. It was in the shape of a person. She rushed up to the it and immediately saw a large stain of blood at one end. Reluctantly, she knelt down and lifted the corner.

There Grant lay, his face in an icy pool of blood. The grotesquely mangled flesh on the side of his neck and shoulder, brought a wave of nausea to her stomach. Her eyes blurred with tears. She immediately dropped the rifle and grabbed Grant's outstretched left wrist. His flesh was extremely cold. Slumped over him and weeping out loud, she searched for signs of life. She couldn't find a pulse.

At 12:23, Linsey Hogan was fast asleep in her spacious queen-sized bed. She was tossing and turning violently, from side to side. Sheets and blankets were thrown to the floor. Her hands slapped and clawed at empty space in the dark room, and her legs kicked out at the air. She was in the middle of a dream, far back in the past, with her first foster family.

In her dream, it was late at night, and the other children were in bed, asleep. The mother was a waitress and was working at a nearby truck stop. The man of the house was drunk. Country music played loudly in the background, as he slipped into Linsey's room and snatched her from slumber—clamping his hand over her mouth to quiet her screams. He took her outside to a small machine shed.

His name was Virgil, and he was a mean evil man with one blind eye that looked cloudy all the time. He was big and had long black oily hair and a large beer belly that hung over his belt buckle by several inches.

His rough greasy hands pawed and probed her small body. Virgil threw her on an old dirty oil-stained car seat that sat on the concrete floor, next to an old oil-burning stove in the corner of the shed. He tore off the man's T-shirt she wore as a nightgown and ripped away her panties. As he leaned over her, Linsey was overwhelmed by the stench of stale booze and cigarettes. It made her vomit. Virgil beat her for that. Then he raped her. Linsey had just turned eleven.

At 12:24, the phone rang and thankfully woke her up. "Hello," she said groggily.

"I'm sorry to call so late and wake you, Linsey," the familiar man's voice said.

"That's all right. I was having a nightmare anyway. What's up," she mumbled, through a yawn.

"Charlie Santord just called me here at home, crying and in hysterics. The Rawlings boy has been attacked by some kind of wild animal. He's all torn up and suffering from exposure. I guess he was lying outside for several hours."

"How is he?" she asked, turning on the lamp next to her bed and lighting a cigarette.

"I don't know."

"Well, is he alive?"

"I don't know that, either," the man answered. "Charlie said she couldn't feel a pulse, and that he'd lost a lot of blood. She's called Doc Phillips in Two Forks, and he's on his way now. I was just heading out the front door myself to go to his cabin, when I thought I'd better call you and let you know what's going on."

"Yeah, thanks a lot. Let me know when you find out if he's dead or alive," she said flatly, her voice lacking any concern. "Either way it doesn't look like we'll have to worry about him interfering with our plans next week."

"Yeah, I guess not. Talk to you later."

Linsey hung up the phone.

Chapter 10

"Boy, do you look like a badly warmed-over meal," Victor said jokingly, as he strolled into Grant's hospital room. His long red braids draped down over his shoulders and lazily swung from side to side.

"Thanks, partner. That makes me feel so much better," Grant muttered, through swollen lips.

It was exactly 8:30, Saturday morning. Victor had just flown up from Two Forks and caught a cab to County General Hospital in Fairbanks, the hospital Victor, Charlie, and Doc Phillips had rushed Grant to, early Friday morning. It had saved his life.

"So, how you feeling this fine morning?" Victor asked.

"Sore," Grant said. "I can hardly turn my head because my neck is so stiff. But I'll be better when I get out of here. I don't like hospitals much."

The whole left side of Grant's face was a deep dark purplish bruise with some yellow feathered around the edges. Because he was so weak from his injuries, and everything happened so fast, he couldn't remember exactly how or when the injury occurred. It could have been when the monstrous dog pounced on his back and slammed him to the ground like a sack of soft potatoes. Or it could have been when the vicious beast violently shook his head and smashed it against the ground.

"Not many of us do, especially when we're the patients," Victor agreed.

"I didn't hear you and Charlie leave last night," Grant said, lifting his head up on the pillow slightly. "I must've been zonked-out. What time was it when you left?"

"Oh, it must've been around seven or so, I guess," Victor answered. "Charlie was right here by your side all day yesterday, worrying, and fussing over you like an old hen with her baby chicks."

"Yeah, I kind of remember her being here, the few times I woke up," Grant said.

"I just saw the doctor leave your room as I was coming down the hall," Victor said as he walked up to the end of the bed and looked down at Grant. "What'd he have to say?"

"Take me home, James. Take me home," Grant replied, as he struggled to sit up and swing his legs over the side of the bed. The large bulky bandage taped to the side of his neck and right shoulder, where the wild dog's fangs had torn into his flesh, pulled at his bare skin. His right arm and hand were numb and in a sling. The move to sit up, initiated several short sharp bursts of pain down the back of his arm, over his shoulder, and up the right side of his neck into his jaw. His face scrunching up in agony, while he wobbled on the bed, very woozy.

"Hey, you all right?" Victor asked, hurrying around the side of the bed. "Maybe you better lie back down and take it easy."

"No," Grant said, waving Victor off with his left hand. "I want to get out of here and go home."

"You've got to be kidding me," Victor said skeptically. "You're in no shape to go home."

"That's right. The young fool is kidding," Linsey Hogan said, standing in the doorway of Grant's room. She had on a tight-fitting pale pink skirt suit, a white blouse, and black patent leather spiked heels. The gaudy attire accentuated her plumpness. He'd only seen the woman a couple of times so far, and each time, like today, her face was ghostly white from too much makeup. And there was a ton of sparkling blue eye shadow smeared up to her brows. If they were at a circus, Linsey could pass herself off as a clown.

"How did you know I was in here," Grant asked, a little embarrassed to see his boss.

"Victor's unpleasant gravelly voice, woke me out of a purely peaceful sleep at 2:00 Friday morning," Linsey said. "But never mind that now." She stared sternly at Grant. "One more round of medications and a hospital meal. Then you can go home, and not minute before, either. I spoke with your doctor at the nurse's station. That's what he told me. After seeing that little demonstration of your recuperative powers just now on the bed, I'm not so sure that quack knows much more about medicine than I do, and I know almost nothing of the profession."

"I'm really okay, Miss Hogan. I guess now that I've had a chance to think about it, the doctor might've said something along those lines," Grant said sheepishly. He eased back onto the bed with Victor's assistance.

"You know good and well that's what he said. You're not stupid, and I doubt that you have amnesia," Linsey scolded, marching into the room, brushing a few strands of the dull, dishwater-blond hair from her face. "You're one lucky young man on several accounts, Grant Rawlings. According to this so-called doctor of yours, the gashes from the feral dog's fangs were only millimeters from your right carotid artery. If that vessel had been severed, we would be at the funeral home viewing your ghastly pale corpse right now. It took thirty-seven stitches in your neck, and seventeen in your thigh, to sew up the damage that dog did to you. No simple matter, mister. And if Miss Sanford hadn't come by when she did, you would have most likely frozen or bled to death. I'm sure I'm not telling you anything the doctor hasn't already said."

"No," Grant answered. His head was down, and he avoided making eye contact with his boss.

"You didn't tell me all this, partner," Victor interjected.

"I didn't think it was important," Grant said lamely.

"Right," Linsey said. "Tell that to your mother. I'm sure she would understand."

"You didn't—"

"No. I didn't call your mother," Linsey said. "But I should. And I should tell her just what a foolish young man you are, like most of the men I've met. Mr. Macho Tough Guy."

"You're right, Miss Hogan. I'll stay until after lunch and the next round of medications," Grant promised. He had the feeling that Linsey was like a bulldog. Once she got her teeth into something, she wasn't about to let it go.

"I really think that's best, Grant," Victor agreed.

"Certainly it's best," Linsey said sharply, cutting Victor off. "That's what the doctor said. Doesn't take much intelligence to figure that out."

Here they go again, Grant thought.

"Thanks for the vote of confidence, boss. You really know how to make a fellow worker feel good," Victor said angrily. He stomped over to the only the chair in the room and dropped into it noisily. Sitting crossways in the chair with his legs dangling over the armrest, he stared out the window at what looked like another beautiful day.

"Well, thank you for the wonderful compliment, Mr. Big Chief Sitting Bull," Linsey said sarcastically. Her eyes blazed, and they could have burned a hole through Victor.

Victor just sat gazing out the window, as if she'd never said a word. He never once looked up at Linsey, but he had a bit of a smirk on his stone-like face.

She glanced back at Grant and cracked a less than genuine smile. "Now that we have the amenities out of the way, let's discuss work. It turns out that this may have happened at an opportune time. There's about a week's worth of paperwork that I need done, maybe almost two week's worth. I was planning on having you two handle it for me at some point. Now that nature boy here, has been incapacitated by one of our local wild animals, he will obviously be unable to go into the field for a while. Since you'll have to stick around your cabin while your wounds mend, your fine partner here can show you how to fill out the forms."

"What kind of paperwork?" Grant hated useless paper shuffling more than anything, and he was less than thrilled about the her idea.

"All the forms, as well as the procedural documentation on the proper way to fill them out, are down in my car," Linsey said. "Victor can come down and get them when I leave."

"Right," Victor mumbled to himself.

"So what about these feral dogs," Linsey asked Grant. "Have you had any encounters with them before? Well of course you haven't. You've been here less than a week."

Grant squirmed in his bed and looked away from Linsey and Victor. He wasn't going to say anything about the other night, but after what had happened, he thought maybe he should. "Actually, I think I may have had an encounter . . . sort of," he said quietly.

"What'd you say?" Victor asked, jumping from the chair. "When? What happened? How come you didn't say anything?"

"Whoa, whoa. Let the boy explain," Linsey said, holding up her hand to ward off the Indian's barrage of questions.

Grant straightened up in his bed, and with a rueful look on his discolored and puffy face, he began to tell the two of them about the night he came home to his cabin after having dinner with Charlie. He explained that he didn't actually see any feral dogs, just scat and urine scent markings. At first he had thought it was the silver-blue wolf, because he'd seen the animal in the road on the way home. But now, after this had happened, he was pretty certain that it was the feral dogs who broke into his cabin, vandalized it, and marked it as their territory. He didn't know why they did it.

As Grant told the story, Linsey had gone over to the chair, pulled it up alongside his bed, and sat down, showing an abundance of leg in white hosiery.

"Okay, that does it," Linsey said. "Those animals have to be found and put down as quickly as possible, before they pounce on some defenseless child somewhere and maim it or kill it."

As she said that, Grant glanced up at Victor, who was now standing at the end of the hospital bed. He recalled what Charlie had told him about Victor and his sister being attacked by feral dogs. For a brief moment, Victor's face went pale and twisted slightly with pain, when he heard Linsey's words. The long jagged scar streaking down the side of his face, flushed a brighter red than the rest of his dark weathered skin.

"You should have told me," Victor said, his tone conveying obvious hurt and disappointment.

"I'm sorry, Victor. I screwed up," Grant said apologetically. "I just didn't want to get something bad started about the silver-blue wolf, until I was sure."

"Okay you two, enough blubbering around here." Linsey said it harshly. She turned toward Victor. "This kind of stuff is bad publicity for me and the organization, and I'm not going to have it happen on my watch. Victor, when you get back to Two Forks, I want you to put the word out to everyone you know. Tell them the AWMC will pay two hundred and fifty dollars for each dead feral dog I see."

"Yes, ma'am. Gladly," Victor said.

A curt smile twisted across Linsey's round face. "Finally, we agree on something. Good. Maybe there's hope for the two of us after all. If you want to participate in the wild dog killing, be my guest. I know what it means to you."

"Thank you, ma'am," Victor said cordially, which was a total surprise to Grant. Twice in a row now, his partner had been civil to his boss.

"But first, after you get Mr. Macho Man here home, get him started on the paperwork," Linsey insisted. She got up from the chair and looked down at Grant. "Now, one more question for you, mister, then I've got to go to a meeting. Have you seen the silver-blue wolf since Wednesday evening?"

Grant cleared his throat and said, "I'm not exactly sure. After one of the feral dogs attacked me, something charged into it and knocked it off my back. All I saw was a silver-blue streak, and heard two dogs, or a dog and a wolf fighting fiercely behind me. I was too weak and too scared to looked back. I knew I was bleeding badly, and all I could think of was getting to the Suburban and going for help."

"What about the woolen blanket?" Victor asked. "Charlie said she found you outside the cabin with a woolen blanket pulled over you. How'd it get there?"

"Yeah, I'd like to know that too?" Linsey asked.

"I don't know," Grant said with a shrug. "I passed out right after the feral dog was knocked off me."

Both stared at him with puzzled expressions. It really was no mystery to Grant about the woolen blanket. The silver-blue wolf had covered him with it. It was all in his dream last night. Of course, he wasn't going to tell anyone. They would think he was crazy.

But now, the majestic predator required something from him. In the dream the wolf had indicated so. He wasn't exactly sure what it needed, and he didn't know how the animal conveyed the message to him. He just knew, somehow.

Charlie sat on a stool at the front counter next to the cash register, staring into her cup of coffee as she stirred it around and around. Yesterday had been a long day, and she was tired and worried sick about Grant Rawlings. It was 2:00 in morning before she, Doc Phillips, and Victor had gotten him to the hospital in Fairbanks. Victor had used the company helicopter to fly them there. Doc Phillips was an old country doctor in his seventies and had done all he could do. Grant was suffering from hypothermia and the loss of a great deal of blood, and in a small town like Two Forks there was no readily available blood supply. Things had looked pretty grim there for a while.

She and Victor had stayed with Grant all day, and part of the evening. Doc Phillips, though, left about nine that morning. He said he needed to leave in case someone else in Two Forks required his services, though he was hoping it was quiet because he was worn down to the bone. He caught a ride with a lumberjack who was heading back to Two Forks, after taking a few stitches in the head after a bar brawl the previous evening. The lumberjack was apparently fixed up enough and sober enough to head home to his wife.

As Charlie sat by Grant, she tried to apologize to him for the way she had acted the other night. But he seemed too groggy from pain medication to understand a word she was saying. She recalled what Edith had said about tomorrow may never come, and the thought of it made her cringe, because that nearly came true for Grant. She felt terrible about the whole mess.

Charlie was still stirring the coffee, which was now cold. She laid the spoon down on the counter and took a sip anyway, not even recognizing how bitter it was. Grant would be here about lunch time. She had told Victor to bring him straight to the Trading Post before taking him to the cabin. When that good looking hunk—bar a few scrapes and bruises on his head—stepped through the front door, she was going to drag him off to the corner where they could have some privacy and a long serious talk.

"Boy, I hope you're not thinking about me, 'cause it sure can't be good with that frown on your face," Billy Jack Boone said as he walked up to the cash register to pay for his breakfast.

"Oh hi, Billy Jack," she said, getting up from the stool and walking to the register.

"Everything's going to work out just fine, Charlie," Billy Jack said as he handed her the check and dug out his wallet from the back pocket of his jeans. "I'm flying to Anchorage Monday morning on some business, and I'm going to take care of that issue we talked about the other day."

"That's great," she said as she rang up his order. "But I wasn't thinking of that. Your total is $5.80, Billy Jack."

"I know. I was just joking with you," Billy Jack said, handing her a ten-dollar bill. "You're thinking of that Rawlings character, aren't you?"

Frank Kicklighter walked up behind Billy Jack, stood in line to pay his check, and overheard the two of them talking. "So how is that young man, anyway?"

"Morning Sheriff," Charlie and Billy Jack said in unison. Frank nodded.

"He gets out of the hospital today," Charlie replied with a sparkle, handing Billy Jack his change. "That feral dog chewed him up pretty good, but I think he'll mend all right. He should be here around 12:30."

"That soon?" Frank asked.

"Yeah. I thought it was a little quick myself," Charlie agreed.

Stuffing his wallet back in his pocket, Billy Jack said, "See you all later. Have to get out to the airport to do a little maintenance on the chopper."

"I'll probably see you out there later, Billy Jack. You know, while making my rounds in the neighborhood to catch those criminals off guard." Frank laughed and handed Charlie his check with a five-dollar bill.

"It's nice to know we have a man like you to protect us, Frank," Billy Jack said with a smile as he went out the door.

"Here's your change, Sheriff," she said, handing him a quarter and two pennies. "It looks like next week before I can get you the money, Frank."

Frank stuffed the change in his pocket and replied in a soft voice, "That'll be fine, Charlie. It'll be next week before I get the rest of the money rounded up, anyway. See you later." He nodded, tipped the brim of his sheriff's hat at her with his right hand, then turned and left.

Whitie Saylor sat at the end of the counter on his usual stool, slurping his coffee, and devouring two-day old donuts Charlie had given him at no charge. "Got any more of them donuts, Charlie," he muttered, licking the sugar glaze from his fingers. "They're real good this morning."

"Sure Whitie. How about some more coffee, too?" Charlie asked, as she picked up the urn full of fresh coffee and the box of two-day old donuts.

"Yup. And some more of them little cream things, too," Whitie answered.

Charlie set the box of donuts on the counter in front of him and said, "Help yourself, Whitie." As she refilled his cup, she struck up a conversation with the old geezer. "Whitie, you were here late Thursday night, when all the trappers were here having their big secret powwow."

"Yup," he said, the word muffled by the donut in his mouth. He opened two small coffee creamers, poured one in his cup and the other in his toothless mouth. No sugar.

"What was that all about, anyway?" she asked.

"If they'd wanted you to know, they'd of told you." He tipped some of the coffee out onto the saucer, lifted the small plate to his lips, and slurped it into his mouth. "Ah-h-h, mighty good coffee Charlie. Maybe the best I ever had," he said with satisfaction, as he sat the saucer back down on the counter. He picked up another donut, dunked it in the coffee, and crammed the entire thing in his mouth.

"Now don't try to smooth talk me and change the subject, you old devil," she said. "This is Charlie you're talking to. Your friend. The one that gives you these free donuts every morning."

Without looking at her, Whitie pushed the box of donuts aside and said, "I'm not for sale, Missy, not at any price. I still have a thread or two of gentlemen's honor left in me. Even though I may not look or act like the Prince of Wales, I've got my pride." Whitie licked both sets of fingers as he finished speaking.

A flare of anger surged through Charlie, like the way a good shot of tequila feels, burning all the way down to your stomach. She reached across the counter with her hands as if her elbows were spring-loaded, snatched up Whitie's face by his long whiskers, and jerked his head up so he had to look at her. She glared into his old eyes and said, "Now listen here, you old coot. You and my father were the best of friends. You used to bounce me on your knee and sing "Tony Boy" to me. Do you remember that?"

"Ye-ah." Whitie stuttered in surprise.

"Now I want to know what the hell is going on here, and I want to know right now," she demanded. "Something strange is going on with these trappers, and I aim to find out what it is. And you're just the man to tell me."

"Charlie, I think you'd better come to the office." It was Edith's son, Jonah, calling her from the kitchen doorway.

"I'm kind of busy right now, Jonah," she said to the young boy, glancing back over her shoulder.

"Mom says it's important. You just got something on that new fax machine of yours. Some guy in Fairbanks says for you to call him right away. Before noon."

She let go of Whitie's dirty whiskers and looked at her watch. It was 11:56. "Oh crap," she said. Spinning around, she ran through the kitchen doors and made a mad dash for her office on the general store side of the Trading Post. The moment Charlie disappeared into the kitchen, Whitie grabbed the box of donuts, gulped his coffee down, and hightailed it out the front door.

Charlie stood over the old marred oak desk and stared at the three fax sheets spread out on top of it. It was from Allen Colbert, the chemist, at the AWMC lab. At the bottom of the last sheet it said: CALL ME AS SOON AS POSSIBLE, BEFORE NOON TODAY. THERE IS A PROBLEM WITH THE SAMPLES.

"What else can go wrong," she said as she punched out Allen Colbert's number on the phone. She remembered that he was going on vacation today. As the phone rang, she glanced the at numbers and list of compounds on the other two sheets. There were numbers like 1 and 2 µg/L, which meant little to her, and compounds like benzene, chloroform, and a host of others that she'd heard of, but didn't know much about.

Charlie prayed she wasn't too late. After several rings, someone finally answered. "Hello, AWMC lab."

Charlie thought she recognized the high-pitched voice, but she wasn't sure. "Could I speak to Allen Colbert, please," she said.

"Is this Miss Sanford?"

"Yes."

"I'm glad you caught me," Allen said. "I was just on my way out the door when I heard the phone ring. My wife and kids are waiting for me out in the car. Going on vacation. Remember?"

"Yes, yes. What's the problem with the samples?"

"First of all, let me tell you the good news," he said. The chemist's voice squeaked over the phone. "The GC/MS for the EPA organic priority-pollutants, and the BODs for microbial activity, were run on all the samples. The GC/MS data showed the water is free of pollutants. However, the BOD data showed higher than normal levels of oxygen uptake in some of the samples, which means there is some type of microbial activity in the lake water."

"What does that mean, exactly? I mean in layman's language."

"All I can tell you, is there are organisms in some of the samples. For anything more definitive than what I've given you, you'll need to have a biochemist or microbiologist look at them under a microscope." There was a pause, then Allen spoke again in a hesitant voice. "Of course that could be a problem."

"What is that suppose to mean?"

"Well that's the bad news," Allen said. "Somehow, all the samples were poured out before I got around to running the ICP-MS heavy metal analysis."

"What?!" she blurted out in frustration. "You mean you didn't do everything Grant asked for?"

"I'm afraid not. Not the metals analysis. I'm sorry Miss Sanford. I don't know how this happened. It just did."

"Wait a minute. The day I saw you, you said something like you may have analyzed water from Broken Eye Lake before. Do you still have those results for the heavy metals?"

There was another pause, longer this time. She was just about to say something, when Allen's voice came back over the line.

"Well, that's another problem. I found the file but the records are missing. It's even been erased from the computer."

"I don't believe this. This is absolutely ridiculous!" Charlie said, completely exasperated.

"Look, my wife and kids are waiting. We haven't been on a vacation in three years. I really need to go."

Charlie was about to scream at the nerdy little man on the other end of the line. She could hardly believe this was happening. But instead, she vented her anger by slamming her free hand down on the desk. Then, very calmly, she wished Allen a nice vacation and hung up.

Linsey Hogan picked up her car phone and pressed the automatic dial button for her man in the field. It rang only twice before the familiar man's voice came on the line. Brushing off his greeting, she said, "This is Linsey. Where are you right now?"

"I'm on my way to the airport. What's happened now?"

"Nothing really. I just wanted to call and ease your mind a little," Linsey said as she pushed in the cigarette lighter on the console of her new red BMW. "I just spoke with our Oriental friends. They're already in Anchorage and hot-to-trot. They're ready to start business early Monday morning.

"Good. The quicker we get this over with, the better I'll feel about the whole thing," the man responded. "What about Grant and his trusty Indian scout?"

"I took care of Grant's water samples, myself. I poured them down the drain before the flaky chemist I have working for me, got around to analyzing them. He doesn't suspect a thing, either." Linsey brought the glowing orange lighter tip up to her cigarette and cracked the window to rid her new car of the smelly smoke.

"Wonderful. I've been really concerned about that problem. If they'd gotten that water analyzed, it could have screwed up the whole thing."

"I know you were concerned," she acknowledged, blowing smoke from the corner of her mouth. "I also destroyed the records from the time you had the lake water analyzed. I even erased any records in the computer that could show they were even in the lab. How's that for efficiency?"

"Oh man. I'd forgotten all about the samples being logged in the computer," the man admitted.

"That's why they pay me the big bucks," she said smiling to herself and feeling good about her accomplishments.

"What about next week? Will Grant and Victor be out of our hair?"

"No problem. Rawlings getting attacked and chewed up by that feral dog, couldn't have happened at a better time for us." She took a drag on the cigarette and blew the smoke toward the open window. "Grant's in no shape to be in the field, and I have him tied up to his eyeballs with paperwork all next week. As far as Victor goes, I've told him to put out the notice to hunt down the pack of feral dogs. I even encouraged him to participate in the hunt himself. He'll be so involved in getting revenge against those dogs, that nothing else will enter his feeble brain until after they're all dead."

"Good thinking. Sounds like next week will be trouble-free after all."

"All you have to do is hold up your end of the bargain, and we'll have us a ringer."

"You can count on it," the man promised. "Thanks for calling. It made my day."

"What are you doing?" Grant said gruffly, as he swatted Victor's hands away from his right arm, which was still in a sling. They had just gotten back to Two Forks and were on the front steps of the Trading Post. Victor was attempting to assist him up the steps. It was 1:20 in the afternoon. "I'm not an invalid. Besides, someone might see you."

"So?"

"So nothing," Grant snapped back. "Are you sure she wanted me to come here? You're not just saying that?"

"No, I'm not just saying that. Charlie was very specific. 'Bring Grant to the Trading Post before taking him to the cabin.' Those were her exact words," Victor said.

"And she really stayed with me all day yesterday?"

"Really. Indians don't tell lies," Victor said very seriously. His weathered face was long and solemn. "It's bad medicine." Then he chuckled.

"One of these days I'm going to get you good," Grant said, patting Victor on the shoulder and laughing. He really liked Victor. At first he wasn't quite sure just how to take him, but now there was no doubt in his mind as to the quality of the man's character.

At the top of the steps, Grant wasn't so sure about not needing Victor's help. His shoulder throbbed worse than an abscessed tooth, and he was slightly dizzy from the three-step climb. He raked his hands through his hair and straightened his shirt. "How do I look?"

"Like Napoleon," Victor said, glancing at the arm in the sling.

The moment Grant stepped into the Trading Post, Charlie sprang from behind the counter and ran toward him. There were only a few customers in the place. Her bright face immediately melted away his nervousness. Forgetting about the throbbing, he straightened up tall and stopped favoring his shoulder. A sharp stinging pain down his right arm, quickly reminded him that his strength wasn't a hundred percent yet. He flinched from the jolt of it, but was silent.

"You're here," Charlie yelled, as she rushed up to him. "Oh, you poor dear. You're in pain. I can see it in your face."

"I'm okay," Grant said, looking around to see if anyone had heard her. He was embarrassed.

"No you're not," she said. "Come on, lets go back in the corner where you can sit and have a little privacy. I've got something to tell you."

"All right," he said, feeling better by the second. He wondered what she had to tell him.

"Can I listen, or is this conversation going to be some of that mushy stuff," Victor asked, smiling. He trailed behind the two of them.

"Hush, and go tell Jonah to come over and take our order," Charlie said. "Grant probably needs a good juicy steak on the house, to help heal his wounds."

Victor rolled his eyes toward the ceiling and then bowed. "Your wish is my command, Your Majesty."

Grant smiled at his partner's silliness.

"Quit egging him on," Charlie ordered. "It'll only make him worse." She gently grasped Grant's right elbow and began to hustle him toward the far corner of the restaurant.

"Oh. It's okay to have *her* help you, but not me. I'm deeply crushed at your lack of confidence in me," Victor said, clutching his chest with both hands as he headed toward the kitchen.

"Stop taunting him or I'm going to strap you to a totem pole and give you twenty lashes," Charlie said, laughing.

"Very good," Grant said to Charlie. "I'll have to remember that the next time I need a good come-back line."

After Charlie got Grant settled at a corner table, he begged off on the juicy steak, saying he wasn't that hungry. But he told her that if she wanted to bring him a cheeseburger and fries after work, he would probably be hungry then and would really appreciate it. With a gleaming smile, she promised to do so.

Jonah brought their drinks. Grant had his usual cherry Coke, Victor had his usual hot tea and honey, and Charlie had coffee. They talked for a little while about what the doctor had said and about Linsey Hogan stopping by.

Then Grant asked Charlie, "So what did you want to tell me?"

"Uh-oh. Time for me to leave," Victor said, getting up. "It's time for the R-rated stuff."

Grant's face flushed. His partner was trying to embarrass him, and he was doing a real good job at it, too.

"No it's not. Sit down. This pertains to you too," Charlie said to Victor, gesturing with her hand for him to sit down. Then leaning toward Grant, she said, "The R-rated stuff will come later tonight at the cabin, when it's just you and me." Charlie fluttered her eyes, leaned back, and pulled out three sheets of folded fax papers from her back pocket. Handing them to Grant, she repeated what Allen Colbert had told her on the phone.

"Well, that's typical government bureaucratic screwups," Grant said, apparently unconcerned. "But all is not lost. I only gave you part of the sample from each bottle we collected. The rest are in the back of my Suburban."

"That's wonderful," Charlie said.

"I do find it a little odd, though, that the records from the earlier samples are missing, and the computer files were erased," Grant said. "But again it's probably nothing more than a typical government screwup. We really won't know for sure if there's a problem, or some kind of cover-up, until we have the samples analyzed for heavy metals."

"You planning on waiting three weeks until this AWMC chemist gets back from vacation?" Victor asked.

"I'd rather not, but I don't know what else to do." Grant said.

"Wait a minute," Charlie said, putting her index finger to her lip, as if she were thinking of something very important. "I have an idea. I'll be back in a minute." She looked at her watch and hurried into the kitchen.

CHAPTER 11

Victor closed the door to the small office in the hangar. He came in early this morning to make copies of the notice he'd written over the weekend. It announced a planning meeting for hunting down the feral dogs, and of course listed the AWMC's reward.

Normally on Monday mornings, the inside of the hangar would be filled with the drone of people talking and the clattering of mechanics working on planes. But at 5:00 in the morning, it was still as quiet as a cemetery at midnight. The only noise, was the echo of his footsteps as he walked across the concrete floor toward the outside door.

He started to step out, bit stopped when he saw Billy Jack pulling a long narrow odd-shaped wooden crate from the back of his Ford Ranger. Billy Jack carried it over to his helicopter and placed it inside the cargo area. Victor stepped back into the building and eased the door shut, leaving a narrow crack large enough to peek through. There were several, maybe ten or twelve, of the crates already in the aircraft. They varied in length and width. The largest was maybe five feet long and four feet wide.

Victor watched, as Billy Jack carried the remaining three crates to the chopper. What's Billy Jack doing here this early? Victor wondered. And what's in those crates?

Billy Jack was acting suspicious, glancing over his shoulder toward the hangar as if he didn't want anyone to see what he was doing. Initially, Victor's instincts wanted him to believe there were wolf hides in the crates, which would explain why the man was here so early and acting so strange. On second thought, however, the crates were much too narrow, and some much too small, to have wolf pelts in them. Plus, Billy Jack was too smart of a person to risk being caught with poached wolf hides here at the airport. "What could he have in those boxes," Victor said to himself.

"Whatcha doin', Chief?" Whitie asked, coming up behind Victor and startling him. "Spying on someone, or got your nose caught in the door?" The old man chuckled.

Victor spun around with a finger to his lips. "Sh-h-h. He might hear you," Victor whispered.

"He who?" Whitie asked, wiping sleep from his eyes.

"Never mind," Victor said. "What are you doing in here, anyway?"

"Ah, some of the mechanics leave a door unlocked for me sometimes when its cold. So I'll have someplace to sleep out of the weather."

"How convenient," Victor said, turning back to the door and peeking through the crack again.

Whitie pulled one of the sheets of paper from Victor's hand and studied it for a few moments. "Two hundred and fifty smackers for an old feral dog," Whitie yelled, slapping his left leg with excitement. "That'd buy a lot of beans."

"Sh-h-h! I told you to be quiet," Victor repeated, continuing to watch Billy Jack.

"I'm going to get me some of that action," Whitie said, but in a lower tone. "Three or four of them old flea bitten hounds, and I'll be set for the summer. Easy pickings too, 'cause I knows just were to—" Whitie stopped in mid-sentence.

Victor let the door close all the way and turned around very slowly, a tight smile across his face. "And just where might that be?"

"Oops," Whitie said. He turned and began to tiptoe off.

Victor reached out, grabbed the old drunk by the collar and pulled him back. "Not so fast, Old Timer. I want to know just where this pack of killer dogs is at."

"Nope, can't tell you," Whitie said.

"Whitie." The volume of Victor's voice began to rise noticeably.

"Nope, nope, nope, not a word out of me," Whitie repeated, clamping his lips tight.

"Come on, Whitie. Tell me something. Please. You know what this means to me."

"Yup, but I can't tell you that. I can tell you what Charlie wanted to know, though. Doesn't make any difference now anyway."

"What are you talking about?" Victor asked.

Whitie looked all around the hangar, to be sure no one would hear. "Well," he said, "Saturday morning Charlie asked me why all them trappers had that big meeting at the Trading Post the other night."

Victor listened, still hanging onto Whitie's collar.

The old man looked around again, then whispered, "There's some big fur buying outfit coming to Anchorage this week. Word is, they're paying prime dollar for every wolf pelt they can get their hands on."

"Who's behind all this?"

"Excuse me," Billy Jack said as he opened the door and bumped into Victor's back.

Victor stepped aside, which gave Whitie his chance to escape. He broke loose from Victor's grip, spun around and scurried through the open doorway like a scared rabbit, shoving Billy Jack up against the door as he rushed by.

"That's the fastest I've ever seen that old codger move before," Billy Jack said. "What kind of burr got under his saddle?"

Walking into the building, Billy Jack looked at Victor and said, "What are you two doing here this early in the morning?"

Victor resented the question. He wasn't the one sneaking around like a common criminal. But he held back his feelings and handed Billy Jack a copy of the notice. "I came in early to make a few copies of this notice about the feral dogs. I want to get them posted around town before everyone wakes up. I guess Whitie's been sacking out here in the hangar in the evenings. Now, what are *you* doing here so early this morning?"

When Whitie had slipped out, Victor noticed through the open door, that the cargo door on Billy Jack's helicopter was already closed. He chose not to mention anything about the crates he had seen Billy Jack loading into the aircraft. He wanted to see how the man answered the question.

"I had to get up with the chickens, because I have an early business appointment in Anchorage this morning," Billy Jack answered.

Victor glanced down at his watch, then looked up at Billy Jack. "What businessman is going to be up this early in the morning?"

"Darn store wasn't open on my way here. I need to get something to drink for the trip down to Anchorage. Excuse me for a minute," Billy Jack said, ignoring the question. He walked off toward the vending machine in the far corner of the hangar.

Victor watched Billy Jack's husky form move across the concrete floor. He carried himself like a man with an abundance of confidence and an assurance of his place in life. Victor was thoughtful.

Why was Billy Jack acting so weird while he was loading those crates in his helicopter, and what was in them? Who was he really going to see in Anchorage, and why so early? Victor was even more concerned, especially after Whitie mentioned that the fur buyers would be there this week. Too many questions and no answers. Things looked awfully suspicious, and they leaned heavily in the direction of Billy Jack being involved in some type of covert activity.

The door cracked open for a second time. Victor noticed the cold air seeping in from outside.

Frank Kicklighter poked his head through the opening. "Hey, what's up, Victor?" the sheriff asked. "You're sure up with the roosters this morning." He opened the door a little wider and stepped into the large building. As usual, he had his bottled water with him.

Victor told Frank about the notice he'd written up and gave the man a copy. This was the third time he'd had to explain himself today, and he was about to explode. He had to get out of here before he went crazy. Victor thought about telling the sheriff about Billy Jack's strange activities with the odd crates, but decided to wait and see what would happen next.

"Help me spread the word," Victor said. "The more we get involved, the sooner we can get rid of these dogs."

"I'll do that," Frank said. "Say, what the heck is going on with old Whitie Saylor. I just saw him running across the field toward Two Forks, as if his rear end was on fire."

As Victor began to explain, Billy Jack came walking back. "That danged vending machine is on the blink again," Billy Jack said to the two of them. "It took two dollars from me. Morning, Sheriff."

"I thought I saw your white Ranger out there," Frank said to Billy Jack. "Seems like everyone is up and at 'em early this morning. I even saw a truck caravan of local trappers, tearing down Highway 3, a few minutes ago."

"Really," Victor said. "That's interesting." Pieces of the puzzle were beginning to come together—the high increase in wolf poaching in the past few weeks; the skinned carcasses he and Grant found the other day; and the hundreds of wire snare traps that had been set lately, indiscriminately snaring any animal that happened by.

"Yeah, I thought so too," Frank agreed.

Billy Jack made no comment about the trappers, or where they might be headed.

"What's the matter, Billy Jack? Need something to sip on while you're buzzing around up there in the air?" Frank asked.

"Exactly. I'm flying all the way to Anchorage today."

"How about a bottle of my water," Frank offered. "It doesn't have the sugar or caffeine you're probably used to, but it's sure a lot better for you."

"Hey, that'd be great. All I want is something wet," Billy Jack said. "All the stores were closed when I came through town." He looked down at his watch. "Man, I better get cranking or I'm going to be late for my appointment."

"I'll get that water from my car," Frank said.

Victor watched from the doorway, as the two men walked toward Frank's police car. They were talking quite a bit as they walked along.

Stepping outside, Victor climbed into his truck and headed for Two Forks. He had to put out his notices.

After pulling himself out of bed Monday morning, Grant, still stiff and sore, fixed himself a cup of coffee. He stretched out on the sofa and began to go over the recent events in his life. Before he'd left the Trading Post Saturday afternoon and came back to his cabin, Charlie had made arrangements to have the lake samples analyzed for heavy metals. That was why she'd left the table so quickly in the middle of their lunch.

She'd remembered that Billy Jack was going to Anchorage today. She also remembered that she had a chemist friend, Henry Danner, who had his own lab in Anchorage. When Charlie came back to the table, she told Victor and Grant about Henry and mentioned he owed her a favor. Her chemist friend said if they could get the samples there by early Monday morning, he would be able to work them in and have the results by noon or so. Otherwise, it would be two weeks before he could get to the samples.

It was Sunday afternoon when Billy Jack came by to pick up the water samples. He was much more civil, in fact, almost friendly. Quite a change from the last time they'd met, when he nearly drowned Grant in Denning Fork.

To his surprise, Billy Jack even said he would be happy to drop the samples off at the lab for him. Billy Jack said he had business in Anchorage early Monday morning, and it wouldn't be a problem. Of course, in the same breath, he also expressed his opinion about how he thought the samples were a waste of time and taxpayers money. "The water in Broken Eye Lake," he said, "was as pure and clean as a new born baby—innocent and uncontaminated by the evils of the world." But again, his tone was civil and non-inflammatory, and it lacked the sound of a dominating bully. Grant wasn't sure what had happened, or who had talked to Billy Jack, but there was definitely a change in the man, for the better.

Charlie came by Saturday evening after work with the cheeseburger and fries, like she had promised. But by then Grant was sound asleep, so she didn't bother to wake him. She left the food on the kitchen counter, with a note saying she'd stopped by, and then headed home. Early Sunday morning, she dropped by again on her way to work, but he was still sleeping.

Around noon Sunday, Charlie finally caught Grant with his eyes open. She'd brought him a cheeseburger, fries, a large cherry Coke, and a huge piece of Edith's homemade pecan pie, his favorite. He was very happy to see her, and particularly happy that she'd brought the food. Since leaving the hospital and getting back to the cabin, he hadn't felt like doing much of anything but sleeping—probably a result of the intense repair work his body was doing. But he certainly hadn't felt like cooking. So by noon on Sunday when she came by, he was starving.

While he stuffed his face, Charlie explained how she'd come by on a couple of occasions. Each time, he was sleeping so peacefully, she didn't want to wake him. Before she left, Charlie promised to come by after work on Sunday evening, saying she had something important to discuss with him.

Grant never knew if she came by or not. After Billy Jack picked up the samples, all his energy seemed to disappear. He went back to the sofa and fell asleep again. He didn't wake up until a few minutes ago. It was now 7:25 Monday morning.

After sleeping for nearly sixteen hours, his body was rested and well on the way to recovery. Much of the stabbing pain in his right arm and shoulder had lessened to a dull ache, and he was able to remove the sling. He wasn't used to just hanging around the cabin, and he was starting to feel fidgety and bored.

He tried to come up with something constructive to do. The thought of climbing in the Suburban and going up to the Trading Post to see Charlie crossed his mind, but then he remembered the paperwork Linsey had sent home with him. He wasn't really in the mood for that, however. He wasn't sure he'd ever be. Besides, he needed Victor's assistance with the forms so they would be filled out properly.

Instead, Grant went outside and cranked up the generator. It had been a few days since he'd made any entries in his personal diary. He got out his notebook computer, placed it on the small round kitchen table, plugged it in, and began to slowly type in the dramatic events of the past couple days. The tips of his fingers were still sore from digging at the hasp on the storage building, but he managed.

About nine, the rumble of an engine and the slam of a car door, broke his concentration. Most likely it was Victor coming to show him how to fill out the silly forms Linsey had given them at the hospital. Grant quickly finished typing in his final thoughts about the feral dog attack, closed the file, and turned off the computer. The next thing he heard was a light peck at the door, followed by the hinges squeaking as the door opened slowly.

"Grant? Are you awake?" Charlie asked, almost whispering as she crept into the cabin.

Grant had moved back over to the sofa. When he heard her soft voice, his heart fluttered, and he immediately stood up. A broad grin covered his face. "Yeah, over here." He was glad it was Charlie instead of the Victor.

"How are you feeling?" Charlie asked. She'd stepped into the room and shut the door behind her, so as to keep out the cold.

"Better than yesterday." And a lot better after seeing you, he thought. A surge of energy rushed through him, and he moved toward her to greet her.

Like the gentleman his daddy had taught him to be, Grant helped Charlie remove her fleece-lined denim jacket, then set it across the back of the sofa. She looked as if she'd just stepped out of a fashion magazine. He was sure she'd gone by her place first to change clothes and freshen up, just for him. The thought of it made him feel good inside.

"You look real nice today, Charlie." It sounded dumb, but he didn't know what else to say.

She looked up at him and grinned. "Thanks. That was sweet. Don't take this wrong, though, but you've looked better." They both laughed.

He noticed how the navy blue skirt fit snugly around her trim hips and stopped just above her knees. Her long legs seemed to be even longer in the skirt. Like a magnet, his eyes were pulled to the white cotton blouse, opened provocatively, to display the deep valley between her firm milky-white breasts. Her nipples pressed against the soft fabric like small protruding buttons in the material. Embarrassed by his carnal thoughts, he shifted his eyes away before she could catch him looking.

In her right hand, she carried a large white paper bag. A tote bag was draped over her left shoulder. "I brought breakfast with me," she said with a pleasant smile. Her blue eyes twinkled. "Eggs, sausage, hash browns, and two large cups of fresh coffee."

They walked over to the kitchen table together, not speaking, just looking at each other. Her auburn hair glistened in the morning sunlight that shined through the front windows. Her heavenly perfume floated up into his nose and reminded him of the lilac bush in full purple bloom in his grandmother's front yard.

Setting the paper bag on the table, Charlie pulled out two large Styrofoam cups and two covered plates. As she removed the lids from the everything, steam rolled up into the air. The aroma was fabulous, and the sight of the hot food made his mouth water.

"You been doing some work this morning?" Charlie asked, gesturing with her head toward the computer.

"Yeah, sort of," Grant replied, as he dug out a couple of forks from the drawer.

As they sat across the table from each other, eating, she asked, "Have you changed your dressings like the doctor said?"

"Well . . . probably. Not exactly," he answered. The doctor had told him to put on a clean dressing, every day.

"I take that to mean you haven't changed them at all," Charlie said pointedly.

Grant was busy watching her eat. Like his father, she cut away the egg whites from the yolks and ate them first, saving the yolks for last. "As a matter of fact," he finally said, "I was just going to do that today." Actually, he hadn't even thought about it. But he figured it was best to act as if he had. Some women seemed to worry about things like that. His mother sure did.

"Men! Some never make a peep about their aliments, no matter how bad they are. Others whine at the first sign of a sniffle. Who can figure them out. It's obvious you're the first type, which is why I came prepared. I assume you don't want an infection to get started, do you?"

"No," he answered, between bites.

"I've got everything we need to fix you up, right in the tote bag," Charlie said. "I'll change the dressing after we finish eating."

They ate and smiled and gazed at one another. Their breakfast conversation was more trivial than anything else—a little bit about work at the Trading Post, how nice the weather had been, and so on—skirting the real issue of why she dropped by to see him.

Thirty minutes later Grant was sitting on the sofa, and Charlie was asking him to take his sweatpants off. He had tried his best to convince her that he would change the dressings later, but she wouldn't hear of it.

"You can either take your sweats off willingly, or I'll go back to the Trading Post and bring back a couple of big burly lumberjacks to hold you down while I take them off myself," she said sternly, cockily standing in front of him with her hands on her hips.

"You wouldn't," he said, not knowing if she was really serious or not.

"Just try me."

"But—"

"But nothing," she snapped. "It's not the first time I've seen a man with his pants off, you know. Besides, I'm just going to change the bandage on your leg, not rape you."

"I can't. I don't have any underwear on," he muttered. This was so embarrassing.

"Is that why you're being so stubborn about this?" Charlie asked. "For crying-out-loud, go put something on. I'll look the other way if that's what's bothering you." She turned her back to him and stared at the fireplace.

As quickly as he could move, he got up from the sofa, rushed over to the dresser next to his bed and dug out a clean pair of underwear. After putting them on, Grant hurried back to the sofa and lay down on his stomach. "Okay, I'm ready now."

Charlie just shook her head and smiled.

After finishing the wound on his leg, Charlie had him remove his shirt so she could do the one on his shoulder. She stood in front of him, bent over, gently loosening the tape around the bandage. Her blouse gaped open even more. He wasn't sure, but it looked as though another button was undone. Her fully shaped breasts were nearly exposed. The smooth taunt skin was tantalizingly inviting. When she moved a certain way, he could just barely see the outer rim of the light-brown areola surrounding her left nipple. His eyes seemed to be permanently fixed on the amazing sight. Grant immediately felt a tightness in his sweatpants, between his legs. He squirmed on the sofa, embarrassed at his fledgling erection.

"Sit still. I'm almost ready to take it off," Charlie said. She was completely engrossed in what she was doing and was apparently unaware of her revealing position or his state of arousal.

He finally tore his eyes loose from the front of her blouse and focused his vision and thoughts on the Chilkat dancing blanket hanging over the fireplace. With all his willpower, he concentrated on the intricate designs in the Indian blanket and tried to keep his eyes off this beautiful woman standing in front of him, graciously tending to his injuries.

After Charlie removed the old bandage, she carefully cleaned the wound with hydrogen peroxide, just as she had done with the thigh injury, and then gingerly applied tincture of iodine to the stitched gashes. It burned like thunder, but he remained still, his eyes fixed on the blanket.

In the process of caring for him, she did most of the talking and finally got around to apologizing for her rudeness the other day at the Trading Post. Charlie was a tough woman, yielding to no one. It was obvious she had difficulty saying she was wrong and apologizing. But she went on and explained about Frank's daughter and how he needed the payment on the Trading Post early. Grant offered to loan her what little he had saved up, which wasn't much. But she declined, saying she'd already made arrangements and would have the money by the end of the week.

Her fingers were soft and gentle as they touched and delicately probed his skin. Once she had finished and the new dressing was in place, Charlie's left hand strayed from its Florence Nightingale duties, and slyly skimmed over the toned, hard muscles of his right arm, exploring his well-kept body.

Surprised, Grant jerked his eyes from the blanket above the fireplace, back to her. But like an addiction, his gaze first stopped, for just a brief second, at the opening in Charlie's blouse, and her beautiful breasts. His eyes continued their slow climb up her long graceful neck to her dainty squared chin, across the thin wet lips that were curled into an inviting smile, over her aristocratic nose, and finally to her captivating eyes that were now . . . staring directly into his.

Oh my God, he thought. Instantly, his eyes darted to the floor and away from Charlie's face. She had caught him looking. How embarrassing. He didn't know what to say to her.

Maybe he shouldn't say anything. What kind of man would she think he was after this?

Charlie's hand slid from his arm, over the contours of his chest, and stopped for a moment at his right nipple. Her warm slender fingers moved in a rotating motion, gently and seductively brushing his nipple.

Like a surprise visit from an old friend, the tightness between his legs returned. His face was flushed, and he could feel the heat radiating through him.

Her hand journeyed up to his chin and gently gripped it as she turned his face toward hers. Their eyes locked for a long moment as they gazed deep into each other's soul. Grant's heart galloped like a thoroughbred racehorse. He began to breath faster and sweat beads popped out on his forehead. Charlie leaned down and pressed her sweet soft lips against his trembling ones. As they met, his heart skipped a beat and a rush of fire flooded through his veins. Their eyes remained open, each lost in the other's, and . . .a car horn honked outside the cabin.

They pulled apart at the same time, as if they were thirteen and had just gotten caught by their parents. Charlie quickly stood up, straightened her blouse, and closed the top two buttons, covering her exposed cleavage. She raked her fingers through her hair, looked down at him with an expression that said she didn't want to leave, and said, "I'd better get back to the Trading Post and take care of business."

"Yeah, okay," Grant said, still in state of confused rapture. He leaned forward on the sofa and looked out the window to see who was coming at such a bad time. "It's Victor," he said lamely. At that moment, he could've strangled the man. "We've got a lot of paperwork to do. Thanks for everything, Charlie. It really meant a great deal to me."

"It was my pleasure, believe me. My daddy always said I should have been a nurse," Charlie said, putting on her coat. "Look, my chemist friend in Anchorage said he would call between 12:30 and 1:00 this afternoon, with the results. So if you want to stop by later, I should have the fax printouts on the lake samples."

"Absolutely," he said, lifting himself off the sofa. He handed her the tote bag. "I'm anxious to see the data. Victor and I'll be up later. I'm sure there's nothing toxic in the water, but it's good to be sure."

"Exactly. See you in a while," she said, smiling sweetly, her face glowing.

Charlie opened the door and was gone.

Grant felt wonderful, full of life, and yes, maybe in love.

The door opened again. He expected Victor, but it was Charlie who poked her head back in. "How about dinner tonight, at my place again?"

"Sure. That'd be great."

"We'll pick up where we left off." She puckered her lips and blew him a kiss, then disappeared behind the closed door.

Grant felt as light as a feather. His eyes were glazed, and he stared into space, recapturing that most wonderful moment of their first passionate kiss. Without even realizing it, he glided over to the front door and opened it.

Victor was halfway between his Suburban and Grant's cabin, when he saw Charlie bouncing toward him. Her face was lit up with a grin as big as all outdoors, and her eyes were twinkling like rare gems.

"Hi, Victor. You look very fit today," Charlie said jubilantly, as if this was the greatest day in the history of mankind.

"Thank you, Charlie, so do you," Victor ,said as she passed him by, humming a merry tune he hadn't heard before. He smiled and continued toward the cabin. This was not the first time he'd witnessed the symptoms of love. He remembered the time when he'd first met Mary Margaret. There was nothing else in life that mattered but winning her heart and love.

Grant stood in the doorway of the cabin, bare-chested in the fresh morning air, wearing the same giddy smile that Charlie had. As he appeared impervious to the cold, Victor decided Grant had been bitten by the lovebug as well.

Grant's glazed eyes followed Charlie as she walked to her car, completely ignoring Victor's presence. They waved at one another, and then she drove off. Grant continued to watch until the truck disappeared behind the spruce trees.

"The president of the United States called me this morning and wants us to go up in the next space shuttle," Victor said to Grant, as he walked toward the stoop.

"That's nice," Grant replied, dreamily.

"Hello in there. Hello," Victor said, waving his hand in front of Grant's face. "Victor to Grant, come in."

"What? What do you want?" Grant said, coming out of his trance. He swatted Victor's hand away.

"So you and Charlie got something going on, huh?" he asked.

"Absolutely not," Grant said emphatically. But his face told the truth. "We're just good friends. That's all." The young man then turned and went into the cabin.

Victor followed Grant inside and said, "Right. Good friends that grin silly lovesick smiles at one another."

"Are you going to show me how to fill out these forms Linsey gave us?" Grant asked, as he slipped on the blue and black plaid flannel shirt that was on the sofa. He hoped to change the subject from him and Charlie, to work.

Victor stared out the kitchen window toward Denning Fork, rubbing the whisker stubs on his chin with his thumb. "I've been thinking a lot about that," he said, turning around to face Grant. "There's something really fishy about all this—the paperwork, letting me be part of the feral dog roundup—the whole thing smells like a week-old salmon washed up on the bank. I've been working for the state of Alaska for fifteen years and never had to fill out these kinds of forms before. This is the kind of moose poop that the administrative people do, not the field agents."

"We really don't have a choice. Linsey said we have to do it," Grant said.

"Look, you're a scientist," he said, walking over to Grant. "Your job is to figure out why the population of caribou is declining every year, not to fill out stupid paperwork that any clerk can do."

"Well, that's a pretty good point," Grant replied. "But Linsey does sign our paychecks."

"Wolves are being poached at a rate that's ten times higher than it's ever been. Oh sure, there has always been poaching around here, but nothing like this," Victor said. He then proceeded to tell Grant what Whitie Saylor had told him about the fur-buyer's consortium being held in Anchorage this week, and what Frank Kicklighter had said about seeing the caravan of trappers heading down Highway 3, obviously on their way to Anchorage.

Grant eased down onto the sofa, while listening to Victor and trying to digest all he'd just heard. "So are you saying that's why there's been this dramatic increase in wolf poaching lately?"

"That's exactly right," Victor said. "But I think it goes much deeper than that. I'm just not sure yet, what it is, though. I still think Billy Jack is involved in this, somehow. But he's too smart of a man to get tangled up in a simple poaching ring, unless the stakes are much higher than selling a few wolf pelts."

"Now wait a minute," Grant said. "Billy Jack is doing us a favor by taking our lake samples to the lab. That has to stand for something. Besides, he was actually pretty friendly when he came by yesterday afternoon. I'm not sure I agree with your assessment of him."

"This business of taking the samples to Anchorage is only a smoke screen. You, better than anyone, should know you never take your eyes off a wild dog, and never, ever, turn your back on one." Victor was silent for a moment, then he told Grant about seeing Billy Jack at the airport, loading the odd-shaped boxes and acting very suspicious while doing it. "Doesn't it seem strange to you, that Billy Jack has a business appointment in Anchorage this particular week? Especially in light of the fact that the fur-buyer's consortium will be there at the same time?"

"I hadn't thought of that," Grant said lamely.

"There is one thing Linsey was right about," Victor said. "You need to take it easy for a few days and heal, before getting back in the field."

"But what about the paperwork?" Grant asked. "You need to help me with it."

"For now, let's forget the paperwork," Victor said defiantly. "You concentrate on getting well, that is if you can keep your mind off Charlie long enough."

"I wish you'd stop that," Grant said, his face reddening.

"Okay, I'm sorry. Oh, by the way, there's an electrical problem with Flutter Butt. I noticed it Saturday when we were flying back from Fairbanks. I checked into it this morning and ordered the part. It should be in this afternoon. I'll fix it then. In the meantime, I'll put my ear to the ground and my nose in the air, to see what I pick up. I'll concentrate on finding out what's really going on around here."

"Hello," Charlie answered the phone in her office.

"May I speak to Charlie Sanford, please?" the voice on the other end of the line inquired.

"This is she," Charlie answered.

"Oh, I—"

"I know. You didn't expect a woman named Charlie," she said. "I'm used to it by now. How may I help you?"

"My name is Kyle Jefferies. I'm a chemist for Henry Danner. He wanted me to call you as soon as we had the results on the lake samples. I have to tell you this water is clean enough to drink. In fact, I've never seen lake water in these parts as free of metals as these samples are."

She looked at her watch. It was 12:45. Just like Henry. Right on time, she thought. "That's great. My friend will be happy to hear the water isn't contaminated. Can you fax or mail me the results, so he can have them for his file?"

"You bet," Kyle Jefferies said. "I'll do it right now. What's your fax number?"

Charlie gave the chemist the fax number for the Trading Post.

"Before I hang up, Henry wanted me to tell you he was sorry he couldn't be the one to call you. One of our major customers phoned and wanted him to come over right away."

"That sounds like Henry, always in the middle of something."

"That's for sure. He also wanted me to tell you, you owe him a beer for this. Come down some time and he'll let you buy him one," Kyle chuckled.

"I'll do that," she laughed. "Thanks for calling, Kyle."

A few minutes later, Charlie was bouncing around in the kitchen with the fax results in her hand. Edith had two chicken steaks in one of the deep-fryer baskets. The other was full of french fries. The hot grease was bubbling and boiling away.

"We've been so busy today, I haven't had a chance to talk to you much since you came back from the Rawlings boy's place," Edith said, turning over one of the hamburgers on the grill. "I gather everything went well, by the way you've been flitting and floating around here like a butterfly fresh out of it's cocoon."

"It went well," Charlie said, knowing Edith was leading up to something. "And before you ask, yes, I apologized for my behavior the other evening."

"That's good, Charlie. But somehow I think there's more to it than that," Edith said bluntly. "He say anything you liked?"

"Well . . . not exactly."

Edith flipped another hamburger. "He do anything you liked?"

"Yes, he took his pants off and laid down on the sofa," Charlie answered, without emotion. Her back was to her friend, and she was struggling not to bust out laughing.

Edith spun around from the grill, dripping hot grease onto the floor from the spatula in her right hand. "Charlotte Sanford, you should be ashamed of yourself. He's just a baby. What would your father think of such a thing. Right there in his cabin."

Charlie turned around, still holding her laughter in check. She wanted to play this out a little bit more with Edith. "A baby, he is not." She rolled her eyes. "I can assure you of that."

"Did you seduce that young boy?" Edith asked, pointedly, her face twisted in disgust.

"No, I did not seduce that young boy. And Grant is not a young boy, Edith. Jonah is a young boy." She couldn't hold back any longer and began to laugh. "I just cleaned his wounds and changed his dressings. That's all. You should get your mind out of the trash bin. I swear."

Edith went back to tending her hamburgers, removing them from the grill and placing them on opened toasted buns spread out on dinner plates. "Where'd that awful feral dog bite him, anyway?"

Charlie reached around with her right hand, grabbed the back of her thigh, and said, "Right here. That's why he had to pull his pants down. And he has the cutest tightest little butt I've ever seen."

"Charlie, hush," Edith said, looking around to see if Jonah was anywhere close by. "That's all. You just changed his dressings, and now you're bouncing around here happy as all get out. I don't think so, young lady. There's more to it than that."

"Well . . . we did kiss . . . kind of, before Victor came driving up and interrupted us," she added.

Edith glanced over her shoulder and smiled. Then her face took on a more serious look. "It sounds to me like you're heading for some stormy weather, girl. This boy is pretty naive when it comes to women. That's obvious by the way he acts around you. Just take it slow and careful, so neither one of you gets hurt."

At first Charlie resented Edith's remarks. After all, she was an adult, and her personal affairs were none of Edith's business. But they had been friends for a long time and knew each other very well. After thinking for a few moments about what Edith had said, Charlie realized her friend was only giving her advice because she truly cared and didn't want to see her get hurt. And there was some wisdom to what Edith had said. Maybe she did come on a little strong at Grant's this morning. But she really liked this guy.

"You're probably right, Edith. I shouldn't rush things between Grant and me. Thanks. Now I'd better get out front and take care of the customers." Charlie went through the swinging doors directly to the cash register, where two customers were already waiting to pay their bills.

Charlie was sitting at the counter drinking coffee, when the bell over the door rang at 1:15. Grant limped into the Trading

Post, with Victor trailing behind him. That fluttering warm feeling flared up in her stomach again. She immediately hopped off the stool and rushed over to assist Grant. "Here, let me help you," she said, pulling his left arm over her shoulder for support.

"That's okay, I can make it," Grant said quietly, very embarrassed. He glanced around the nearly empty diner. Apparently, the lunch crowd had already come and gone.

"Maybe we should get him a wheelchair, Charlie," Victor chuckled.

"It's not funny, Victor," she snapped. Sometimes his jokes could really get on her nerves. "Grant has been through a traumatic experience. You could be a little more sympathetic—" Charlie looked up at Victor, as she helped Grant into a chair at a table near the counter. That's when the long ugly scar on Victor's face came into view. She had forgotten that Victor had also been attacked and maimed by feral dogs. "I'm sorry, Victor. I guess you understand better than any of us, other than Grant, just how traumatic the experience is."

The tall Indian brushed the comment aside as if it had never been spoken. "How about a cup of coffee and a piece of Edith's chocolate pie," he said as he sat down in a chair next to Grant.

"Besides a cherry Coke, can I get you a piece of pie, too, Grant?" she asked.

"Cherry Coke is fine. I want to save my appetite for tonight," he answered, smiling.

"I'll be back in just a sec," she said, walking over to the counter and picking up a manila folder.

Jonah came through the swinging doors from the kitchen just then. She gave their orders to the boy, then walked back to the table and sat down on the other side of Grant, across from Victor. Grant's stiff leg was stretched out under the table.

"The chemist from Anchorage faxed the results from the heavy metals tests on those lake water samples, just like he promised," she said, handing the folder to Grant. She'd even labeled the tab on the folder with a black marking pen. It said BROKEN

EYE LAKE. "He said the water was clean enough to drink. The cleanest he's ever seen for around here."

Grant opened the folder and scanned the two fax sheets for a few seconds, then said, "Boy, he was right about that. As far as dissolved metals go, this water is really clean." Grant closed the folder and laid it on the table. "Well, now we know it isn't contaminated. That's one piece of the puzzle we don't have to worry about any longer. But we still have to solve the problem of why the caribou's population keeps declining."

Charlie laid her hand on Grant's arm and said, "You'll figure it out. I know you will."

"I certainly hope so," Grant said. "The wolves are getting all the blame for this, and I have a gut feeling there's something else going on besides a predator/prey problem. Especially with the increased poaching activity of the wolves in this area, it seems to indicate there's something else that's at least part of the problem with the caribou."

"I think Whitie Saylor knows something about all of this," Charlie said.

"He does," Victor said. He told them what the old man had said to him earlier that morning.

"So that's why all those trappers were in here late Thursday night," she grumbled. "They were planning a trip to Anchorage."

"That's the way I figure it," Victor said.

"I think the sheriff has been suspicious too, that something funny is going on," Charlie added. "I've seen him talking to most of these guys. I haven't heard what he's said to them, but what ever it is, it's serious, judging by the expression on Frank's face."

Victor then told her about Billy Jack loading odd-shaped boxes into his chopper and how he was acting real suspicious while doing it.

"Well, I don't know what was in those boxes, but I know two things he was going to do in Anchorage—take your water samples to the lab, as a favor to me I might add, and conduct some very important business for me," she said firmly. "Victor, I know you don't think very much of Billy Jack, but he's a honorable man. I would stake everything I own on his not being involved in any of this."

Jonah brought their drinks and Victor's pie. He carefully set everyone's order in front of them and politely asked, "Will there be anything else?" The boy was staring at the seat of Grant's chair as he spoke, and seemed to be preoccupied with something about the way Grant was sitting.

"What in the world are you looking at?" Charlie asked.

"The gossip around town is, Grant has the cutest tightest little butt in Two Forks," Jonah said. Then he ran toward the kitchen, laughing.

Grant looked at her with unforgiving eyes. Her face was beaming red. She swallowed and said, "I don't know what he's talking about. I'll talk to Edith about him."

Victor was leaning over, gawking at Grant's jeans-covered butt. "I guess I'd never noticed before, how cute and tight your butt is," he said. "It's amazing what a person can learn every day, if he just listens closely enough."

"Okay, okay. I don't think I want to hear any more of this," Grant said, glaring at Victor, then at Charlie.

"Just kidding, partner. Don't take offense," Victor said, smiling. He had already finished his pie and half of his coffee when he stood up. "I'd better go out to the airport and see if that part came in. What do I owe you, Charlie?"

"It's on me."

"Thanks. See you two later." Victor turned and left.

"I'd better get going, too. I've got some things I need to do," Grant said, getting up from his chair. "Is there anything I can bring tonight?"

"Just yourself," Charlie said as sweetly as she could. Noticing Grant's solemn face, she asked, "You're not angry at me, are you?"

He looked at her for a moment, then cracked a smile. "Of course not. How could I be angry at someone who thinks I've got the cutest tightest little butt in Two Forks."

Chapter 12

At 7:45, Grant sat on the back steps of his cabin, drinking his morning coffee and watching the tumbling water of Denning Fork roll by. White clouds drifted lazily in the sky. Even though steam swirled from his cup into the brisk air, the temperature was warmer than yesterday. Summer was slowly easing its way into the north country. The soreness in his shoulder, arm, and leg had improved since Monday. He felt more like himself, maybe seventy-five percent recovered.

His dinner with Charlie last night had been wonderful. She left the Trading Post early and let Edith lock up. To his surprise, Charlie came by and pick him up around 6:30, so he wouldn't have to drive and irritate the bite wounds on his shoulder and leg.

As before, they talked nonstop from the moment he got in the Jeep, to the moment she brought him home at 11:30. Charlie apologized for Jonah's outburst at the Trading Post, and admitted she had playfully said those things to Edith. But she didn't think Jonah had heard. And besides, deep down she really meant them.

Of course he was flattered that she thought he had a cute butt, but he was also embarrassed. As they talked, he grilled the steaks, while she cut up the salad and tended to the baked potatoes. The evening had been easy, comfortable, and very pleasant.

Charlie was dressed a bit more conservatively than when she had changed his dressings yesterday morning. She wore jeans, but not skintight, and had on a loose-fitting blue and white plaid long-sleeved blouse. There was no cleavage showing this time. For some reason, Charlie's aggressive nature had eased. He much preferred the slower pace of their blossoming relationship.

His mind wandered back to the lake samples. Earlier, he'd poured out what remained of them. Proper scientific protocol required that whatever was left of the samples be kept until the final results came in. Since he'd gotten those from Charlie, and even had them in a special folder labeled "Broken Eye Lake," there was no point in keeping them.

He entered the faxed results from the lab in Anchorage, and his comments about the samples, into the notebook computer. The water was clean, which was no surprise to him or anyone else. In a way, he'd almost hoped something had been in the water. Then he'd have something he could put his finger on and say that was the culprit. Like DDT. The damage caused by that chemical, was clear. It caused the egg shells of eagles to soften, allowing them to crack open prematurely, killing the chicks. It clearly endangered the survival of the species.

But that didn't seem to be the case here, because the water was clean. There must be something else. But what? He could hardly wait to get back in the field. To solve this problem, he had to continue his investigation and research the predator/prey relationship of the wolves and the caribou. He wondered where would he look next.

The numbers of caribou in Unit 20A were decreasing every year for some reason. There was a strong enough supply of plant life from Denali National Park all the way to Broken Eye Lake, to support three times the current numbers of caribou in the area.

From everything he'd seen so far—wolf scat, trails and tracks, evidence of dens, and the remains of wolf-kills—there didn't seem to be a large enough population of wolves in the area, to account for the continuing decline of the caribou.

Maybe the animals were not reproducing normally, as Victor had suggested. But why not? There was nothing in the water to indicate such a thing. The plant life in the area did not appear to be deformed, or dying from some type of contamination. Besides, he had not seen any indications in the area, of stillbirths or miscarriages. There didn't seem to be enough evidence to support Victor's theory.

Could the trappers be poaching caribou in 20A, as well as the wolves, and was that why their numbers were declining? He then recalled what Victor had said about how strange it was for Billy Jack to be going to Anchorage the same week the fur buyers were there. It was odd, but he just didn't know. Again, there didn't seem to be enough evidence to support Victor's claims.

Grant took a sip of the rapidly cooling coffee. His eyes wandered toward the storage building. Like a nervous tick, his left cheek muscle and eyelid twitched, as brief terrifying images of his near-death experience, flashed through his mind. If he'd remained up on the cache platform, the cold plummeting temperatures would have quietly sapped the life from him. Based on the dreams he'd been having since the attack, he was positive the silver-blue streak he'd seen that evening, was the silver-blue wolf. He was convinced it dashed from the forest shadows, rammed the feral dog, and saved his life. He was also certain that the wolf had covered him with the woolen blanket from his bed in the cabin, saving him yet again. But even then, if Charlie hadn't come by when she did, he would have bled to death.

With a troubled look on his face, Grant tore his frightened eyes from the storage shed and glanced back toward Denning Fork. His coffee cup shook in his trembling hand. Like a vision from heaven, the silver-blue wolf stood regally on an outcropping of rocks on the other side of the stream. It was staring back at him.

The moment the animal realized Grant had seen it, it leaped down from the jagged rocks and began to pace along the water's edge. As the silver-blue wolf paced urgently, its piercing golden eyes glared at him as if it was agitated and upset about something. He set the coffee cup down beside him on the stoop, eased down the steps, and gently moved toward the wolf.

The place where he'd been attacked by the feral dog, was directly in his path to the stream. Halfway there, he noticed a dark area on the ground, the size of a large saucepan. It was a dried pool of his own blood. Another shiver crawled down his spine. He carefully, but deliberately, sidestepped the spot and continued toward Denning Fork, and the wolf.

The impatient animal was still pacing back and forth, head held high, ears alert. The scene reminded him of a Lassie movie that he had once seen as a child. Lassie paced back and forth, just like the silver-blue wolf was doing now, trying to send the little boy, Timmy, a message to follow her to the man who'd been injured after he'd fallen from his horse.

When Grant came to the edge of the stream, he stopped and watched the wolf gracefully prance in one direction, then swiftly spin and prance in the other. He reached down and gently squeezed the back of his injured thigh. The leg felt okay, just a little stiff with a slight residue of pain. It crossed his mind that he probably needed to exercise his leg anyway. Or was he just trying to find an excuse to follow the wolf?

The local doctor, the doctor at the Fairbanks hospital, Charlie, Victor, and Linsey, had all told him to take it easy for a week or so, to give his leg and shoulder a chance to start healing. Maybe it wouldn't be wise to go traipsing off into the woods.

But the animal is trying to tell me something, Grant thought to himself. The silver-blue wolf wants me to follow it somewhere, so something must be wrong. Since it saved my life, our spirits are now intertwined and connected forever. He stood there for a moment, unable to quell the thought running through his mind— the animal is in trouble and needs my help.

Charlie closed the large ledger checkbook and sighed loudly in disgust. She shoved it in the corner of the old wooden desk in her office and flopped back in the ancient wood swivel chair, exhausted. It had taken her over an hour to write out the monthly bills. She had been here since 6:00 and now it was 7:30. It was going to be a long day, and she was already worn out. Pushing away from the desk, she said, "I guess I'd better go help Edith with the breakfast crowd."

At that moment, the phone rang. Quickly answering it, she heard, "You owe me two beers now, Charlie."

She immediately recognized the husky voice on the other end of the line and said, "Henry Danner! I didn't think a man of your stature got out of bed before ten in the morning. What in the world are you calling for, at this hour?"

"Got some bad news, girl," Henry said seriously. "Or someone is playing a sick joke on you, which I don't appreciate. Especially, considering all the work I've done for you on these lake samples, as a favor. All the time I've spent analyzing them, is out of my own pocket, you know."

"What are you taking about?" Charlie asked, totally confused.

"Those water samples you sent me, are bottled water," Henry explained.

"What do you mean bottled water? There must be a mistake," Charlie said.

"Definitely not," Henry responded, firmly. "I looked at the results late last night. The same ones Kyle faxed you, yesterday. That's when I realized it was Alaska Sparkle water, which happens to be bottled right here in Anchorage. The reason I know that's what it is, is because they are my largest customer, and we analyze several of their water samples daily. The analytical data profile of what is in their bottled water, is exactly what showed up in the samples you sent me."

"Are you sure your chemist didn't get our samples mixed up with theirs, somehow?"

"Positive. I reran your samples myself, this morning. Directly from the containers you sent them in, I might add. In fact, that's why I'm here so early this morning."

"That's good enough for me, Henry," she said. "I don't know what's going on, but something is really fishy here, and I'm sure as heck going to get to the bottom of it. Oh, by the way, you're right. I do owe you two beers. The next time I'm in Anchorage I'll pay my debt. Thanks, Henry. I've got to go."

Charlie hung up the phone, grabbed her jacket from the back of the swivel chair, and ran out the door.

Fifteen minutes later, Charlie's right foot stomped down on the brake pedal of her Jeep Cherokee, preventing the vehicle from slamming into the cluster of spruce trees in front of Grant's cabin. Before she got out, she caught a glimpse of movement from the corner of her eye. Unbelievably, there was Grant at the back of the cabin, in full dress, including backpack, hiking boots, and rifle, preparing to cross the foot bridge over Denning Fork. What she hadn't noticed though, was the silver-blue wolf across the stream that had darted into the underbrush undetected when she drove up.

Charlie was furious. "What's wrong with men, anyway?" she asked, of no one in particular. "Is part of their brain missing? They obviously have a defective gene." She angrily jumped out, ran as fast as she could to the corner of the cabin, and yelled at the top of her lungs, "What in the hell do you think you're doing? Get your butt back up here in this cabin right this minute, mister."

Grant had heard a vehicle bouncing and bumping down the old logging trail, long before he saw Charlie's Cherokee barrel around the corner of the makeshift road. At first, as he watched her wildly maneuver the Jeep down the slope toward the cabin, he was sure she was going to crash through the stand of spruce trees and go right on through the front door. But just at the last moment, the brake lights popped on, and the Jeep slid to a dusty halt. Before the vehicle quit rocking back and forth from the violent stop, the door flew open and she emerged from the brownish cloud, yelling.

He reluctantly ambled up toward Charlie, like a scolded pup with its tail between its legs. Even when he was a little kid, he was never good at getting away with anything, with his parents or teachers. He knew he shouldn't be wandering off into the forest with the injured leg, but the silver-blue wolf needed his help. "I was just going for a little walk," he said.

"A little walk? In full dress, hiking boots, backpack, and rifle? Are you crazy? You're suppose to stay off that leg and keep the strain off your shoulder. Where were you going to walk to, the North Pole? Just what in the world are you thinking of, anyway?" Charlie was still furious.

"Well . . . actually, I was going to follow the silver-blue wolf," he said meekly, turning and pointing to the other side of Denning Fork. The wolf was gone.

"Right," she said with a suspicious look on her face. "You know you're not supposed to be out gallivanting all over the countryside with your injured leg."

"I know," he said sheepishly, deciding to not pursue the issue of the silver-blue wolf. "What are you doing here, anyway?"

"Come on in the cabin and take that garb off," Charlie said in a lighter tone. Gesturing with her hand, she added, "I'll tell you inside. You need to be sitting down, when you hear what I have to say."

Inside the cabin, Charlie helped Grant off with his backpack, while he laid a Savage .30/06 on the kitchen table. "Nice rifle," she said, then asked, "Where'd you get it?"

"Victor loaned me the rifle and a dart gun until I get a few bucks saved up to buy my own," he replied. "He said this is a bad time of year to be in the woods without a rifle. You know, in case I run across a protective grizzly with her cubs. I don't like to carry it, though. The thought of shooting any animal makes me ill. I'd rather use the dart gun and put them to sleep."

"It might make you ill, but it might save your life, too," Charlie said while walking over to the sofa and plopping down on it. "There's been more than one photographer, hiker, camper, hunter, you name it, that's been clawed to death in these parts, by an old mama bear. I don't think the dart gun would do you much good against an angry grizzly. Doesn't work fast enough."

"Yeah, I suppose you're right, but just the same, it doesn't make me feel any better," Grant said.

"Come over here and sit down," Charlie said, patting the sofa cushion next to her, "and let me tell you the bad news."

He couldn't imagine what she had to tell him that was so bad he had to take a seat. "I don't think I'm going to like this," he said as he sat down beside her and carefully looked into her eyes.

"Henry, my chemist friend in Anchorage, called me this morning," Charlie said with a woeful look on her face. "After looking at the results Kyle faxed me yesterday, he thought there was a problem with your samples and reran them this morning." Charlie sighed, looking away for a moment, then continued. "Someone poured out the lake water and replaced it with bottled water."

"What? That's ludicrous! Someone must've gotten the samples mixed up."

"That's what I thought, too," Charlie said. She then proceeded to tell him everything Henry Danner had told her, earlier on the phone.

"Alaska Sparkle water. That's the same bottled water Frank Kicklighter is always sipping on," Grant said.

"You're right, it is. I hadn't thought of that."

"Yeah, but it was Billy Jack that took the samples to Anchorage. He's the only one who could've switched the water. I sure as heck didn't do it," Grant said.

"I know you didn't switch the water," Charlie said, patting him on the leg. "How is your leg this morning?"

"It's fine and don't change the subject on me," he snapped. "This is important."

"I know it's important, but I just don't believe Billy Jack would do something like that," Charlie said.

"Well, somebody did."

Charlie's face winced.

"I'm sorry. I don't mean to take it out on you, but this is absolutely unbelievable." He reached over and caressed her hand with his for a moment, then pulled it back and continued. "Lets try to look at this logically and see if we can figure out why anyone would do such a thing. Can you think of any reason why Billy Jack or Frank would want to do something like this?"

There was a pause while Charlie thought for a few seconds and massaged her temples with her finger tips. Then she brought up the compelling issue of Frank's daughter's terrible illness, and his desperate need for money to pay for her operation. The fact that he had asked for the payment on the Trading Post several months in advance, was clear evidence of his dire situation. "But Frank is the sheriff and a pillar of our community. He was one of my father's best friends, and mine. He's one of the nicest men I have ever known," she said emotionally.

"I haven't been around here long enough to know anyone very well, certainly not long enough to make that kind of judgment. But when it comes to Frank, I'd have to agree with you," he said. "That leaves Billy Jack. Lets just look at the facts. He did take the samples to Anchorage. He did try to slit me open with his hunting knife. And he has threatened me more than once, to stay away from you. Maybe this is his way of getting back at me, because I didn't listen to him. Victor thinks he is involved in the wolf poaching around here, and may even be the ringleader. After all, he did go to Anchorage the same week the fur-buyer's consortium was there—"

"Okay, okay, you made your point," Charlie said, obviously upset. "I'll admit that Billy Jack is a bully and arrogant as hell. But to sneak around like an adolescent and play some foolish prank, is just not his style. He's like a bull in a china closet. He doesn't hold things back. He takes them head on, straightforward, and he's a large enough man to do just about whatever he wants.

"Yes, he took your samples to Anchorage, as a favor to me. And you should be thankful. And yes, he got a little over-rambunctious with you about me. But I spoke to him about that, and he promised to leave you alone. Billy Jack has never broken a promise to me, or anyone else, that I know of. He just watches out for me like a big brother, that's all. Lord knows, running a place like the Trading Post, with all the horny trappers and lumberjacks stomping in and out every day, a girl needs a little extra protection. Billy Jack has made sure no one gets out of line with me. That's all there is to it, and I'm thankful for his help.

"And as far as the wolf poaching is concerned, he loves wildlife as much as you do. He stopped guiding hunters several years ago, even though many people don't believe it, including Victor. All Billy Jack takes out now in his helicopter, are tourist and wildlife photographers, and photojournalists. He even has his own camera equipment and takes a ton of pictures himself. So where's that leave us. Nowhere."

"I have no reason to not believe you," Grant said. "After all, you know Frank and Billy Jack and everyone else around these parts, much better than I do." Grant wondered in the back of his mind, just what Charlie had said to Billy Jack about him. Whatever it was, it explained why Billy Jack had made a 180 degree turn and was so friendly yesterday afternoon.

"I'll even admit that the suspicions Victor has about Billy Jack and the wolf poaching, I find hard to believe myself," Grant said. "But the fact remains, someone, for whatever reason, has switched the lake water with bottled water. It may have been a prank, or . . . there may be a more sinister reason why someone doesn't want me to know what's really in the water at Broken Eye Lake. So the real question is not so much, who, but why."

Grant and Charlie heard someone pull up outside and slam a truck door hard. Moments later Victor stormed through the front door of the cabin, his face red with anger.

"Edith just told me about the lake water results," he barked. "What the hell is going on around here, anyway?"

Grant had never seen Victor in such a worked up state. After a few minutes of calming him down and persuading him to take a seat, Grant and Charlie began to explain to Victor what they had been discussing.

When they finished, Victor leaped up from the kitchen chair as if stabbed in the rump with a needle and began to pace in front of the fireplace. His face was flushed again. "That may be all well and good, but I saw Billy Jack take a bottle of Frank's water this morning," he said flatly. "He said the vending machine wasn't working, and he needed something to drink on the way to Anchorage. A likely story, I'm sure."

"He did?" Charlie said with a slight inflection of doubt in her voice this time. "You saw him take the water?"

"With my own two eyes," Victor said, pointing to them. "I've been watching this character for quite some time, and I don't care what you think, Charlie, I believe Billy Jack is right in the thick of this wolf poaching business. And for some reason, it has been worse in the past week or so, than ever before. Something is up. Something big is going down."

Charlie was silent, her eyes blank, face drawn with disbelief. Grant wondered what was going through her mind. He glanced over at Victor, who'd begun pacing back and forth again, twisting one of his braids around his finger.

"Well, there's only one thing we can do now," Grant said. "Get more samples."

"What about the samples we already have?" Victor asked.

Reluctantly he answered the question. "Once I had the results, I didn't see any need to keep them any longer. I poured them out first thing this morning. So I have to go get more. That's all there is to it."

"I don't think so, buckaroo," Charlie said sternly. "Not with your leg and shoulder. Victor can go collect them."

Ignoring Charlie, he stood up and moved in front of Victor, to stop the man's annoying pacing. Facing him, he asked, "Do you have the electrical problem fixed on Flutter Butt yet?"

"No, the part won't be in until this afternoon," Victor answered.

"How long do you think it will take you to fix it, once you get the part?"

"About an hour, maybe two."

Okay. That'll work out just about right," Grant said. Then he revealed his plan. "Go fuel up the chopper and call Dr. Barlow, my professor in Fairbanks. I'll write the number down for you. Tell him everything, and that we'll be at the university sometime late this afternoon, with water samples to be run on the ICP-MS."

"That's my boy," Victor hollered, displaying a thumbs up.

Charlie hopped up from the sofa, furious, and said, "Wait just a minute here. The doctor said—"

Grant turned to her and interrupted. "I don't care what the doctor said or anyone else. I'm going to get more water samples. Pardon me for being abrupt, Charlie, but Victor is right. Somehow, the wolf poaching is connected to the reason someone don't want us to know what's in that lake water. Something very smelly is going on here."

Unconsciously, Grant began to pace too, staring down at the floor. "From Linsey Hogan dumping paperwork on us, to why in the hell, excuse my language, we can't get these samples analyzed for heavy metals, the whole thing stinks worse than vulture vomit. First the samples were poured out at the AWMC lab, supposedly by mistake, something I'm now beginning to doubt. And then the chemist up there found the file where the lake water had been run before, but all the records were mysteriously missing. Now the samples have been switched with bottled water. One thing Johnny Boy Jackson, my professor back at Minnesota, taught me, is that coincidence is not a coincidence. I don't know who's behind this, but I'm going to get to the bottom of this if it kills me."

"I understand all that. But what about your leg and—"

"Forget my leg and shoulder. There's a little discomfort and a few aches and pains. It's no big deal," Grant said. "I'm going after those samples, and that's all there is to it."

"Not without me, you're not," Charlie said firmly."

"She right, Grant," Victor said. "It's not a bad idea to have Charlie go along, with your leg and all. She's pretty tough when it comes right down to it. Besides, by the time you head back it will be late in the day, and it won't hurt to have an extra pair of eyes to keep a lookout for grizzlies. They like to roam around a lot at that time of day."

"Okay, you've ganged up on me," he said, realizing that he was also pacing. He immediately stopped in his tracks. "And you're probably right, too."

Charlie's face broke out in a huge grin. "Thanks." She leaned over and kissed him on the cheek. Their eyes met for just a second. It was wonderful. "Give me fifteen minutes to go home and change into my hiking duds." With that she bounced across the room and charged out the front door.

"That gal is sweet on, Bub," Victor said after Charlie had left. "Now write down that professor's number so I can go take care of business."

Grant walked over to the kitchen table, pulled a notepad from his backpack, and wrote down Dr. Barlow's number at the university. When he handed it to Victor, he said, "I'll tell you something else, partner. I'm sweet on her, too."

Chapter 13

It was 9:30 when Victor wheeled into his normal parking place at Two Fork's small airport. To his surprise, Linsey Hogan was standing outside the hangar, smoking a cigarette as usual. Off to the right of the hangar, in the field next to Flutter Butt, was her private AWMC helicopter. A fuel truck was parked alongside, topping off the chopper's tanks. Her pilot and the fuel truck assistant were standing close by the aircraft, talking.

The moment Linsey saw his Suburban pull up, she began to walk quickly toward him, as if she had something important to tell him. The expensive leather coat with the wolf fur collar that she always wore, was cinched tightly around her waist. A narrow stream of gray smoke trailed from her large mouth, as she struggled to walk on the white gravel walkway in high heels.

Victor turned off the engine, jerked the keys out of the ignition, and casually stepped out. Under his breath he said, "I wonder what that witch wants."

He strolled around the front of the Suburban and fortuitously walked toward Linsey. She had stopped. A cigarette dangled from the corner of her mouth, and she was anxiously waving at him to hurry over to her. Victor grinned to himself and continued at his slow pace. He knew it was childish and immature, but one of his greatest pleasures in life, was disobeying and infuriating this woman.

About halfway to Linsey, Frank Kicklighter came walking out of the hangar, with a white Styrofoam cup in each hand. He hadn't seen the sheriff's car when he came driving up. By the time Victor reached Linsey, Frank was already there and had given her the cup. She left deep red lipstick stains on the rim of the cup, as she sipped the coffee.

Linsey stared at him with arctic eyes and snapped, "Didn't you see me waving at you?" She took another sip of coffee, then sucked deeply on her cigarette again. "Of course you did. All you Indians have the sight of an eagle." Smoke spit from her mouth as she talked. "Its just that all Indians have lead in their ass and can't move any faster than a crippled snail." Linsey tossed the cigarette butt to the ground.

Victor maintained his cool and didn't respond Linsey's caustic remarks. He just looked at her with a playful grin on his lips. Victor had succeeded in raising her hackles. Now he was content.

He directed his attention to Frank. "Morning, Frank. I didn't see your vehicle when I drove up."

"It's in the hangar," Frank replied. "Darn thing has a thumping sound in the engine. One of the mechanics is having a look at it—"

"I hate to break up your manly conversation about nuts and bolts," Linsey butted in, "but I'm busy." She then turned to Victor and asked, "Where's Grant?"

"At the cabin doing the paperwork you sent back with us. Just like the good employee he is," Victor lied.

"Then how's the feral dog hunt going?"

"Not very good, I'm afraid. All the trappers are in Anchorage this week."

"Really," she said sarcastically. She handed Frank her cup, lit another cigarette, then took the cup back. "So no one's out hunting these wild dogs?"

"The town drunk, Whitie Saylor, is the only one, so far, that I know of," Victor said, knowing there was more to Linsey's visit than wanting to know what was happening with the feral dogs. "Just why are you down here, Director Hogan?"

"O-o-o-u, I like the sound of that. 'Director Hogan'." Linsey's tone got serious again. "You've finally realized I'm your boss. That's progress. There may be hope for you after all." She took a long drag on the cigarette and glared at him as she exhaled smoke through her nose. "I heard about Grant's lake water samples being switched with bottled water, and thought I'd better come down here to be sure you two don't do something stupid."

"How did you find that out so quickly?" he asked, shocked that she was even aware of the samples being re-analyzed. "Charlie just found out about the samples herself this morning."

"I have my sources, Victor," Linsey said coolly. "There's not much that goes on in my territory that I don't know about. Don't forget that, either, mister. I even know that it was Billy Jack Boone who took the samples to the lab in Anchorage."

"Billy Jack. Huh," Frank mumbled, thoughtfully. "Yesterday morning, early, I gave him a couple of my bottled waters to drink on the trip down to Anchorage."

"Well, there you go," Linsey said. "But I'm not here about who did the switching. I could care less about that. I'm here to tell you and Grant to stop this foolishness about getting more lake water analyzed. For Christ sakes, Alaska has the cleanest water in the country, compared to the lower forty-eight. This state has very few industries that would pollute the water or air with hazardous substances. Especially in my area."

Frank was standing beside Linsey, looking at her intently, nodding his head affirmatively as she babbled on. Occasionally, he would unscrew the cap from his bottle of water and take a sip, then continue to bob his head up and down as he listened.

Linsey continued to ramble on. "So there's no reason to analyze the water. It's a waste of time and taxpayer's money. With shrinking budgets, there just aren't enough dollars to go around for this kind of birdbrained idea, especially when we know there's nothing in the water to begin with."

"I think she's right, Victor," Frank said, shifting his eyes toward to him. "We all know there's nothing in the water at Broken Eye Lake that's going to harm the wildlife."

What was Frank doing, Victor wondered. This was none of his business.

"So, when you see Grant again, remind him that his job, and yours too, is to substantiate that the wolf is the reason the caribou population is declining," Linsey commanded. "Not to irresponsibly spend taxpayer's dollars on silly scientific schemes. Do you understand what I have said, or do I need to repeat it?"

"It's pretty clear what you've said. Even for a brainless Indian like myself. I believe I understand," he said without emotion, staring resentfully into Linsey's steely eyes.

"Excellent. To give both of you the incentive to follow my orders and not stray out of line again, let me leave you with this to mull over, Victor. If I find that either, or both, of you, have disobeyed my orders, you will be terminated immediately." An evil grin crawled across her face, and she pointed her finger at him. "I will see to it that you, Victor, will never work at anything in this state again. And I will enjoy every moment of ruining your life." She pulled her finger out of his face. The fiendish grin stayed though.

"And tell our new man, Grant, that if he disobeys my orders, I'll be very disappointed in him. I truly have high hopes for that boy. However, his higher learning opportunities in this state will be over with, and I will equally enjoy ruining his chances of ever getting into another graduate program anywhere in the country." Linsey tossed her cigarette butt to the ground. "It's always a pleasure talking with you, Victor. Have a nice day."

She motioned to Frank with her left hand. "Come with me, Sheriff. I have a few things to speak to you about, too." Like an obedient dog responding to its master's commands, Frank jumped to attention.

Anger pulsed through Victor's veins like a raging river. His face remained like granite, as he watched the two of them walk off. He wondered what he should do. Actually, he knew exactly what he was going to do, no matter what *Director Hogan* said. But he wasn't so sure what path Grant would take.

Grant was more than happy that Charlie volunteered to come along and collect lake samples with him. They were nearly halfway back to the cabin, at least timewise. But they still had quite a way to go in distance. Though the difficult terrain was behind them, the rest of the way was still no cake walk. His leg was holding up fairly well, but the agonizing pain in his shoulder and arm, ached something fierce. The weight of the backpack had finally become too much strain on his injured shoulder, and he now dragged it on the ground beside him.

Charlie had taken the lead on the way back. She stopped for a moment at the top of the ridge, to let him catch up. Turning, she hollered, "How you holding up?"

"I'll be fine," he panted. His feet kept slipping on the loose rocks as he struggled to get up the steep slope. "Thanks for asking, though."

Charlie had insisted they tie a safety line between them, just in case one of them slipped. She was now taking up the slack on the forty foot length of rope.

"You want to rest for a few minutes?" she asked. She had already sat down on a flat rock and slid off her backpack.

"No, it's almost six, and I want to get to Fairbanks this evening." The moment he said that, he wished he hadn't. Struggling up the slope, he knew he could really use a few minutes rest.

He had brought along his field notepad, and because of the meticulous notes he had taken, they were able to collect the water from the exact locations he and Victor had sampled before. Victor was right, he thought. Charlie was a tough gal. She had carried the empty sample bottles in her backpack on the hike to

Broken Eye Lake. She was carrying those same bottles in her backpack again, only now they were full of water. They had to weigh at least twenty-five pounds, maybe more. Charlie never complained, though.

By the time he reached the top of the ridge, his body ached all over. The pain pulsing from his injuries, was almost unbearable. He gasped deeply for air. "How about you?" he asked Charlie. "You want to take a break for a few minutes? I think we have enough time to take a few minutes," he said, wiping the sweat from his brow with his coat sleeve.

"Yeah, I think we both could use a break," Charlie agreed. "How about fifteen minutes."

"Okay," he said, and plunked down beside her. "How about taking this safety line off now? I don't like this thing tied to me. Makes me feel like a dog on a leash."

"Definitely not. Not until we get back to the cabin," she said firmly.

"Yes, mother," he replied, snidely.

Charlie glanced at him with a cross look, then her face went pale. "Oh no, you're bleeding," she cried.

Blood from his leg wound had saturated the bandage and seeped through his jeans. "It'll be all right," he said confidently "We'll change it when we get back to the cabin, before we go on to Fairbanks."

"That's not what I'm worried about," Charlie said gravely, rotating her head as she scanned the area, searching for movement. "If there are any grizzlies close by and they get a whiff of fresh blood, your blood, they'll literally come running." She stood up, anxiously looking around, and tugged at his coat,. "I wished you'd brought your rifle. Come on, we'd better go. We can rest when we get home."

She helped him up from the rock, and they hurried off in the direction of the cabin. Ten minutes later, they came upon the dead feral dog he and Victor had seen the other day. Its decaying appearance hadn't changed much in six days.

"God, that stinks," Charlie groaned, holding her nose as she walked by the rotting animal.

"Good. Maybe it will mask the scent of my blood," Grant said jokingly.

"Not hardly," she muttered. "A bear can smell fresh blood for miles. Lets get away from this wretched thing."

They moved on, but this time, he took the lead. "All right, but first let me show you this spectacular view at the end of the ridge."

"We can see it some other time. I think we should keep moving," she urged.

"It'll only take a second," he pleaded, playfully tugging on the safety line as he headed out toward the narrow spur at the end of the ridge.

"Okay, but only a second, and no more."

By the time Grant reached the lone spruce tree that angled off into the air at the very point of the ridge, Charlie had reeled out all of the safety line, and it was taut between them.

"Are you sure this is safe out here?" she asked, nervously, slowly sidestepping her way along the center of the ten-foot wide spur. She stretched and craned her neck, apprehensively glancing to each side, as she made her way out to Grant.

"Yeah, it's solid rock underneath us," he said as he looked down at the tiny thread of Denning Fork, winding its way below them toward Broken Eye Lake. "Come on, this is beautiful."

A few moments later, Charlie was standing beside him, clutching his left arm with both hands and hanging on for dear life. She strained to peek out over the edge, then quickly jerked back and said, "Yeah, that's beautiful all right. Now lets go."

"Okay, we'll go. I just wanted you to see—"

From behind them came a horrific, deafening roar, that vibrated the rock they stood on. Charlie shrieked, released her death grip on Grant's arm, and spun around. Her eyes were wide and her face was twisted in fear. At the same instant, Grant swung to his left, instinctively taking a crouched position to defend himself.

In front of them, no more than ten feet away and towering eight feet high, was the largest omnivore land mammal in the world . . . a grizzly. Huge glistening drops of saliva hung from the creature's large teeth, as it violently shook its massive head in anger at them, snarling and growling viciously. The beast bent over slightly and lashed out with his mammoth left paw, stabbing at Grant's head.

The four knifelike claws, which were each about six inches long and protruded from the bear's paw, sliced through the air, whistling inches from his face. He ducked and dodged to one side, the heel of his left hiking boot slipping dangerously close to the edge of the ridge. A few loose smaller rocks dislodged and fell away, plummeting to the gorge far below. Close behind was his backpack, which slipped from his shaking hand and tumbled over the edge.

Charlie screamed and lurched backwards, bringing her close to the edge as well. "What are we going to do?" she yelled at Grant, in panic. "There's no place to go. The spur is too narrow to get around him. If we stay here, this monster is going to kill us for sure."

Grant didn't answer. He was too busy watching twelve hundred pounds of grizzly inch toward them. The bear's large hungry eyes were intently focused on him. He glanced over his shoulder. Nothing but air, and it was a hell of a long way down. He quickly brought his stare back to the advancing grizzly.

Tears streamed down Charlie's terrorized face. She was hunched over and shaking. The grizzly had dropped to all fours and was now springing directly toward Grant, displaying unbelievable ease of movement for such a tremendous hulk. At the same time, a bloodcurdling scream pierced Grant's ears. He jerked his attention toward Charlie, just in time to see her topple over the edge of the ridge, her arms flailing.

Before Grant had time to think, sharp pain bolted down both his legs. The pointed tips of the bear's razor-sharp claws, had slashed across his knee caps, slicing through his jeans and into his flesh. Blood spurted through the shredded material. The monstrous body of the bear slammed to the ground with a loud thud. Fortunately, the creature's grip was just shy of being able to grab him and haul him over to be devoured.

Unfortunately, the force of the bear's attack was enough to push him over the edge, into empty space. He plunged toward the jagged rocks several hundred feet below, and certain death. The last thing Grant saw as he fell backwards, was the grizzly's cavernous mouth as it leaped from the ground and charged toward him.

It seemed like an eternity, floating through space, even though he was descending at a very rapid rate. It was so fast, the face of the rock cliff was a dark gray blur. He was going to die.

Strangely, a peacefulness came over him. A warmth oozed through his body and into his flailing limbs, calming him. Images of Grant's life, moved in slow motion in front of his eyes. The closeness and strong bond he'd with his parents, comforted him. He thought of them and how much he loved them.

"Be sure and find a good church when you get there, hon," his mother had said to him, at the airport. Huge crocodile tears were in the corners of her eyes, spilling onto her deeply lined cheeks. "We love you. Be sure to write," she said with a broken voice. She waved as he walked down the tunnel, to the airplane that would bring him to Alaska, and the greatest adventure of his life.

His father was by her side, arm around her waist, squeezing her tight. The glistening tears in his father's eyes, were evidence of the man's heavy heart as his beloved son left home once again. That was his last memory of his parents. He would never see them again in this life.

Grant's racing heart quieted to a gentle pace. His heaving lungs slowed to normal breathing. His lengthy hair wrapped around his head and fluttered in his face, dimming his view of the pale blue sky above him. The raging wind roared in his ears, as he fell closer to his death. He closed his eyes and began to recite the Lord's prayer. "Our Father, who art in heaven, hallowe—."

As if he'd been snatched from the sky by the giant claws of a prehistoric flying dinosaur, his rapid plunge to the perilous boulders below, suddenly jerked to a halt. Air exploded from Grant's lungs, as the safety line snapped taut, cracking like a whip and cinching around his mid-section. Grant's eyes immediately popped open. He gasped for air, not yet realizing what had happened.

A second later, on his right, Charlie's limp body swished by him in a blur, as if she were swinging on the end of a pendulum. She was slightly higher than he was and appeared to be unconscious . . . or dead.

Two more seconds passed. Charlie swung back from the other direction. Her arc was not quite as high this time, and the speed of her swinging motion had begun to diminish and lose momentum.

Five seconds had gone by since his reprieve from death. He had caught his breath, and the cobwebs in his head were beginning to clear. He realized Charlie had saved their lives, even though she didn't know it.

When they had been forced over the ridge by the monstrous grizzly, the safety line Charlie had insisted on, had gotten caught on the lone spruce that angled out from the end of the ridge. It was a small tree, with a circumference roughly the same size as Grant's thigh. The rope was straddling it and holding them over several hundred feet of empty air, far above Denning Fork and the deep rocky gorge below. Grant was on one end of the rope, while Charlie swung from side to side on the other end.

He noticed she was heading back toward him. His mental faculties were nearly under control, and a plan was forming that might save their lives. The adrenaline began to pulse through his veins again, and he reached out to grab her as she drew closer.

She was spinning slowly on the tether, limbs splayed out and angled down. Her head was back, and her neck was stretched tight from the weight of her head. Just as Grant's outstretched fingers began to close around Charlie's wrist and he was sure he had her within his grasp, the rope gave way.

He dropped six inches, while she jerked upward an equal distance. He missed her, and she swung on by. Then he dropped another three inches. She moved up three. It suddenly dawned on him, what was happening here. He outweighed Charlie by thirty-five to forty pounds and was acting as a counterweight. She was now a good two feet higher than he was, and maybe out of reach. If he didn't grab hold of her, they were doomed for sure.

Charlie swung back to his right this time, which was his weak and injured side. Thank God the rope was holding, he thought, and he hadn't slipped any farther.

Grant waited until the last moment to make his move. Then with his left hand tightly clenching the safety line, he pulled and strained to lift himself, so he could meet Charlie's oncoming body. He stretched out with his right hand as far as he could, praying his fingers would touch something other than air. Pain exploded in his injured shoulder, shooting up his neck and fanning out over the back of his head. His face twisted

"Oh God, please," he screamed.

Charlie's dangling left boot and then her left hand, swept by his extended fingers. Both were out of reach. That was it. He was too far below her. There was nothing he could do now. His strength was depleted, and the pain in his shoulder was too great.

Grant's grip gave way on the rope, and he began to slip back down the safety line. With his hopes nearly extinguished, he felt Charlie's dangling auburn hair dance across the tips of his outstretched fingers. He immediately clenched his hand into a fist, reached, and had her in his grip.

Moments later, he had pulled himself up to Charlie's level. By then, he was greatly relieved to see that her eyes had fluttered open, and she had begun to come around. But she was still very groggy.

"What's going on?" she asked, looking over at him with glazed eyes and reaching up to rub the top of her head. "Why does the top of my head feel like someone tried to pull my hair out by the roots? Where's the bear?"

For the past two or three minutes, the grizzly had been the furthest thing from his mind. "It's going to be all right," he said to her, holding on to her free hand as the two of them dangled in the air. "Just take some deep breaths—"

Before he finished the sentence, they began to spring up and down, as if they were attached to the end of a long bungee cord. Grant's eyes reluctantly lifted upward, to see just what was going on.

"Oh no. Is there no end to this?" he asked, more to himself than to Charlie. Twenty feet above them, the grizzly was leaning out on the spruce that held their safety line. The monstrous animal grasped the tree with its front paws and was shaking it up and down, violently. The small tree began to give way under the tremendous weight of the bear. Dirt, dust, and small rocks fell from the cliff and onto their faces.

Charlie tilted her head up and screamed when she saw the bear on the small spruce. It was dangerously close to breaking. Her eyelids fluttered, then closed. Her scream stopped. She had passed out again.

The crack of a rifle shot rang out above them. The grizzly quickly jerked back from the tree and disappeared from sight. Two more shots blasted away in quick succession. A few seconds later, a loud roaring growl rumbled down over the ledge, followed by a series of wild yelps and screams.

"What in the world is going on up there?" Grant asked himself, in a low tone.

The roaring stopped abruptly, but the yelping and screaming continued for another minute and a half. Then there was a long silence. Grant's eyes were glued to the rock ledge above them.

Finally, Whitie Saylor's scruffy old bearded face, popped over the edge. "How you two young pups doin' out here in the wilderness?" he asked, with a large smile plastered across his face. "Need a little help?"

Chapter 14

Whitie Saylor had set the grizzly packing, then helped Charlie and Grant back up to the top of the ridge. Grant had never been so happy to see anyone in his whole life. By then, Charlie had regained consciousness and swore never to go hiking in the woods again, without a rifle. In fairly short order, they regrouped, anxious to leave the area before the bear recovered his courage and came back for dinner.

Whitie had been out hunting the feral dog pack, hoping to collect the bounty. But so far, he hadn't seen hide nor hair of a single wild dog. By the time the three of them left the ridge and headed back toward the cabin, it was late in the day. Whitie decided to tag along with them. Even though they moved over the rough terrain as fast as they could, with Grant's gimpy leg and slashed knees, it still took them better than two hours. By the time they reached the cabin, the pain in his shoulder and leg was excruciating. He could barely walk, and he finally draped his left arm over Charlie's shoulder, for support.

Once they arrived, and Charlie helped him into the cabin, Charlie hopped in her Jeep and rushed back to her place to change clothes. Grant did the same, with the old codger's help. Then

Whitie drove Grant to see Doc Phillips, picking Charlie up on their way.

The gray-haired barrel-chested family practitioner first cleaned and bandaged the deep gashes in Grant's knee caps, then changed the bandages on his leg and shoulder injuries. Fortunately, none of the new wounds required stitches, and they were on their way in twenty minutes.

Doc Phillips was a kind and gentle man, but he scolded Grant severely for gallivanting in the woods before his leg and shoulder had properly healed. The old-fashioned doctor read the agonizing pain in Grant's face and insisted that he take medication to relief his suffering. Grant flatly refused, partly because Charlie was there, and he didn't want to look like a wimp. However, he mostly refused the painkillers because he needed to be sharp and alert when evaluating the analyses of the lake samples.

They stopped at the Trading Post long enough for Charlie to take Whitie inside and tell Edith to cook the old man the largest steak she had in the refrigerator, and anything else he wanted to eat—all on the house. She quickly explained where they were going and that it would be late that evening before they got back from Fairbanks. Without complaint or question, Edith said she would be glad to lock up and said she'd open first thing in the morning. Charlie accepted the offer and thanked her longtime friend.

At 7:25 that evening, Grant slid the Suburban into a parking place next to Victor's vehicle, at the Two Forks airport. Victor was pacing back and forth alongside Flutter Butt. His arms were crossed, and he wore a frustrated expression. When he saw them pull up, he ran toward them. His face changed to one of relief.

"Where in holy hell have you two been?" Victor asked, as he stormed up to the Suburban. "I was just about ready to crank up old Flutter Butt and come looking for you."

Grant had already gotten out of the vehicle and was limping toward his partner. Charlie was by his side, carrying the backpack that contained the lake samples. "It's a long story," Grant said. "I'll tell you on the way to Fairbanks."

Inside the chopper, seated next to Victor, Grant proceeded to tell his partner the amazing story of how Whitie Saylor had saved their lives from the gigantic grizzly. "I never saw a prettier sight in all my life, than Whitie's burly old face peering over the edge of that rock ledge," Grant said.

"That's amazing," Victor said, speaking into the tiny microphone of the headset in his helmet. "Just how did he scare that old grizzly off, anyhow?"

"All I know is, I heard three rifle shots and a whole lot of whooping and hollering up on the ridge." Grant went silent for a moment, staring down at the wilderness below. The helicopter's whirling blades had a hypnotic pulse to them, and he sat there thinking about how close he and Charlie had come to plunging to their deaths. Finally, and with a weaker voice, he answered Victor. "Whitie said he grinned the bear down like Davy Crockett."

Victor chuckled to himself, then glanced over at Grant and said, "There could be more truth to what he said than you realize. With all the liquor that old geezer drinks, his breath alone was probably enough to run the grizzly off."

Charlie was strapped in a fold down seat in the cargo hold, next to the cockpit. Like Victor and Grant, she had on a helmet with a headset and was listening to everything they were saying. She leaned toward the cockpit and said, "And Miss Macho Broad here, fainted and was out colder than an arctic gale, during the whole blame thing."

All three burst out laughing, then Grant glanced over his shoulder at Charlie. Her blue eyes sparkled in the waning sunlight. "That may be, but if you hadn't insisted on the safety line, neither one of us would be laughing about it now."

"He's absolutely right," Victor chimed in. "At least one of you was using your noggin." He glared over at Grant. "And you, my young friend, are an idiot for going into the woods without a rifle, especially at that time of day and this time of year. That's like a death wish in this part of the country."

"I know. Charlie hasn't let me forget it, either. I've learned my lesson. I promise," he said meekly. "I'll take firearm protection with me the next time I go into the forest." He said it, but it left a bitter taste in his mouth. The thought of shooting an animal was just against his nature.

Victor cleared his throat, squirmed in his seat, then nervously said, "Before we get to Fairbanks, I need to tell you something. Something I probably should have mentioned before we left Two Forks." Victor's voice sounded serious.

Grant looked over at the tall man next to him. The late afternoon sun was casting a dim shadow over Victor's strong-featured face, and Grant wondered what was wrong now.

"When I got back to the airport this morning, Director Hogan was there," Victor said reluctantly.

"What did she want?" Grant asked.

Victor told Grant and Charlie the threat Linsey had made, should he and Grant continued to pursue getting the lake samples analyzed. "If you want to go back, I'll understand," Victor said.

"That bitch," Charlie said, shaking her head in disgust. "Sorry for the language, guys. It's just that I never have liked that woman much, and now, I like her even less."

"Go back? Are you kidding? That makes me want to get these samples analyzed more than ever," Grant said in a rebellious tone. "You've been right all along, Victor. For Linsey to fly all the way down and threaten us with our jobs, tells me she is involved in this whole stinking mess. Whatever this mess is, I'm not sure yet. But it's more than the wolf poaching, and it's big."

"I agree," Charlie added.

"That's the spirit," Victor yelled with excitement.

"I think from this point on, we should be very careful about who we talk to, regarding these lake samples," Grant said seriously. "Someone in Two Forks has to be informing Linsey about us, for her to know our every move."

Thirty minutes later, they pulled into the university faculty parking lot, in Dale Barlow's minivan. Grant had called his professor before leaving Two Forks to say they were on their way, and asked if he would pick them up at the Fairbanks airport. On the ride from the airport, he explained their dilemma, and the urgency of getting the samples analyzed. After listening to him, Dale used his portable phone to call a colleague of his in the chemistry department. Dale asked him to meet them at the university.

Waiting for them in the lobby of UA's science building, was a short balding man with horn-rimmed glasses. What hair he had left, was pulled together into a stubby ponytail that stuck straight out from the back of his head. Standing next to the short man, also wearing horn-rimmed glasses, and a forced smile, was an extremely skinny woman with an enormous abundance of curly hair that encased her thin gaunt face. He guessed both to be in their early to mid-forties.

"Grant, this is Dr. John Evans," Dale said. "He's the head of our spectroscopy lab. When I called him to see if one of his grad students could run your samples this evening, I passed along the story you told me. He immediately took interest in your little mystery and volunteered to run the samples himself." Dale then motioned toward the woman. "And this is Dr. Maggie Foust, head of the microbiology department, and a close friend of John's."

Dr. Evans leaned forward, smiled kindly, and extended his hand. Grant shook it and said, "Pleased to meet you, sir." He was amazed at the power in Dr. Evans grip.

"Likewise, young man," Dr. Evans said. "I'm always interested when I suspect environmental skullduggery. I'll bet a pitcher of beer, we're going to find some nasties in that water."

"Yes, sir," he responded, to the strange character. Then he reached over and shook the Dr. Foust's hand. "Pleased to meet you, too, ma'am."

In a gravelly voice, Dr. Foust said, "Call us by our first names, son. Just plain old John and Maggie. You're probably wondering why I'm tagging along. It's certainly not because I've got goo-goo eyes for this old coot, I'll tell you that. I just happened to be at John's house when Dale called. When I heard these lake samples had elevated BOD values, I just had to take a look at this water and see what kind of microbial critters were causing all that activity."

"I appreciate that. We'll take all the help we can get," Grant said to Maggie. Then to both, he said, "It's awfully kind of you both, to come on such short notice." Each nodded their heads cordially. He then introduced Victor and Charlie to the two professors.

Charlie was beside Dr. Evans, as they entered his lab. "My God!" Charlie said with astonishment. "This place is amazing."

Victor, who was right behind her, simply said, "Wow!"

"Thank you," Dr. Evans said. "But I'll let you in on a secret. We scientists keep it that way for job security." Chuckling, he sat down at an instrument and started pushing buttons and flipping switches, to turn it on. Within seconds the large machine lit up like a Christmas tree. Red, green, blue, yellow, and white lights blinked all over it.

"I know this thing measures the concentration of metals in water. But what does ICP-MS stand for?" Charlie asked Grant.

Before he could answer, Dr. Evans piped in, "Ah, a questioning young mind—the elixir, the lifeblood, of higher education. It's what we professors live for. ICP stands for inductive coupled plasma. MS stands for mass spectrometry, the most powerful analytical tool known to mankind. And this little sweetie can be whimsical at times."

Dr. Evans reached out and lovingly stroked the large instrument, as if it was his favorite canine. "But she is pure beauty, and the demonstration of man's achieved brilliance." The strange little man swayed back and forth in his chair in front of the impressive instrument. His slender fingers floated over the computer keyboard, as if they were masterfully playing a Bach classical.

Dale leaned toward Grant and whispered, "John's just a little eccentric."

From the other side, Maggie leaned toward him and whispered, "And besides that, the old fool is missing a few marbles."

Grant didn't reply because he didn't know what to say. He just nodded his head.

"Bring on the samples, laddie. This magnificent piece of equipment is ready to do her stuff," Dr. Evans said merrily.

Grant obeyed, quickly retrieving Charlie's backpack, which contained the lake water samples. He lined them up in numerical sequence, on a small sample prep table next to the instrument.

Maggie stepped forward with a small polyethylene vial and said, "I've seen this thing operate a zillion times before. Sometimes I think he cares more for this bucket of electrical wires and screws, than he does for me. I'm going to take some of your sample and look at it under the microscope in my lab." She poured a small amount of the first sample into the vial and left.

They all watched anxiously, as Dr. Evans introduced sample number one into the ICP-MS. A yellow graph on a blue background appeared on the computer monitor. Within seconds, thin red horizontal lines began to appear on the left side of graph.

"What are those red lines?" Charlie asked.

"That's what's in the water," Grant answered. "The y axis of the graph, is the intensity of the signal, or how much of the metal is in the sample. The x axis, is the molecular weight of each element, or metal. As you move from left to right on the graph, the molecular weight increases."

Grant pointed to the large chart on the wall of the lab. "That's the Periodic Chart of the Elements. It lists important information about all the elements. The Na, in the left-hand column, is the symbol for sodium. The number beneath it, 22.98977, is its molecular weight. Each element has a unique molecular weight. Now on the monitor, the first red line halfway up the graph, at 23, depicts the amount of sodium in the sample."

"Okay. That makes sense," Charlie said with interest.

"Now if you want to know about the hardness of the water, you check for calcium and magnesium. Their symbols are on the chart near sodium," Grant ,said pointing to the Ca and Mg symbols. "And do you see how the molecular weights of the elements increase as you go down and across the chart?"

Charlie and Victor nodded.

"Now, look at the red lines on the monitor. Next to the first red line, sodium, is magnesium, at 24, then calcium, at 40. See how they're displayed, as the molecular weight increases—"

"Bingo, bull's-eye, and there she blows at 52! Chromium's off the scale!" Dr. Evans yelled, as he leaped out of his chair, waving his arms over his head like a madman. "What'd I tell you? What'd I tell you?! You owe me a pitcher of beer, laddie!" The little man was prancing around in circles.

Charlie looked at Grant. "What's he talking about?"

At that moment, Maggie hurried through the door of the spectroscopy lab. She had a microscope slide in her hand. "I'll tell you what he's talking about, my pretty," she said. "Chromium is the nasty, Jonathan is talking about. A real bad actor, environmentally speaking. It's toxic as hell, and at levels higher than the EPA limit of 0.500 parts-per-million, it's a carcinogen and most likely a mutagen."

"What's a mutagen?" Charlie asked.

"Good question, my dear," Maggie replied. "A mutagen is an agent, such as ultraviolet light or a radioactive element, that induces or increases the frequency of mutation in an organism. An organism can be anything from a microscopic germ, to a human being. So the caribou would definitely be affected."

"So that's in the water from Broken Eye Lake?" Charlie asked, shocked.

"Ten thousand times higher than the EPA limits," Dr. Evans spurted out, as he stared at the monitor, enthralled at the red lines that continued to appear on the graph.

"Where could it have come from?" Grant asked.

"I think I might have an answer to that question," Maggie said, holding up the microscope slide in front of her face. She confidently strolled over to the white board on the wall, picked up a green marking pen, and wrote $FeCr_2O_4$ on the board. "That's the formula for chromite," Maggie said as she turned to face the group. Dr. Evans continued to analyze the samples, as she explained about chromite. "It's a brownish-black iron-chromium ore mined in the Alaska interior, mainly for it's chromium value."

"Let's not make a major theatrical production out of this, Maggie. Don't hold us in suspense," Dr. Evans yelled over to them. "You know, and so does everyone else, that chromite is not soluble in water. So how did it get from the solid state of ore, to the liquid state in water?"

Maggie leaned over and cupped one hand over her mouth. In a low voice, she said, "The old poop gets upset when someone steals his thunder."

"Come on, Maggie, spit it out!" Dr. Evans hollered.

Maggie held the slide up again. "The answer is on this slide," she said with certainty and an edge of excitement. "In this lake water, are the little demons of pollution—extremely rare bacteria, and some very common algae. They're partners in the intriguing mystery I'm about to unravel for you all.

"First, there are the bacteria. These particular bacteria exist only in deep underground reservoirs. They can only survive in a very narrow pH range, from 6.0 to 6.4."

She wrote the numbers on the board, while she explained what pH was. "It's the measure of acidity or alkalinity in solutions. The middle of the pH range is 7.0, which is considered neutral. A pH around 6.0 is on the acid side, which is how these little critters like their water."

Grant and the others listened intently, as Maggie proceeded. Tapping the white board under the pH numbers with her marking pen, Maggie said, "Now if this pH gets out of balance, say it drops to 5.6 or jumps to 6.8, the bacteria will die. In fact, that may be one way to get rid of them. But for the moment, they're still kicking, so let's go back over here and take a look at the iron.

"These bacteria have a colossal appetite for iron." She then pointed to the Fe, in the $FeCr_2O_4$ formula she had written on the white board. Now, there's iron in the chromite. Right?" Maggie circled the Fe in the formula with the green marking pen.

"Right," Grant answered.

Maggie's voice was crackling with excitement as she continued. "The bacteria attack the ore—the chromite. When they do, they free the iron for their metabolic needs. You might say they eat the iron. At the same time, the chromate ions are freed." Maggie circled the Cr_2O_4 with a red marking pen.

"So that's how the chromium goes from being a solid in the ore, to being soluble in the water," Grant said. "I do know that chromium is found in nature in two forms, chromium-3, and chromium-6. I also know they are both toxic, but chromium-6 is the worst. Which form is this one in?"

"Excellent question, young man. Very astute of you," Maggie said to Grant. "That's where the algae comes in. When the chromate ions are first liberated by the bacteria, they are in the form of chromium-3. However, the common algae that we have in our waters here in Alaska, metabolize the chromate ions, that is they eat them, and then discard them as by-products, in the form of chromium-6."

Grant rubbed his chin thoughtfully. "Okay," he said. "I understand everything now, except for one thing. If these bacteria only inhabit deep underground reservoirs, then how did they get into Broken Eye Lake?"

"That's a very good question, and I'm not sure I can answer that one," Maggie replied. "I can only postulate a reasonable theory. With as many earthquakes as we have here in Alaska, it's possible that the earth cracked open, deep underground, and allowed the water containing these bacteria to escape from one of these reservoirs, possibly into an old chromite mine shaft."

"Or gold mine," Dr. Evans yelled. "Look at the monitor. We have gold at 197. These samples are loaded with it. At first, I thought it was a fluke. But I've just finished analyzing the fifth sample, and it's like the previous four—loaded with gold. Somebody is going to be a very rich person if they can find the source of this water."

As if a sealed door had suddenly sprung open in Grant's brain and a brilliant light came shining through, the pieces to the puzzle started to fall into place. He swung around, grabbed Victor by the shoulders, and began to shake him. "That's it, Victor," he said excitedly. "Greed. The old dependable desire that will lead you straight to corruption. That's why we've had all this trouble trying to get these samples analyzed for metal content. Now, I'm more convinced than ever, that Linsey is at the bottom of all this."

"Your right," his companion replied. "And someone in Two Forks is in on it with her. Now can you stop shaking me before the fillings rattle out of my teeth?"

"Oh yeah. Sorry," Grant said, not completely aware of what he was doing. His mind was zooming with ideas, putting the pieces together. "That's why the chemist at the AWMC lab couldn't find the records from the last time the lake samples were analyzed. Linsey saw the results and realized that the samples were loaded with gold and chromium."

"Precisely, laddie," Dr. Evans said, jumping into the brainstorming as he swung around in his chair. "With the pollution of chromium being on such a massive scale as we see in these samples, no average citizen could afford to clean up that mess. Not an entire lake, the feeder streams, and the rivers that have been contaminated. My guess is, this Linsey person you speak of, is blackmailing the individual that brought the samples to her lab in the first place."

"Exactly," Charlie added. "And I'll bet that individual is someone from Two Forks."

Grant walked over to the white board and picked up a marking pen. "But this doesn't explain two things." As he spoke, he wrote on the board. "Wolf poaching, and the decline in caribou population."

"Maybe the poaching is nothing more than a diversion, to keep us too busy to see the real problem. Just like Linsey encouraging me to ramrod that feral dog hunt. It would divert my attention," Victor said.

"Very perceptive," Maggie replied. "As far as the decline in the caribou population is concerned, I think I can answer that question if you get me a semen sample from a mature caribou bull. Chromium-6 is most likely a mutagen, especially at these high levels. It's possible, and most probable, that the sperm cells of the caribou bulls, have mutated and been deformed, to the point of affecting the reproductive process. Fewer babies, fewer caribou."

Grant turned to Victor and said, "Once again, it looks you may have been right, partner." Then he turned to the rest of the group and said, "Victor told me from the very beginning that he thought the number of calves born in the Unit 20A area, seemed to be dropping with each season. He's noticed this for the past three or four years."

"Get me a semen sample, and we'll know for sure," Maggie said.

It was after midnight when Flutter Butt left Fairbanks International Airport and headed back toward Two Forks. Grant had thanked Dr. Evans and Dr. Foust again for their assistance. When his professor, Dale Barlow, brought them back to the airport, he warned Grant that Linsey Hogan was a very powerful woman, and if he was wrong about any of this, it could ruin his career in wildlife management.

In the helicopter, Grant pondered the warning Dale had given him. He was completely aware of the consequences. No matter how high the stakes, he would never be able to live with himself, if he didn't pursue this until the truth was revealed. A plan of what to do next, had already begun to develop in his mind. He spoke into the small microphone in the helmet, "Victor, I think the most important thing to do first, is to determine where the source of this chromium contamination is coming from. Once we know that, we'll get a semen sample and send it up to Dr. Foust."

"Okay," Victor answered, as he maneuvered the control stick and leaned the chopper toward Two Forks. "That field kit Dr. Evans made for you to check for chromium, should come in real handy."

"Yeah, just how does that work?" Charlie asked. "I mean, why does he have a huge instrument in the lab, if this tiny little field kit can analyze the water?"

Grant glanced back into the dark cargo hold where Charlie sat strapped in the fold-down seat. Her face had an eerie green glow from the helicopter's instrument panel. "The ICP-MS is a thousand times more sensitive than the field kit, and it will measure all the metals in the sample at the same time. The field kit will only measure higher levels of chromium-6," he explained.

"You'll have to show me how to operate that thing before I go out in the morning," Victor said.

"You won't be going out in the morning. I will. By myself," Grant said.

"I don't think so," Charlie fired back. "Not with your injuries. Are you crazy? We nearly died yesterday. Have you forgotten that already?"

He knew Charlie would resist his going back out into the woods this soon. But he had another reason for wanting to go alone. The memory of the last time he saw the silver-blue wolf, stuck in his mind like an annoying gnat. He was certain the animal needed his help for some reason. Hopefully, it wasn't too late.

"Just calm down, Charlie. It'll be okay. Trust me on this one," Grant said.

"The famous last words of every man I've ever known," she said sourly.

"I don't know if that's such a good idea, Grant. Charlie's probably right about this," Victor said. "Besides, this time of year with the snow and ice melting, there are hundreds of streams feeding into that lake. It could take you weeks to find the right one."

"First of all, this is not open for discussion. This is something I have to do," Grant said firmly, hoping he didn't offend either one of them. "I was hoping that we could narrow it down some. Do either of you know anyone in Two Forks who has or has had any kind of a mine in the area?"

"There are several old mines in the area, but I don't know of any that are still active," Victor replied. "The only person I know of that still has a mine, is—"

"I'll tell him, Victor," Charlie interrupted. "Billy Jack's father had an old gold mine that he abandoned years ago. Even before he died. I think Billy Jack still owns it, though."

"Do you know where it is?" he asked.

"Yeah. Billy Jack took me there once, when we were kids," Charlie answered. Her voice was low and reluctant. "I'll mark the location on the map, when we get home."

"That guy's name keeps popping up, just like dead fish stink," Victor muttered.

"Yeah, well, we'll find out later today if this trail leads back to him," Grant said with an edge to his voice. Victor was right, Billy Jack's name kept cropping up wherever trouble seemed to poke its head out of the garbage. "I'll get a little sleep first, then head out about seven in the morning. I'll check out the feeder streams coming from the direction of Billy Jack's mine, first."

"Sounds like a good plan to me," Victor said.

"While I'm trying to find the source of the chromium contamination, I would like for you two to try and trace anyone else that might own any kind of mine in the area. It's possible, Victor, that the problem is not with Billy Jack." He made the last statement more for Charlie's sake, than anything else.

"Wilma Adams," Charlie said.

"What?" Grant and Victor said in unison as they glanced back at her.

"Wilma works at the county records office," Charlie said. "She'll be able to give us a list of everyone that has a mine, or has filed a claim for a mine, in the last fifty years. I'll call her first thing in the morning."

"Now we're cooking," Grant said enthusiastically. "Victor, if anything important comes up, you can fly out to me in the woods in Flutter Butt, put her down in a clearing, and give me the information. One last thing, and this is really important. We don't want to discuss any of this with a single person in Two Forks. Agreed?" He held out his hand, palm up.

"Agreed," Victor and Charlie said together, each laying a hand in his, sealing their agreement.

Moments later, Flutter Butt's skids touched down at Two Forks Airport. When Grant stepped from the helicopter, a stiff northerly gust nearly knocked him to the ground. Since leaving Fairbanks, the temperature had plunged to twelve degrees, and there was a strong angry wind.

Twenty minutes later he was standing with Charlie, on the front stoop of her cabin. She'd marked a map for him, showing the location of Billy Jack's mine.

The wind screamed under the eaves and whipped dust around the corner of the cabin. Charlie leaned up and kissed him gently on the lips. Before she pulled away, she let her warm wet lips slide to his ear. Whispering seductively, she said, "I wish you'd let one of us go with you in the morning. Especially since this cold front has moved in." She pressed her wonderful lips to his ear and said, "I've just found my knight in shining armor. I don't want to lose him."

He drew back and looked at her. Tears had welled up in her blue eyes. "I'll be back, Charlie. You can count on it," he said softly. Then he kissed her on the forehead. "Please try to understand. This is something I have to do by myself."

CHAPTER 15

Grant had left his cabin at 7:00 A.M., sharp. It was now 8:15. The weather was unbearable. The temperature had dropped like a fallen tree, into the single digits. The wind howled and ripped down through the gorge, fiercer than anything he'd ever seen in his life.

So far, he had tested the waters of thirteen small feeder streams that flowed into Denning Fork from the northeast. All had given a negative response for chromium-6. He hovered behind a group of willows, to protect himself from the cutting wind that raged around him like an angry banshee. He folded the map and slipped it into his backpack. If Charlie was correct, the feeder stream from the ravine where Billy Jack's mine was located, was just ahead about a hundred yards. He pulled his parka back over his head, stepped out from behind the willows, and continued walking along Denning Fork. The moment he was free of the trees, a blast of wind hammered at his backside, shoving him forward.

Even though his mission was to find the contaminated source of chromium, he couldn't shake his thoughts of the silver-blue wolf. He had seen no sign of the magnificent creature so far this morning, and disappointment haunted him. With a great deal of uneasiness, he had lied to Victor and Charlie—something that was almost as painful as his throbbing shoulder and leg were, in this unforgiving weather. Grant had promised both of them, he'd bring his rifle along for protection against any grizzlies he might encounter. But he hadn't done so. He feared that just the sight of a firearm, might frighten the wolf away.

Last night he'd had another disturbing dream about the silver-blue wolf. All he could remember were some fragments and partial images. There was a man in a gray coat with a rifle, aiming it at a wolf. He wasn't sure if it was the silver-blue or not, as there was another wolf, maybe two, in the dream. It was deathly cold, and the man's parka was pulled up over his head, his face blocked from view by the fur trim. Even though Grant couldn't recognize the man, he sensed it was someone he knew. The faceless man pulled the trigger, and as the roaring boom of the shot resonated in his ears, Grant jerked awake and sat up in bed. He was covered in sweat. His insides churned with an overwhelming desire to go that very instant and search for the silver-blue wolf. He still didn't know why the poor creature desperately needed his help, only that it did.

Slate gray clouds raced across the gloomy sky like an evil flying carpet. Willows, and black and white spruce trees, bowed to the relentless power of the wind god, as it marched down from great arctic north. Grant's knees had begun to stiffen from the torturous cold, where the grizzly had raked his claws over the knee caps. His youthful mobility had deteriorated to that of a man three times his age. The going was slow, but he trudged on.

Grant finally reached the next feeder stream, which was ironically name Hazard Creek. Before testing the water, he moved up the narrow ravine, far enough for its sloping wall's to protect him from the wind. The stream was larger than the others he had come across so far this morning. It was considerably wider and deeper, and impossible to cross at this point. However, he expected this, because it was fed by two smaller streams that had merged farther up the ravine, about a quarter of a mile. Large jagged boulders bordered the treacherous white-water rapids as far as he could see up the chasm. Based on Charlie's map, Billy Jack's mine was less than a quarter of mile up the ravine, on the left side.

Before traversing the treacherous terrain up the gorge to Billy Jack's mine, he would first test the water here for chromium. If it was negative, as the others had been, he would move on down Denning Fork to the next feeder stream and try again. If it was positive, as he hoped it would be, he would continue up the ravine to where it forked and then test the two individual streams.

The bulky black snowmobile suit he wore, was rated for temperatures down to sixty degrees below zero. Surprisingly, even in this terrible wind, his body had remained reasonably warm. The only exceptions were his gloved fingers and his knees. He slipped the backpack off, knelt down on one knee, and removed the small blue plastic index-card box that contained the testing materials for chromium.

Grant opened the lid and lifted out an empty twenty milliliter glass vial that had a long tether of nylon fishing line attached to its neck. He unscrewed the black cap, laid it back in the box, then stood up and walked toward the stream. After maneuvering up and over on a large boulder at the water's edge, he dropped the vial into the swirling stream. The rushing water immediately swallowed the small bottle and filled it. He reeled it back in by its tether and took it back to where he had left his backpack and the small blue box.

This time he dug out a second vial, of about the same size. The bottle contained an amber colored reagent solution, diphenlycarbazide, that was specific for detecting chromium-6. Dr. Evans had prepared the solution in ethanol, so it would not freeze in the low temperatures. He unscrewed the eyedropper cap, squeezed the bulb to fill the dropper, then pinched two drops of the solution into the water he had just collected from Hazard Creek. The reagent, a liquid that was heavier than water, slowly spiraled down through the frigid liquid, leaving in its wake, thread-thin deep purple streamers.

Grant capped both the vials, placed the reagent bottle back in the blue box, labeled the Hazard Creek vial, HC1, then shook it vigorously to mix the reagent with the water. The stream water immediately turned a deep purple color, indicating it was loaded with chromium-6.

"I'll be darned," he said to himself, as he put everything back into his backpack. "Just like Victor said, 'wherever there is trouble, Billy Jack's name seems to always pop up.'" He slipped the backpack on and began his journey up the ravine.

Charlie sat on the stool closest to the cash register, sipping her morning coffee and pondering all the crazy things going on in her life right now. Her curiosity about who owned the mines in the area, had kept her awake most of the night. She finally gave up on sleep at 5:00 A.M. and called her friend from the county records office, at home, before the woman had even gotten out of bed. Wilma was surprised by the call, but happy to hear from her. Charlie asked her friend if she could get her a list of who had mines, or had filed claims for any type of mines, in the Unit 20A area in the past twenty years.

The bell over the front door rang, bringing Charlie back to the present. Frank Kicklighter came striding in, carrying his usually bottle of water. Before Frank reached the counter, she jumped up and had a steamy cup of coffee waiting for him. "Morning, Sheriff. How do you like this weather?"

"She's a cold one, that's for sure. Especially for this time of year." Frank replied. "Thanks for the coffee. I'll need it this morning. Anything new going on?"

"You wouldn't believe it if I told you," she said.

"What's that supposed to mean?"

She hesitated for a moment, recalling what Grant had said about not telling anyone what the three of them were up to. But this was Frank, the most trustworthy person she knew. Plus, Frank might have a good idea who Linsey's spy was. She leaned over the counter toward the sheriff and said in a low voice, "I'm not supposed to tell any one, so this has to be strictly between you and me, Frank."

"I'm the sheriff, remember. Your friend and public protector against the bad guys." Frank smiled and sipped his coffee.

"Broken Eye Lake is contaminated big-time, with chromium," she said flatly. "We think that's the main reason the caribou population in 20A has been declining for the past few years. Not because of the wolves."

Frank set his cup down and stared at her for a moment. "That's crazy. We have the cleanest water in the whole country up here. Who told you such nonsense?"

"No one told me, I know." Charlie proceeded to give Frank a full account of all the events from yesterday morning to the present.

"But at the airport yesterday morning, Victor said Grant was home in bed. I don't think Miss Hogan is the type of woman who would appreciate being lied to."

"Probably not, especially since we think she's involved in all this, somehow," Charlie said.

"No way. That's ludicrous," Frank insisted.

"We think she has a spy down here in Two Forks, too. Feeding her information on everything Grant and Victor are up to."

"I think someone's been feeding you some bad information. Someone that has a creative imagination or has read far too many mystery novels," Frank scoffed. "So where's Grant this morning?"

"He's hiking down along Denning Creek, checking every feeder stream for chromium contamination," she answered.

"By himself?! In this weather?! That's crazy!"

The bell over the door rang again. Victor dashed in, shuddered from the cold outside, and slowly wandered over to a table. It wasn't ten seconds later that Billy Jack burst through the front door, rubbing his hands and blowing on them, to warm them. With a lively spring in his step, he marched toward the counter.

When Charlie saw Billy Jack enter, she leaned close to Frank and whispered in his ear, "Do you know of anyone that has a claim on a mine around here?"

"No." Frank turned around part way to see who had come in the Trading Post. "No one but—" He nodded his head toward Billy Jack, turned back around, and took another sip of coffee. Standing up, he said, "Best be on my way. Thanks again for the coffee, Charlie." Frank picked up his bottle of water and headed for the front door.

Billy Jack strolled up to the counter, passing Frank on the way. "Didn't mean to run you off, Sheriff," he said cheerfully. "I'll buy you a cup of coffee."

"Thanks, Billy Jack, but I've got to be going," Frank replied, stepping out into the raging wind.

The phone by the cash register started ringing. Charlie answered it.

Billy Jack seemed to be in a good mood, almost skipping up to the counter as if he were a little boy again. He plopped down on a stool, pulled off his watch cap, and raked his fingers through his dark hair. Victor rose up from the table, came over to the counter, and sat down next to Billy Jack. He didn't look at or speak to the man, just stared straight ahead.

"Morning, Chief," Billy Jack said cordially, which was totally out of character for him. It had been a long time since Charlie had seen Billy Jack in such good spirits.

Victor grunted. His jaw muscles flexed like taut rubber bands, and his eyes stared at the swinging kitchen doors in front of him. Tension oozed from every pore in his body.

Charlie put her hand over the mouth piece of the phone and said, "Be with you guys in just a sec." Victor looked like he was going to explode like Mount Saint Helens, if she didn't get over there and depressurize him. She turned her back to the two men and talked low into the phone. "I'm back, Wilma. What'd you say?"

"I have your list of names ready, but I'm having trouble with this new fax machine," Wilma complained.

"That's okay, Wilma, send it when you can." Turning her back on Billy Jack and Victor, Charlie whispered into the phone.

"But let me ask you one thing. Is Billy Jack Boone's name on that list?"

"Yup," Wilma replied, immediately. "It was transferred to his name, shortly after his daddy died. That was in the good old days. Now with all the budget cuts and everything, we're so far behind it takes us a good year and a half to get a mine transfer recorded in the county books. So this list I'm sending you, is not really current. It's the best I can do right now."

"Whatever you have will be fine, Wilma. Thanks, you're a doll. I owe you one." Charlie hung up the phone just in time to hear Billy Jack ask Victor something.

"Well, Chief, looks like you're in your usual festive mood," Billy Jack scoffed. "Tell me, did Wonder Boy find any bad stuff in those lake samples I so graciously delivered to the lab for him?"

"Damn you, Billy Jack. You know good and well there was nothing in that water," Charlie said, her face lit up with anger. There was no doubt in her mind now that he was guilty of all of it—the wolf poaching, the polluting of Broken Eye Lake. How could she have been so wrong about him?

"What's the matter with you?" Billy Jack asked, a stunned look on his face. "Well of course I knew. Everyone knows there's nothing in that water," Billy Jack replied, cockily.

Victor stood up, his face like a granite statue. "There was nothing in it because it was bottled water. The same bottled water Frank gave you Monday morning. I was there. Remember?"

"I don't know what you're talking about," Billy Jack said, standing up. His eyes darted from Victor's rigid face to Charlie's angry one. He stepped back from the counter, wearing a look like a cornered animal, preparing to defend itself. "You're crazy. Both of you are plumb loco."

Charlie cut in. She wasn't going to let Billy Jack get off that easy. "Just what kind of business did you have in Anchorage, huh?"

Billy Jack looked at her in disbelief. "For one thing, I went to the bank and did *you* a big favor. For another, I took lover boy's lake samples to the lab."

So much had been happening the past couple of days, she had forgotten all about the money she was going to borrow from Billy Jack, to pay Frank. Before she could say anything, Victor butted in.

"Are you saying you knew nothing about the fur-buyer's consortium in Anchorage this week? Or about all the wolf poaching that's been going on around here?" Victor's voice was rising as he demanded answers.

"You were going to Anchorage for another reason, weren't you?" Charlie burst out, her lower lip trembling and fury pulsing through her veins. "What was it? To sell wolf pelts? You're pathetic, Billy Jack. How could I have been so blind?"

Billy Jack's face went slack, as if he were confused, then it began to contort. His upper lip curled into a snarl, like a mad dog. "I don't know wha—"

Dashing from behind the counter, Charlie shook her finger in Billy Jack's face. "Grant is probably at your mine right now, getting proof that it's contaminating Broken Eye Lake and all the wildlife that drink from it. God knows how much damage you've done to those animals."

Billy Jack slapped her hand away from his face. The motion made a loud smack that cracked through the room. Victor promptly stepped between them. He raised his hand and began to poke Billy Jack in the chest with a finger. "That's why you switched the water samples, isn't it?" he shouted, staring him down with warrior-eyes.

From nowhere, Billy Jack's enormous right fist bolted up from his side and smashed against Victor's left jaw. There was a loud, wet crunch. Victor's head snapped back and to the side. Blood spewed from his mouth and splattered across Charlie's face. It even got into her eyes and mouth. She began to wipe at her eyes and sputter frantically. Like a giant timber, the tall Indian slammed into her, hard. They both toppled to the floor, with Victor on top.

Billy Jack stormed out the door, yelling, "You're crazy! The whole lot of you are completely out of your minds! That cheechako will pay for this!"

With Victor sprawled on top of her, Charlie never saw Billy Jack leave. She just heard the bell ring, and the front door slam shut.

Grant understood now, why they called this Hazard Creek. The treacherous ravine was narrow and crooked, like a sidewinder rattle snake, and just as dangerous. He went up the left side of the raging stream. Twice, it was necessary for him to scale steep slopes to get around rock bluffs that plunged straight into the water.

A long laborious hour later, he was finally at the place where the stream forked. His lungs burned, as if they were on fire from inhaling the cold air. The only good he could see about coming up here, was the protection from the fierce wind. Large plumes of steam billowed from his nose and mouth, as he stopped for a moment to rest on a flat rock.

Looking around, he noticed several trees had been uprooted from some past disturbance. On closer inspection, he noticed the land on the right side of the fork looked odd, almost unnatural. There were jagged rock outcroppings that seemed out of place, as if the earth had cracked opened and vomited them to the surface.

He'd tested the water in three different places on the way up the stream, to be certain the chromium contamination was not seeping into Hazard Creek from an underground feeder. All three had been positive, indicating the source was farther up. Every step he took, the more it appeared that the pollution was indeed coming from Billy Jack's mine. In a way, for Charlie's sake, he almost wished it wasn't so.

According to her markings on the map, the mine was located about 150 yards up the left branch of the stream. Once Grant had caught his breath, he hiked twenty feet past the point where the two smaller creeks merged, to ensure he would get a sample that truly represented water from only one tributary. Thank God, both streams had narrowed down to where they could be easily crossed without getting his boots wet.

The terrain had improved since he'd reached the fork in the streams, and the ravine had begun to widen. If only the weather would give him a break, this hike wouldn't be half bad. In a way, snooping about in the wilderness like this, he felt like Sherlock Holmes trying to track down clues to convict the dastardly villain. It was all elementary, he thought, chuckling to himself.

He anxiously collected a sample of water from the left stream, added the chromium reagent, capped the vial, and shook it vigorously. Holding the small bottle up in front of his face, he stared at it, dumbfounded. The water in the vial remained colorless. The test was negative. The source of chromium contamination did not come from this stream. This meant it had to come from the stream on the right, instead.

Grant hurriedly crossed over to the right tributary and tested it. The water in the vial turned a deep purple, the color of a ripe plum. Had Charlie made a mistake, and Billy Jack's mine was to the right of the fork in Hazard Creek? He hastily put away the test kit and continued his journey up the ravine.

Fifteen minutes and seventy-five yards later, he eased along a narrow path that rounded a steep rock bluff, near a bend in the stream. When the other side came into view, Grant froze at the devastation. It started twenty yards in front of him. Standing there next to the rapidly flowing creek, he hugged the face of the rock bluff and stared in disbelief. Near the water's edge, a six foot shift in the earth's crust cut a crooked diagonal swath up the right slope of the ravine. Thirty feet on each side of the fault, up-rooted trees sprawled in all directions, twisted, mangled, and snapped in two, as if they were nothing more than toothpicks.

He moved slowly around the buff, never removing his eyes from the scene. Large and small boulders alike, were scattered down the side of the gorge, below the fault line. Many of the larger ones had crashed down to the small stream, crushing anything in their paths. In one location, a single huge monolithic boulder had plunged all the way down the slope and landed across the stream, damming up the water and creating a small reservoir. The boulder was at least fifteen feet taller than he was. Water trickled over the top, forming a beautiful waterfall in the midst of all the destruction.

Finally, Grant came out of his stupor. He recalled the tremor at his cabin, on his first day in Two Forks. "Victor said Alaska had more earthquake activity than any other state," he mumbled to himself. "And that they had a big one just five years ago." His eyes panned the area.

From the rate of decay on the fallen trees, he guessed the devastation here had occurred in that time frame. He rubbed his chin while thinking out loud. "Victor told me the epicenter was three miles southeast of my cabin. That would put it just about here."

That's when it hit him, and it all came together in his brain. Pacing back and forth, and talking to himself, he ran through the scenario:

"Five years ago, a major quake takes place, cracks open the earth, and allows the water from a deep reservoir or river, to come to the surface. The water has a rare bacterium in it. That bacterium breaks down the ore, chromite, into a form, chromium-3, that is soluble in water. An alga that is common to the waters of Alaska, converts chromium-3 to chromium-6, one of the most toxic metals known to man, and a carcinogen and a mutagen. The chromium-6 is then carried in the streams, down to Broken Eye Lake. Since you can't see it, smell it, or taste it, no one knows it's there, and the caribou drink it. They continue to do this for five years—a long enough period for the sperm cells to mutate. The caribou bulls become impotent and there's a dramatic decline in their population."

He stopped pacing, went silent for a moment, and shook his head. "That's it," he said to himself. "My gut feeling was right all along. The wolf packs in 20A aren't responsible for the high decrease of caribou over the past few years."

From the corner of his eye, he caught a quick movement high up on the slope, just above the fault line. He turned his head and saw the silver-blue wolf standing there, peering down at him from its lofty height atop a huge boulder. He headed up to meet it.

Ten minutes later, Grant stood in awe, face-to-face with the magnificent creature that had haunted his dreams for the past several weeks. The animal pranced anxiously, next to the opening of an old mine shaft. From where he'd stood a few minutes ago, he'd been unable to see the mine, because the large rock the wolf had been standing on, blocked his view of it. Bubbling from the mine's depths, was the source of the contaminated stream that trickled down the ravine's slope and fed Hazard Creek.

He cautiously worked his way around the pacing wolf. Reaching the mine opening, he looked inside. The shaft had partially collapsed, probably from the earthquake. Rock and bracing timbers littered the mine floor. And there, carpeting the bottom of a small pool of water, was a brownish-black ore. Based on Dr. Maggie Foust's description, he guessed it to be chromite. He shed the backpack, retrieved the test kit, and stepped inside the mine.

While collecting a sample of water from the pool, he noticed a yellow glitter mingled in with the brownish-black ore. Gold! For a moment, Grant almost forgot his mission, feeling the urge of greed. But he quickly recovered and analyzed the sample he had collected. As he suspected, the water was loaded with chromium. For the sake of good science, and for evidence, he plucked a few dark ore pebbles, and a few tiny gold nuggets, from the pool. He'd have them analyzed later in the lab, to confirm his findings.

Outside, the silver-blue wolf was still nervously pacing back and forth. It's golden mesmerizing eyes were constantly on Grant, as he packed away the samples and test kit in his backpack. Her stare was intimidating, and he wasn't quite sure what the animal's motives were, yet he didn't really feel threatened.

After Grant slipped the backpack on, the wolf darted off, trotting up the side of ravine. The beautiful creature stopped and looked back at him, an odd expression on her face. The wolf turned and slowly pranced back toward him, stopped and looked at him, then turned and ran up the slope. She stopped again a short distance later, glaring at him with a desperate helpless look.

"You want me to follow you, don't you girl," he said to the wolf. "Just like Lassie, you want me to follow you."

Linsey Hogan was celebrating. Sitting in her office with the door closed, she leaned back in the plush black leather chair and propped her feet up on her desk. She was smoking a cigarette and sipping wine.

The head of the fur-buyer's consortium had just called her and said he was staggered by the number of quality wolf pelts he had gotten so far. He assured her he was paying top dollar for every one of them, too. The only thing he wished for now, was the silver-blue wolf fur.

The phone rang and she leaned forward to pick up the receiver. "Hello, Linsey Hogan."

"It's over," a man's voice desperately spewed over the phone. "They know everything—the gold, the pollution of the lake, they even know about the fur-buyer's consortium in Anchorage." He took a deep breath to catch his wind. "It's over. I told you we couldn't get away with this."

Her feet slammed to the floor. "Would you stop saying that. It's not over," she snapped, angrily stabbing out the cigarette butt in an ashtray on the desk. "Get a hold of yourself and stop acting like an immature ass. You know what needs to be done now."

"What are you taking about?" the man whined.

"That pesky little SOB I hired, needs to be stopped. That's what I'm talking about. I don't care how you do it, but put an end to the problem. Now! And get me that silver-blue wolf's hide! This guy in Anchorage is foaming at the mouth for it."

"I don't know if—"

"Remember, Jackass, it's your mine that's polluting the lake. It's been you that's made all the contacts with the trappers, on the wolf poaching deal. My name is clear of everything, and if you say anything to the authorities about this, I'll deny every word of it. Besides, you have a great deal more to lose than me, and you know exactly what I mean. It depends on the success of the mine, the money from the wolf pelts, all of it. So take care of business."

With that, Linsey slammed the phone down. She swiveled around in her chair and stared out her office window, at downtown Fairbanks. An uneasy feeling began to grow inside her.

A few moments later she picked up the phone and called Peter Worley at the bank. "Peter? This is an emergency. I need to talk to you about my finances."

Chapter 16

Grant's body screamed with pain as he tried to keep up. He'd been following the silver-blue wolf, up the steep wall of the Hazard Creek ravine, over the top of the ridge, and down into the adjoining ravine, which had no name assigned to it on the map. As she neared the bottom of the second gorge and moved alongside the unnamed feeder stream, the female wolf had increased her gait to a blistering pace. Wherever she was taking him, there seemed to be a dire urgency to it. Streaking through the brisk frigid air with extraordinary ease, she was now ahead of him by twenty-five to thirty yards. It was all he could do to keep up with her.

His burning lungs heaved as he jogged down the treacherous incline through the woods. He was constantly dodging low hanging limbs, or weaving to avoid the maze of huge boulders and trees that seemed to be rushing toward him. Large clouds of steam rushed from his mouth and streamed past his face, with every jolting step he took. The injuries to his shoulder, leg, and knees ached with debilitating pain. He wasn't sure how much farther he could go at this brutal pace.

The pounding of his heart filled his ears and prevented him from hearing the drone of the low flying helicopter, until it was directly above him. When the chopper zoomed overhead, the loud beat of the rotor blades startled him, and he ducked. He recognized Billy Jack's aircraft before it quickly dropped out of sight and flew on down the ravine, toward Denning Fork.

In the brief moment it took to glance at the helicopter, he lost sight of the wolf. She had cut around a bend in the ravine and disappeared behind a large clump of willows. A few seconds later, as he raced around the drooping limbs of the trees, huffing and puffing, he saw the wolf again. She stood about ten yards in front of him. But it was the scene beyond her, that caught his eye. He came to an abrupt halt and gazed in utter anguish.

In front of him was a small clearing, where the gorge had widened, and the sharp incline they'd been speeding down, had leveled off. It went on for a short distance, maybe twenty yards, then dropped to a steep slope once again. The nearly flat surface of the clearing slowed the narrow feeder stream to a trickle, allowing it to gently meandered through the center of the treeless opening.

Scattered around the perimeter, were dozens of self-locking wire snares. They looked like the same ones he and Victor had observed a few days ago, where the moose cow and her calf had been caught. On the other side of the stream, a red fox and hoary marmot were snared and dead. In another wire trap, the paw and lower hind leg of a wolf, or feral dog, remained, sticking up in the air as a reminder of the animal's terrifying capture. The creature's desire for life and freedom had been so strong that it had chewed and gnawed on the entrapped limb, severing hide, tendons, and bone, to escape. Once freed, the animal hobbled off on three legs into the bitter cold, to finish out its days as a cripple in the unforgiving wilderness. Grant's stomach lurched up into his throat. He gagged as he jerked his eyes away from the ragged bloody end of the poor creature's leg.

But the worst, was right in front of him. Caught in the deadly self-locking snares were three yearling wolves. The harder the helpless animals jerked and twisted to escape the wire death traps, the tighter the cable cinched around their bodies. Now he understood why the silver-blue wolf needed his help, and why she had brought him here. These were her pups.

The swinging doors suddenly burst open and Charlie came blazing out of the kitchen. She held some fax pages in her hand. "You're not going to believe this," she hollered.
Victor sat slumped over the counter, holding an ice bag on his left jaw, where Billy Jack had cold-cocked him. He raised up his head, sluggishly. "What now?" he asked.
"Billy Jack has two mines," she said.
Victor's eyebrows raised with interest, and he lifted his head up more attentively. He laid the ice bag on the counter and asked, "Two? Where's the other one at?"
"The only thing it says here on the list Wilma sent me, is that the second mine is on the east slope of Hazard Creek," Charlie said, studying the sheet of fax paper.
"That would put it on the right side of the ravine," Victor said, gently touched his swollen jaw. "I thought you said his mine was on the left."
"The one Billy Jack took me to, was on the left side. I know that as well as I'm standing here," she explained. "That's the whole point, he has two mines and they're both located in Hazard Creek." She watched Victor test the soreness in his jaw, as he lightly poked the outer edges of the purplish bruise forming on the side of his face. "How's the jaw?"
"It hurts," Victor said. "There's no telling what that maniac is going to do."
That struck a chord within her, and she began to recall the ugly scene earlier, when Billy Jack became violent. He said something when he stormed out of the Trading Post, but was it? Her forehead creased as she concentrated. She stared at the floor,

nibbling on her lower lip, trying to mentally dig open the memories of just a few hours ago. At the time, she'd been pinned under Victor and was too preoccupied with getting Victor's blood off of her, to be worrying about what Billy Jack was saying. Finally, a fragment of that moment came to her.

"Cheechako." she said.

"What?" Victor asked, confused.

"Cheechako," she repeated. "That's the last thing Billy Jack said before he stomped out the front door this morning. Don't you remember? That's what he calls Grant."

"So?" Victor said.

"Give me a second. I'm trying to remember all of what he said."

Whitie Saylor sat on his usual stool at the end of the counter, hunched over, with his head resting on his arms. He turned toward Charlie and Victor. As if on cue, his eyes lazily opened, still glazed from last night's booze. He barely lifted his head and said, "That's easy. 'That cheechako will pay for this.' That's what Billy Jack said," the old drunk mumbled. Then he dropped his head back down on his arms.

"That's right," she hollered, then paused. A few moments later horror washed over her face like a white veil. "Oh no!" she yelled. "Billy Jack's going after Grant. Victor, you have to take Flutter Butt and get out there before it's too late!"

His face was twisted in anger, and his teeth were gritted like they always were when he was raging mad. Stepping wide and fast, Billy Jack climbed the slope next to the narrow stream that cut through the steep gorge. Luckily, the terrain had cleared and leveled off enough, so he could land the chopper close to where he'd seen Wonder Boy and his precious wolves. In a few short minutes Grant Rawlings would wish he'd never been born.

"That cheechako has been a pain in my butt every since he showed up in Two Forks," Billy Jack mumbled to himself. The sounds of his grumbling blended with the sounds of his large boots crunching pebbles along the stream. "Everything was fine with me and Charlie until a week ago. Now its all screwed up because of that twerp. Even after I went to Anchorage and did her a huge favor, she turned on me. I can't believe it. We've known each other all our lives."

When he flew over, he'd seen the three wolf pups caught in snares and the silver-blue wolf standing close by. Grant might be a cheechako but at least he wasn't blowing smoke about the elusive silver-blue wolf. He could hardly believe it. Billy Jack's pulse quickened at the very thought of actually seeing the mythical animal. The wolf's legend was rich and deeply rooted in the native folklore. Its magnificent pelt was priceless and had been sought by thousands of hunters, for decades. Now it was finally going to be his. He would capture it and display its majestic essence for all to see, forever.

Billy Jack's pace picked up, as he began to formulate a plan. Before he tore this greenhorn apart with his bare hands, he would approach Grant and the wolves very quietly. They would be distracted and not notice him, concerned about the welfare of the pups caught in the snare traps. There was a large boulder at the far end of the clearing, close to where they were located. He could hide behind it, allowing him sufficient time to take careful aim for the perfect shot.

Grant slowly slipped the backpack off, carried it by the straps in his left hand, and eased closer to the first yearling wolf. Stretched out on the hard cold ground, the pup was stiff . . . and dead. The wire snare had done the job it was designed for, lassoing the pup around the neck and strangling it. It was a slow and miserable death.

Grant stood there in a daze, staring down at the gray yearling wolf. Its eyes were bulging and glassy, devoid of the sparkle of life. Its tongue, blue-purple and partly coated with dirt and tiny pebbles, dangled from its mouth. A heavy pain wrenched at Grant's insides, almost dropping him to his knees. His vision blurred from tears.

The dead wolf's mother, the silver-blue, slowly circled her deceased baby, smelling the ground around it, and smelling the cold lifeless body that would never play with her again. She gently rested her right paw on the pup's rib cage and began a mournful whine. Then, lifting her head toward the wind, she let loose an eerie howl.

Chills of sorrow rippled down Grant's back. He wiped his eyes. After three grueling trips around her pup with her head hung low, the wolf stopped and stared up at him. The sadness in her eyes tore at Grant's heart. He took a deep breath and had to glance away. He was close to weeping, himself, and guilt flooded his insides. He recalled his encounter with the silver-blue wolf the previous morning, when he'd seen her pacing back and forth on the shore across Denning Fork, acting as if she wanted him to follow her. If only he'd followed her then . . . maybe he could've saved her pup. It had only been dead a day or two. "How could anyone with even a drop of compassion or humanity, want to kill these animals for pleasure or money?" he asked, out loud.

He tried to shake the guilty thoughts and focused on the other two yearlings. One was black, with flecks of white and gray in its pelt, and the other was solid white. Like their brother, they were also caught in snare traps. Though they were in a great deal of pain, they were still alive.

The wire was tightly cinched around the black wolf's chest, just behind its front legs. It laboriously gasped for air, as the murderous self-locking snare slowly squeezed the life from its lungs. Seven feet beyond the black pup, the white pup sat with its left leg caught just above the paw. The wire was cutting into its flesh, and the paw was raw and bloody where the poor creature had chewed away fur and skin, exposing the crimson stained white bone in its leg.

The silver-blue wolf submissively moved away from her dead pup, apparently accepting the reality of its death, and trotted over to the black yearling. Grant cautiously eased in that direction, being careful not to make any quick movements that would spook the animals. The two wolves affectionately rubbed their heads together, a common display of greeting for the animals. The pup wagged its tail and whined, obviously happy to see its mother. They lick each other's face for a few seconds, continuing the greeting. Then the silver-blue moved on to the next pup. The white wolf had joined in with its sister's whining. When its mother came up to it, the pup held out its injured paw and waited for it to be caressed. Without the slightest hesitation, the silver-blue wolf began to lick her baby's bloody wound.

"Good girl. Everything is going to be all right," Grant said to the black wolf, as he knelt five feet away. He took off his gloves and pushed the sleeves of the snowmobile suit up to his elbows. As he spoke gently to calm the animal, he shuffled through the backpack and dug out the wire clippers. Thank God he'd listened to Victor's advice and put a pair of clippers and the dart gun in his backpack.

The mother wolf backed away from the white yearling and stood there watching him intently, evaluating his every move as he eased closer to her black pup.

He held out his hand toward the black wolf. "It's going to be okay. I'm going to help you." He tried to speak as soothingly as he could, but his emotions were high and his voice cracked.

Startled, the pup lurched back. It was immediately yanked to the ground by the wire restraint around its chest, which squeezed even more air from its lungs. Instantly, the yearling wolf jerked back to its feet and slunk into a defensive posture, with its fangs bared, ears dropped, and fur up on the back of its neck.

Grant ignored the display and inched closer, continuing to speak to the frightened animal. He held his free hand out toward it, both as a friendly gesture and for the pup to smell his scent. So as not to spook the young wolf, he held the wire cutters in his other hand, which was behind him and out of view. When he drew close enough, he leaned forward and made an attempt to clip the strangling wire. But the scared animal lurched forward and viciously snapped at him, weary of the intruder and wanting nothing to do with the wire cutters.

All he saw was a silver-blue blur streak toward the defiant black pup, like a magical phantom. He heard the growl, and in the next blink of his eyes, he saw the mother wolf clamp her mouth onto the back of the yearling's furry neck. She was snarling, her lips were curled, and her large teeth were showing. Cowering in submission, the young black wolf became obedient and whined for forgiveness.

After the mother wolf released the pup and stepped back, he tried to clip the wire a second time, and once again it snapped at him. That was it. He had to take the young wolf down to free it from the snare trap, or it was going to die, too. While he prepared the dart gun, the silver-blue wolf paced anxiously, watching him closely, her penetrating yellow eyes trained specifically on the shiny chrome firearm. As the spectacular animal strode just a few feet beyond him, the tips of her claws clicked against the water-smoothed pebbles along the creek.

Without hesitation, Grant stood up, aimed, and fired the tranquilizer dart at the black wolf. The young pup jumped and yelped, both from the sound of the gun, and the sting of the needle, as it penetrated her left shoulder and injected the sedative. Like a concerned mother, the silver-blue wolf immediately ran over to her and began to smell the dart sticking from her baby's body. She glanced up at Grant with an expression of confusion and doubt, leery of his intent.

"It's all right girl. Your baby is going to be okay. Just calm down." Grant was sure the adult wolf was feeling a sense of betrayal. He could see the suspicion in her eyes. Before she had second thoughts and charged him to protect her young, he reloaded the dart gun, walked over to the white wolf pup, took aim, and squeezed the trigger.

It didn't fire. He cocked it and tried a second time. And a third. And a fourth. And a fifth. The gun would not fire.

The sedative had begun to work on the black pup, and the silver-blue wolf was becoming more anxious as she watched her baby stagger and slump to the ground, as if it were dying. Her eyes darted between the pup and Grant, hatred, anger, and fury spewing from them.

"Your pup is going to sleep for a while. Just trust me. I'm going to help it," Grant said as calmly as he could. He knew he had to act fast, because if the silver-blue wolf perceived him as a threat to her family, she was going to do what came natural to her—kill him.

Grant turned to face the adult wolf, preparing for the worst, when he heard the white pup behind him whine. He glanced quickly over his shoulder. The young animal sat on its haunches, with a pitiful expression on its face, and the bloody snared paw lifted in the air. Grant looked back at the mother. Her body was crouched low to the ground. Her ears were set, lips were spread and fangs were displayed. She was ready to spring at him. The black pup was completely down now, motionless.

"It's all right, girl. Just keep it together for a couple more seconds."

He eased backwards toward the white wolf. He held his left hand held out in front of him for protection, in case the silver-blue wolf charged. With the other hand, he frantically dug in the back pocket of his snowmobile suit for the wire cutters. Was it possible that the white pup would let him cut the wire from its paw without having to put it down? He was counting on it, for the young wolf's sake, as well as his own. That would be a sign to the mother, that he was here to help and not harm her pups.

The white pup continued to whine, as if begging him to release it from this horrible human contraption. Grant was close enough now and knelt down beside the tortured young creature. It didn't flinch, jerk away, or snap at him, as its sister had done. It just held up its injured paw and stared at him, helplessly.

Very carefully, he reached over with his left hand and gently grasped the pup's ensnared leg. For a fraction of a second, he had taken his eyes off the silver-blue wolf and looked down at the white pup. Immediately, and before he was aware of what was happening, the silver-blue wolf sprang forward and clamped her powerful jaws tightly around his left wrist. She applied just enough pressure for the fang stabbing into his forearm to initiate a trickle of blood.

Even though he was frightened out of his mind, Grant knew better than to jerk his arm back and startle her. Her eyes were steady, intense, and locked on his. He knew she could bite completely through his arm in an instant, with little effort. He also knew her grip on his wrist was insurance. If he hurt her baby, she would hurt him, and most likely kill him.

His right hand trembled as he raised the cutters to the white pup's paw and clipped the wire. The moment he released the yearling's leg, the silver-blue wolf released his wrist from her mouth. For just an instant, there was a look of acceptance, maybe even appreciation, in her eyes. She backed away slowly, then quickly pranced off to join her freed pup, which had limped a few feet away. It had stopped and was licking its injury.

While she was still distracted with her freed baby, Grant hurried over to the young black wolf. He quickly clipped the wire around its chest, before it revived from the tranquilizer, and removed the dart from its shoulder.

As he knelt beside the sedated pup, he watched the silver-blue wolf bounce around the white pup with total elation. Grant thought about the people who say animals in the wild have no feelings and cannot express themselves with emotions like humans. He knew that to be pure bunk. If those skeptics were here now watching these two magnificent creatures interact with one another, he knew they would be skeptics no longer.

Smiling, he, at that moment, understood completely why he'd chosen a career in wildlife management. For a moment, his eyes blurred as he watched the two wolves in their joy. Just as he reached up to wipe away the happy tears, a loud boom rang out from behind him.

The silver-blue wolf's head snapped back with great force, then her whole body followed, as she tumbled, end over end, across the creek-bed pebbles. He thought he saw a glistening crimson liquid on top of her head, right between her ears.

Before she stopped somersaulting across the ground, Grant leaped to his feet and began to run toward the wolf. "No! No! No! This can't be!" he cried, his voice quivering as it echoed through the gorge. As he ran full out, he glanced over his shoulder to see who had fired the shot and killed the silver-blue wolf. A film of tears obscured his vision, and all he could see was a blurry outline of someone stepping out from behind the large boulder at the end of the clearing.

In all the commotion, the young white wolf skittered for cover as best as she could on three legs, heading toward the tree line. A second loud boom burst through the air, painfully ringing in Grant's ears. The bullet kicked up a large patch of dirt and rock, just as the pup darted behind a clump of willows and out of sight. Thank God the bullet missed the little guy, Grant thought to himself.

Sliding on his knees through the gravel, he slammed into the silver-blue wolf's limp body. The hair on the top of her head was plastered down with blood. He wiped his eyes and nose on the sleeve of the snowmobile suit and stared for a long time at the wolf sprawled out on the ground. That's when Grant noticed the deep scar on her leg just above the paw. It was at that moment he realized she'd been caught in a snare once before. He now knew this was the same silver-blue wolf the animal activist had taped last November, the one he'd seen on TV. It was the same silver-blue wolf he'd been dreaming of, for the past six months.

Grant reached down and lifted her into his arms, stared at her for a moment, then pulled her tight to his bosom. Her head dangled lifelessly, while her pink tongue hung out of her gaping mouth. He glared down at the gorgeous creature. His heart was heavy with sorrow.

After a few long seconds, the shroud of dark clouds winked out the sunlight, and the day became gloomy again. He glanced back over his shoulder, this time his vision clear, and he recognized who fired the shots. "It's you. How could you do this?"

Billy Jack was close now, maybe fifty yards away. He could see part of the boulder he was going to hide behind. It wouldn't be long now. He'd take his shot at the silver-blue wolf, then kick that boy's butt back to wherever he came from.

Like the crack of a giant bullwhip, the sound of the rifleshot reverberated off the walls of the narrow ravine. Billy Jack came to a dead stop and looked up the gorge. Just what was going on up there? Had the silver-blue wolf turned on Grant, and he had to shoot it? Like a grizzly, a wolf bitch will do just about anything to protect her young.

Almost immediately after the rifle shot, he heard Grant's echoing voice saying, "No! No! No! This can't be!" Then he heard a second shot.

Like a race horse sprung from the starting gate, Billy Jack shot into action. His large thigh muscles tensed, his boots dug into the loose gravel, and he charged up the steep slope of the gorge.

Grant gently set the silver-blue wolf back on the ground, carefully stood up, and faced Frank Kicklighter. The sheriff stumbled incoherently toward him, erratically waving the rifle in front of him. His face was tortured with despair, and his eyes were wild, puffy, and red from weeping. The man was completely distraught and large clouds of steam billowed from his mouth.

"I told her this wasn't going to work, but no-o-o-o, she had to have her way," Frank muttered, wobbling around as if in a daze. "She's evil you know. All eaten up with greed and her fancy career."

"Put the rifle down, Sheriff, and lets talk about this," Grant said with a steady tone, while his insides trembled with fear.

"I didn't want to do it, you know," Frank said. His voice was like that of a crazy person. "I had to. You know what that animal's pelt will bring me on the black-market? Enough money to make my baby well." Frank lifted his head skyward and cackled insanely, his flushed cheeks slick with tears. "That's why I had to do it. Have dollars will operate. That's the doctors' motto today. Greedy bastards."

"We can talk about this. I'll help you. Put the rifle down on the ground," Grant said to the despondent man. If only he could get close enough to overpower Frank and take the rifle away, he might have a chance at surviving this situation. He eased forward, taking each step very slowly.

Like a startled wild animal, Frank leaped high into the air drawing his knees to his chest, and landed low to the ground in a crouched position. The rifle was slung between his open legs and aimed directly at Grant. "You found the mine, didn't you? And the contamination and the gold?" Frank asked. The inflection in his voice went up and down. "The mine belongs to me, you know. And you can't have it." He cackled insanely, again.

"I don't want your mine, Frank. Now put the rifle down, and let's talk about all of this." Grant stopped moving forward for a moment, but maintained eye contact with the disturbed man. He didn't want to push the sheriff over the edge.

"Talk! You want to talk! I can talk!" Frank yelled. "It's all Linsey Hogan's fault, you know. Miss Greedy Bitch." He stood up straight, and while continuing to face Grant, he walked over to the dead yearling pup that had been strangled by the snare trap. He kicked the animal's stiff carcass. "The wolf poaching was all her idea, so we could raise the initial money to open the mine. She made the arrangements with the fur buyers, and I made the arrangements with all the trappers. And the mine, that's what started this whole stinking mess. I bought it from Billy Jack about a year ago. When I had the water analyzed, Linsey found out that it was loaded with gold and polluted with chromium. She blackmailed me, knowing all along that Broken Eye Lake was contaminated and affecting the caribou population."

While Frank rattled on, Grant inched closer to him. The barrel of the rifle was pointing toward the ground. Another couple of feet and Grant would be close enough to try to disarm the man. "I know all that, Frank," Grant said softly. "It doesn't matter now. Everything is going to be all right. Just put the rifle down."

"I switched the water in your samples. Did you know that? To make it look like Billy Jack did it," Frank rambled on. "I even jimmied the vending machine in the hangar, so Billy Jack would need my water to drink on the way to Anchorage."

"That's okay, Frank," Grant said. He was almost there. "No one is mad at you. Just put the rifle down, and let's talk about it."

"I had no choice but to kill the silver-blue wolf," Frank said, speaking as if he was in a trance. "It's for my daughter, you know. I love her so much. She means everything to me. You understand, don't you?"

"Yeah, I unders—"

Frank snapped the rifle up, jamming the butt of the walnut stock to his shoulder. Bringing the sights up, he aimed directly at Grant's chest and yelled, "You're a liar! You just want to hurt me so I can't save my baby. My sweet Nina. You know everything. Now you have to die!"

Grant's vocal cords froze with fear, and his eyes locked on the trigger guard of Frank's rifle. His eyes went wide at the same moment he saw Frank's finger jerk. He heard the loud boom and saw the flash of fire from the rifle barrel. Instantly, the bullet pierced his chest, kicking him into the air and backwards, slamming him to the ground on his back.

The pain was terrible. He couldn't catch his breath. The bullet had torn through his right lung. Bright red blood foamed from his mouth. His right arm was paralyzed and he rolled over on his left side so he wouldn't gag on his own blood.

Grant could still see Frank. The sick man had slumped to his knees. The rifle slipped from his fingers and fell to the ground. Dropping his face into his hands, the sheriff began to weep and moan, "Oh dear God, what have I done?"

During all this, the drugged black wolf pup had come to. It stammered to its feet and wobbled toward the woods, to join its sister who was peeking from a cluster of willows.

Grant gasped desperately for air. His eyes began to wander and finally lifted up toward the sky. A silver-blue streak flew over him. His eyes weakly followed the movement. It was the wolf. She was alive! In spite of the pain, his lips crept into a smile.

The silver-blue wolf's front feet hit the ground with a quiet thud. Almost immediately, her back feet landed and pushed off again, springing her into the air.

Frank lifted his head from his hands, a look of disbelief forged on his face.

The silver-blue wolf sailed through the air. Before Frank's screams of terror could be heard, the wolf's front paws crashed into the middle of his chest, knocking the man to the ground. Her huge wide-open mouth tore into Frank's neck. She shook her head violently, back and forth. Flesh, veins, and bones ripped apart under the force of her large teeth. Fountains of dark blood spewed in all directions.

Grant's head rolled back, and his eyes closed. Darkness overtook him.

Billy Jack silently slipped through a stand of willows and cautiously approached the back of the large boulder. He didn't know what to expect in the small clearing on the other side. Having run full speed up the steep incline of the gorge, he was exhausted. His heart slammed against his ribs as he sucked in air, trying to catch his breath.

He was close when he'd heard the third rifle shot. The sound of the firearm's discharge was much louder than the previous two shots. It had rumbled down through the ravine like a runaway locomotive. God only knew what kind of trouble that young man was in.

Right after the last shot, he thought he'd heard another voice yelling, besides Grant's. It sounded almost Frank Kicklighter's voice, but it was different somehow. Why would the sheriff be out here, anyway?

By the time Billy Jack had made it up the gorge to the clearing, his anger toward Grant had completely dissipated. He had totally forgotten about his revenge and beating the cheechako to a bloody pulp. His thoughts were more on the silver-blue wolf, and what was going on.

Reaching the rock, he leaned against it, resting for a moment. He readied his Nikon camera and focused its 28-80mm telephoto zoom lens. This might be his only opportunity to shoot the legendary silver-blue wolf, he thought. He might get only one good shot, and he wasn't going to blow it on some stupid mistake like no film in the camera, or forgetting to remove the lens cap. Just as he completed his check of the camera, he heard the familiar sound of a helicopter's rotor blades slicing through the air. No doubt it was Victor and his famed Flutter Butt, he thought.

Billy Jack carefully peeked around the boulder, the camera held up to his right eye. His index finger was lightly pressing on the shutter button, ready to snap a picture. Moving the camera from left to right, the scene in the small clearing came through the viewfinder.

The first thing he saw was two yearling wolf pups, one black and the other white, poking their heads around a clump of brush. He snapped two quick photos and moved on.

Next there was a gray wolf pup caught in a snare. It was dead. Again he snapped two more pictures.

When Frank Kicklighter's body came into the viewfinder, his heart skipped a beat, his mouth dropped open, and he stopped breathing. Stunned, his finger remained on the shutter release, taking picture after picture. It looked as though there'd been a massacre. Blood was everywhere. There was no doubt the man was dead. Frank Kicklighter's throat had been savagely ripped away. His eyes were wide open and devoid of life. His face was frozen in an expression of pain and terror.

"What the hell are you doing?" Victor yelled over the bullhorn, from the helicopter hovering above. "Grant looks like he's hurt bad. Get your butt out there and help him."

Victor's voice startled Billy Jack and jolted him out of his shock. He held his breath for several seconds, and gasped deeply for air. Billy Jack swung the camera around to his right. There in the viewfinder, was the most extraordinary scene he had ever witnessed in his life.

The silver-blue wolf stood over Grant Rawlings bloody body. Her lips were peeled back, displaying her large, vicious-looking fangs, and it appeared as if she were protecting the young man. Billy Jack snapped several shots, then lowered the camera.

As if the clouds had erupted into a stampede, they moved quickly across the sky and momentarily opened a gap in them. A single white ray of sunlight streamed down from the heavens, encasing Grant and the silver-blue wolf in a shaft of brilliant illuminating light.

Billy Jack dropped to his knees and adjusted the lens to a wider angle, so he could get the entire magnificent scene on film. He began to snap several photos of the wolf, Grant, the majestic shaft of light, and Victor hovering above in the helicopter.

In less than two minutes, he had finished the entire thirty-six-exposure roll of film. When he laid the camera down on the ground and stood up to go to Grant, the silver-blue wolf stepped back, as if she knew Billy Jack was coming to help her new friend. He didn't know what had taken place up here, but this was the damnedest thing he had ever seen. It was obvious that the wolf had accepted Grant as a member of her pack. The spectacular animal turned and trotted off toward the edge of the woods to join her pups, looking back at Billy Jack as she went.

Billy Jack hurried to Grant and knelt down beside him. The boy was still alive, bleeding from the mouth and chest, and breathing shallowly. He leaned over and gently scooped the young man up in his powerful arms. Grant was going to die unless he got some medical care in a hurry. The clearing wasn't large enough for Victor to land Flutter Butt. There was only one way to save Grant—carry him down the slope to his own helicopter and fly Grant to the nearest doctor.

The silver-blue wolf and her two pups looked on as Billy Jack carried Grant off, cradling him in his arms. Moments later, the two men dropped out of the wolves sight, as they descended down the nameless ravine.

Chapter 17

On this ninth day of June, there would be more than twenty-one hours of daylight. The temperature had climbed to seventy-three degrees, which made it the warmest day since Grant had come to Alaska. It was quite a contrast from the bitter cold winds of nearly a month ago, when he was shot and almost died.

It was a little after eleven in the evening, and the glow of the waning sun painted an orange-pink postcard spectacle across the western horizon. As the brilliance of the sun began to fade, an exceptionally large and bright full moon ushered in the oncoming night, by slipping its silvery globe over the mountain ridge that looked down on Denning Fork.

Grant had spent twelve long days in the hospital in Fairbanks, four of those in ICU. Since bringing him home two weeks ago, Charlie had stuck to him like flypaper. When she did leave to get groceries or check on the Trading Post, she made sure that Victor was there to keep an eye on him. There was no way she was going to let him out of her sight, until old Dr. Phillips stamped the good seal of health on his forehead. Grant knew she was fearful that he might wonder off into the woods again, in search of the silver-blue wolf. And to be quite honest, she was probably right. No one had seen the wolf and her pups since the day he was shot. Even the dreams of the magnificent creature had stopped.

Grant sat on the sofa, his back propped against the armrest and his legs stretched out over the cushions in front of him. His fingers floated over the keyboard of the notebook computer, writing in his daily diary. Victor pulled up outside in his new AWMC Suburban. A few minutes later, he and Charlie came through the open front door of the cabin, chattering away at each other.

"I'm afraid Victor has some bad news to tell you, Grant," Charlie said with a serious tone, as she walked up behind him.

Grant stopped typing, closed out the computer, and set it on the coffee table. "What's that? I've been fired?" he snickered, as he rose from the sofa to face Charlie and Victor.

"It's worse than that," Victor said with a mischievous grin. "I'm your new boss."

"What?" Grant asked.

"I just finished speaking with the Governor at Two Forks Airport," Victor said. There was a touch of excitement now in his voice. "He flew up here from Juneau, to inform me that I'm the new director of the Alaska Wildlife Management Commission."

Grant was truly happy for his partner and friend. He rushed around the end of sofa with his hand held out. "Congratulations!" He grabbed Victor's hand and pumped his arm vigorously. "Man, that's best news I've heard since I've come to this place. What about Linsey Hogan? Have they located her yet?"

"Nope," Victor answered. "The same day Frank Kicklighter came after you, she converted any of her assets into cash that she could on such short notice, and split. No one's seen her since."

"As the old saying goes," Charlie added to the conversation, "what goes around comes around. It'll sneak up on her one of these days, when she least expects it, and it'll bite her right on her fat butt."

"Yeah, I believe that too, Charlie," Grant agreed.

Victor nodded his agreement.

"I heard that obnoxious banker, Peter Worley, was fired," Charlie said. "The authorities could never actually prove he did anything illegal, but I guess the bank felt he may not have been above board in his dealings with Linsey and Frank, so they canned him. Bad image for the bank and all. Last I heard, he moved out of state."

"Serves him right," Grant said.

At that point, Victor turned his attention to Grant and said, "As your new boss, the first assignment I'm going to give you is to get yourself completely healed before continuing your study on the caribou population."

"Amen," Charlie said.

"That, I don't think you are going to have to worry about," Grant said. "I think I've learned my lesson. Besides, Charlie's been sticking to me like glue on a postage stamp."

"And don't you forget it either, Bub," she said jokingly.

"The thing I'm especially interested in, is whether the number of caribou calves will increase next season, since we took Professor Foust's advice," Victor said.

"I remember her saying something about that, when we went to Fairbanks to get the water samples analyzed. But I'm not sure I got it all," Charlie said, more to Grant than to Victor. "What did she say?"

"Well," Grant started, "if her theory is correct, slightly lowering the pH of the contaminated water system feeding into Broken Eye Lake, will kill the algae and bacteria that changed the harmless ore, chromite, into a toxic chromate form."

"Change the pH in the whole lake? Charlie asked. "That's a lot of water. How in the world are you going to do that?"

"By altering the water at the source of the problem, at the mine, with a mild solution of nitric acid," Grant said.

"Won't acid harm the aquatic life in the lake, like the fish?"

"Actually," Grant said, "it should have just the opposite effect. For one thing, we'll use a low concentration of acid. Also, the nitrate part of the nitric acid will be useful as food. Many of the organisms in the water, plant as well as animal, can metabolize nitrates."

"So how will you actually do all this?" Charlie asked, persisting in her questions.

"Dr. Foust helped Victor rig a device that we'll set up at the mine. It will meter in the dilute acid anytime the pH goes above 5.5. This will immediately kill any further growth of algae and bacteria at the mine. Since the mine water feeds into the lake, with time, the pH of the lake water will lower to the point of killing any bacteria or algae there, too."

"Good," Charlie said. "Eventually, maybe things will get back to normal around here."

"What about the chromium that's already in the lake?" Victor asked.

"With the millions of gallons of water that run in and out of that lake, it won't take long before the remaining chromium is diluted to a level that won't be toxic. By the end of summer it'll be so low, we'll most likely not even find a trace of the metal in the water."

"That'll be good," Charlie said. "In fact, almost everything about this whole mess is turning out good."

"Yes, it is," Grant replied. "The only thing I hate, is that Frank had to die. But at least the community came together and donated money for his daughter's operation. There are some real nice people around here."

"That's true," Victor said to Grant. Then he looked at Charlie. "I understand that next to Billy Jack, you were the largest contributor."

"Well, that's a little misleading," Charlie said. "Frank held the second mortgage on the Trading Post. He came to me about a month ago, and said he needed the payment early for his daughter's bone marrow transplant. The problem was, I couldn't get another loan to pay him back. No one wanted to give me one, because my credit was already extended up to my eyeballs. But a good friend of mine came through for me. I guess it doesn't make any difference now, if I tell you where I got the money. Billy Jack loaned it to me."

"That's what I thought," Victor said, his face beginning to flush slightly. "I have to admit that you were right all along, Charlie. Billy Jack is one fine fellow. I don't know how I misjudged him so."

Charlie reached over and clasped both of Grant's hands in hers. "And . . .the night I was so ugly to you at the Trading Post . . .that's when he told me he would help me out with the payment. I can see now how my behavior with Billy Jack must've looked to you. It's just that I was so happy to be able to keep the place. But I still haven't forgiven myself for the way I acted that night."

Grant squeezed her hands gently and only smiled. His eyes said everything that needed to be said.

He was quiet for a moment longer, then said, "I don't remember it, because I was out cold. But according to what everyone has told me, if Billy Jack hadn't carried me down that ravine as quickly as he did, I wouldn't be here right now."

"Thank God, he is as big a man as he is," Charlie added. "No one else I know of, would have been strong enough to carry you all that way without collapsing." She was quiet for a moment, then said, "I guess it was my fault. If I hadn't told Frank all about the gold and chromium in the lake water, none of this would have happened." Charlie's eyes met Grant's for just a second, then dropped back to the floor. "I'm sorry. You were nearly killed because I—"

Grant put his finger on her lips, smiled, and shook his head. "Forget it," he said.

There was a light knock on the open front door. "My ears are burning. Someone must be talking about me," Billy Jack muttered, standing in the doorway, holding a long narrow rectangular object in his right hand. It was covered with a light cloth material that looked like an old sheet.

"Speak of the devil," Grant said. Victor and Charlie turned toward Billy Jack and greeted him with a nod.

"What's that in your hand?" Charlie asked.

"It's a gift for my new friend, Grant," Billy Jack said, his eyes focused on him, as if asking for acceptance. "At least, I hope he is my friend."

Grant grinned, feeling the heat rise in his face from embarrassment. "Well of course you're my friend. You saved my life. But you didn't have to buy me anything."

"He didn't buy it, he—" Victor started to say.

"Lets not ruin the surprise, Victor," Billy Jack interrupted. "I've kept my passion a secret for all these years because I had this foolish macho pride thing going. I thought people would make fun of me and think me less of a man. I don't care anymore what people think. It's time to come out of the closet.

"First, before I show you what I have, I would like to mention a couple things. Victor here, has taken official steps to name that ravine, where you saved the silver-blue wolf's pups and nearly lost your life. It will be called Rawlings Gorge."

Grant was shocked. "I can't believe it. Really?" He looked first to Victor, in disbelief, then to Charlie. "Did you know about this?"

Charlie nodded her head with a smile, walked over to him, and gave him a peck on the cheek.

"Victor also helped me select a name for my latest creation." He turned his back to the three of them, to unveil the rectangular object. He held it up in front of him, then turned around so all could see. "It's called, *Messenger to the Spirits*."

Grant was completely astounded. It was an oil painting of the silver-blue wolf crouched over him in a defensive stance, as if protecting him. Her lips were curled, and her teeth were bared for action. The two of them were shrouded in a beam of white light shining down from the slate gray cloud-covered sky. In the far right upper corner of the painting, hazily painted into the clouds, was a bust of an Indian. Just barely visible, was a long scar down the left side of the Indian's face, a face that slightly resembled Victor's. Standing in the background next to a gently flowing mountain stream, watching the majestic spectacle, were two wolf pups, one black and one white.

"You're the one that's done all those beautiful paintings of Alaskan wildlife and scenery, aren't you?" Charlie asked, with amazement. Not even she knew of Billy Jack's hidden passion. "They're so real, they just seem to draw you into them. And they seem to be everywhere. I saw a small one in the chemist's office in Fairbanks, and at least two larger ones at the bank, when I went to see about the loan."

"And I think Dr. Barlow had a couple of your paintings in his home, too," Grant added. "There was one in the den and another in the bedroom. In fact, I saw a couple of paintings at the Fairbanks airport that I'm sure are yours. Are you the artist?"

"One and the same," Billy Jack answered, lowering the painting to the floor and leaning it against the wall. "My agent in Anchorage calls quite a bit, and she's been on me like a bear after honey to get reproductions made of this one. But when she called the other day, I flatly told her there would be only one *Messenger to the Spirits* painting, and it's all yours, Grant."

"That's what all those crates were, that I saw Billy Jack was loading into his helicopter, the morning he took the lake samples to Anchorage," Victor said. "He was taking them to his agent to sell for him."

Grant was still speechless, staring at the gorgeous painting. It was so lifelike. He moved over to it, kneeling to get a better view. That's when he heard the howl of a wolf coming from the back of the cabin.

The four of them rushed to the open back door. Grant and Charlie hurried out to the back stoop, her arm tightly holding his waist. Billy Jack and Victor stood behind them, looking over their shoulders.

There, across Denning Fork, standing high on a large rounded rock, was the silver-blue wolf, flanked by her two pups. Her regal head was tilted toward the stars, now glimmering brightly since night had overtaken the day. The two younger wolves lifted their heads and began to howl, joining in with their mother's serenade. All three animals were silhouetted in the silver glow of the full moon, which had now risen above the tree tops on the far mountain. It was a once in a lifetime scene.

A shiver of excitement ran down Grant's back. He loved this country. Just then, a shooting star arched over the face of the moon.

A smile crawled across his face, and his lips parted as he said in a low reverent tone, "Messenger to the spirits."

About the Author

Michael J. Whitaker has been a research chemist for the last sixteen years and is internationally recognized as a world expert in Flow Injection Analysis, an analytical technique he helped pioneer and develop.

His urge to write and share his work with the science community began early in his career with several publications as a student and graduate of Florida State University. Since then, he has published numerous articles in journals such as *Analytical Chemistry, Talanta,* and *Analytica Chimica Acta,* and is a member of the American Chemical Society. He has lectured widely on his research at international conferences, universities, and industries, in both the US and the UK.

Over the years he has also become a fierce advocate for nature and wildlife, a passion that led to writing this novel. He is a member of the Defenders of Wildlife, the Audubon Society, and the International Wolf Center. An avid sailor and fisherman, he is a member of the Augusta Sailing Club. He lives with his wife and two dogs in South Carolina.